VALUING CARE WORK:
COMPARATIVE PERSPECTIVES

Edited by Cecilia Benoit and Helga Hallgrímsdóttir

Health care systems encompass many forms of paid and unpaid labour, including home care for the elderly or disabled, community health services, and the care family members provide for loved ones. *Valuing Care Work* is a comparative study that examines economic organizations as well as home and institutional environments to show how personal service work is shaped by broader welfare state developments.

Tracing the relationships between gender, labour, and equity in health care, the essays in this volume analyse the rules and practices that shape care work. The contributors highlight how national configurations of the welfare state shape the gendering of paid and unpaid intimate labour in a range of settings and discuss how the policies and practices associated with neoliberalism have focused on efficiency and accountability to the detriment of other policy agendas. Together the essays explore systems and strategies that promise to increase dignity and equity for both recipients and providers of paid and unpaid health care.

CECILIA BENOIT is a scientist at the Centre for Addictions Research of British Columbia and a professor in the Department of Sociology at the University of Victoria.

HELGA HALLGRÍMSDÓTTIR is an assistant professor in the Department of Sociology at the University of Victoria.

EDITED BY CECILIA BENOIT AND
HELGA HALLGRÍMSDÓTTIR

Valuing Care Work

Comparative Perspectives

UNIVERSITY OF TORONTO PRESS
Toronto Buffalo London

© University of Toronto Press Incorporated 2011
Toronto Buffalo London
www.utppublishing.com
Printed in Canada

ISBN 978-1-4426-4182-2 (cloth)
ISBN 978-1-4426-1092-7 (paper)

Printed on acid-free, 100% post-consumer recycled paper with vegetable-based inks.

Library and Archives Canada Cataloguing in Publication

Valuing care work : comparative perspectives / edited by Cecilia Benoit and Helga Hallgrímsdóttir.

Includes bibliographical references.
ISBN 978-1-4426-4182-2 (bound).   ISBN 978-1-4426-1092-7 (pbk.)

1. Care of the sick.   2. Caregivers.   3. Home care services.   4. Medical care.   I. Benoit, Cecilia, 1954–   II. Hallgrímsdóttir, Helga, 1969–

RA645.3.V34 2010   362'.0425   C2010-906335-X

University of Toronto Press acknowledges the financial assistance to its publishing program of the Canada Council for the Arts and the Ontario Arts Council.

 Canada Council   Conseil des Arts
for the Arts   du Canada

 ONTARIO ARTS COUNCIL
CONSEIL DES ARTS DE L'ONTARIO

University of Toronto Press acknowledges the financial support for its publishing activities of the Government of Canada through the Canada Book Fund (BPIDP).

Contents

Acknowledgments

The editors would like to acknowledge the generous support of the B.C. Women's Health Research Network, as well as the Canadian Institute of Population and Public Health, the Canadian Institute of Gender and Health, and the University of Victoria. Funding from these organizations allowed us to organize the international network of scholars who are contributors to this volume. We would also like to thank the Aid to Scholarly Publications Program for funding to bring the product of our international collaboration to publication.

Contributors

Cecilia Benoit, PhD, Centre for Addictions Research of BC and Department of Sociology, University of Victoria

Kristín Björnsdóttir, PhD, Faculty of Nursing, University of Iceland

Ivy Bourgeault, Interdisciplinary School of Health Sciences, University of Ottawa

Debra Brown, MA, Department of Sociology, University of Victoria

Leslie Brown, PhD, School of Social Work, University of Victoria

Marilyn Callahan, PhD, School of Social Work, University of Victoria

Lauren Casey, MA, Centre for Addictions Research of BC, University of Victoria

Christine Ceci, PhD, Faculty of Nursing, University of Alberta

Holly Dolan, PhD, Guelph, Ontario

Þorgerdur Einarsdóttir, PhD, Department of Sociology, University of Iceland

Rachel Eni, PhD, Faculty of Medicine, University of Manitoba

Laura Funk, PhD, Centre on Aging, University of Victoria

Helga Kristín Hallgrímsdóttir, PhD, Department of Sociology, University of Victoria

Karen Kobayashi, PhD, Department of Sociology, University of Victoria

Chris Leischner, Prostitutes, Empowerment, Education and Resource Society, Victoria

Patricia Mackenzie, PhD, School of Social Work, University of Victoria

Anne Martin-Matthews, PhD, Department of Sociology, University of British Columbia

Muriel Mellow, PhD, Department of Sociology, University of Lethbridge

Rachel Phillips, PhD, Centre for Addictions Research of BC, University of Victoria

Mary Ellen Purkis, PhD, School of Nursing, University of Victoria

Joanie Sims-Gould, PhD, Department of Sociology, University of British Columbia

Kathy Teghtsoonian, PhD, Studies in Policy and Practice, University of Victoria

Deborah Thien, PhD, Department of Geography, California State University

Rachel Treloar, MA, Department of Sociology and Anthropology, Simon Fraser University

Barbara Whittington, PhD, School of Social Work, University of Victoria

Sirpa Wrede, PhD, Swedish School of Social Science, University of Helsinki

PART ONE

Theoretical Considerations

1 Conceptualizing Care Work

CECILIA BENOIT AND HELGA KRISTÍN HALLGRÍMSDÓTTIR

Work, understood in its broadest sense, involves creating and serving for either one's own or one's dependants' direct consumption, in exchange for pay and/or other support (Applebaum 1992). Unpaid work is that which is carried out for personal consumption or for others (e.g., household work, child care, attendance to the needs of the disabled or elderly, community service) and may be (but not always) accompanied by non-monetary rewards such as companionship, opportunities for creative growth, and so forth. Most of the activities that fall under unpaid work are in some way or other connected with the social reproduction of human beings on a daily and generational basis (Folbre 1994) or what others call 'care work' (Glenn 1992; England 2005) or 'care labour' (Folbre 1995). In this book we use the terms *care work* and *intimate labour* interchangeably.

Care work has always been gendered work. In pre-industrial, agricultural societies, care work tended to fall on the shoulders of girls and women. However, girls and women in these societies often also played a central role in farming and other productive types of labour, as is still the case in low-income countries around the world today (Benoit 2000). One of the significant cultural and social changes associated with industrialization is the increased segregation of private and public production. The private sphere, where the daily and generational social reproduction of family and community members takes place, became a women's sphere, and a site of non-economic, non-instrumental activities. Thus, over time, caring activities became to be seen less and less as economic and more and more as if they were not work at all (Folbre 2001). The gendering of care work, that is, the bearing, raising, socialization, and education of children, the care for other dependants in the population (disabled, sick, elderly) inside homes, and the care work that is done by volunteers in formal institutions such as schools and hospitals or in volunteer agencies and non-governmental organizations (Prentice & Ferguson 2000), in effect has led to its devaluation.

The rise of the welfare state has been accompanied by increasing 'commodification' of care (the gradual shift of caring from the private sphere back into the public sphere), and an accompanying marketization of care work. Paid care work includes the so-called caring professions, such as dentistry, medicine, teaching, nursing, social work, and midwifery (Abbott & Wallace 1990), as well as an assortment of other jobs that are associated with low pay and little by way of prestige (these include work in call centres, restaurants, nursing homes, nurseries, as airline attendants, hairstylists, and paid private attendants in other people's homes). Jobs within this latter category share the characteristic of being located on the 'front line,' involving face-to-face interaction with clients or what Arlie Hochschild (1983) aptly terms 'emotional labour,' without the buffer or front person, for example, a secretary or office clerk (Zemke & Schaaf 1989; Kerfoot & Korczynski 2005). Some scholars refer to these latter personal services provided in the private and public sectors as the 'care economy' (Durano 2003).

Care Work – Degrading or Dignifying?

As Arlie Hochschild (1983) and others have noted (Ehrenreich & Hochschild 2002; Zimmerman, Litt, & Bose 2006), paid emotional labour or care work involving the delivery of services through direct contact between recipients or clients or customers and service providers has surpassed work in the primary and secondary industries in North America and is increasingly common at the global level. Whether or not providing care work for others – paid and unpaid – awards satisfaction for workers and contributes to the worker's psychological and physical well-being is a subject of much debate among academics. Personal service employees not only expend physical labour but are routinely compelled to manage their own and others' emotions by, for example, producing an overtly visible facial and bodily display that is pleasing to the recipient. Commercial organizations require workers to use their emotional skills to exaggerate positive feelings towards clients (e.g., kindness) while suppressing negative ones (e.g., anger). Indeed, these workers are expected to feel and display sympathy, trust, and good will – to 'bow from the heart' – even when clients are disrespectful or rude, because their continuing loyalty to the establishment means increased commercial gain (Hochschild 1983). In such jobs, workers are expected to follow particular 'serving scripts' that involve giving 'good service' to clients so that they leave satisfied and will return (Hall 1993). For many jobs, these serving scripts are, at times, explicitly mandated by a company or manager to encourage workers to 'self-manage' their emotions in acceptable ways. Importantly, these serving scripts are both gendered and sexualized; emotional labour that is incorporated into jobs becomes thus part of the production and reproduction of gendered work hierarchies and gendered occupational structures.

These conditions, in particular, gendered devaluation and gendered expectations around emotional work, place considerable challenges to workers in the health care workforce in their efforts to achieve *dignity* in their work (Hodson 2001). Dignity in health care is a complex phenomenon that is at once rooted in ideas around patients' rights (to receive care, quality of care, and continuity of care) and workers' rights (job satisfaction, responsible autonomy, job security, and opportunities for advancement). Dignity in care and work thus consists of many overlapping aspects that involve rights of both the recipients of care and the providers of care to respect, privacy, autonomy, self-worth, and self-respect (Stacey 2005), and while they may not always be treated as such by policy makers, dignity for care recipients is nonetheless closely tied to dignity for the provider. This is because the requisites for dignity in work, such as good working conditions, respectful colleagues and managers, job security, and being valued both economically and socially, are important factors contributing to the recruitment and retention of health care workers. Conversely, health care workplaces that are understaffed and face high staff turnover are unlikely to be able to ensure patients' rights to continuity and quality of care (Diamond 1992).

Recent scholarship, however, asks us to nuance the relationship between care work and dignity. In particular, this literature argues that the emotional work that is embedded into care work is not automatically alienating nor does it necessarily have negative consequences for workers' physical and psychological health. As Amy Wharton and Rebecca Erickson (1993) have noted, studies examining the consequences of care work on the worker's feelings about her or his work have typically been case studies where the emotional costs are high for the worker, thereby making it impossible for the researcher to control for important work features (e.g., worker autonomy, involvement in tasks, self-monitoring abilities, balance between work demand

and control, etc.) that are likely to affect job satisfaction and other psycho-social outcomes. At the same time, there is a significant body of literature that points towards the potential rewards and benefits of engaging in this kind of care labour (Leidner 1993; Owings 2002). For some workers, performing paid care work for others has been shown to be an important source of personal fulfilment, enhancing workers' sense of self-worth and lowering their personal and professional levels of stress (Sharma & Black 2001). A case in point is Owings' (2002) ethnographic study of the work of waitresses. Female waiters in establishments that offer dignified working conditions described deriving personal pleasure and substantial job satisfaction from being able to teach clients about food and wine, facilitate memorable and special occasions, and create a warm and friendly atmosphere in which to dine. Thus, caring for another human being can be rewarding, even when one is being paid to do so (Messing 1998). Much depends on the characteristics of the worker to be sure, but also to the social context of the work itself. Others studies have shown that personal service jobs can sometimes serve as pathways for workers to gain recognition and legitimization in jobs that are commonly regarded as unskilled and/or low status (Bolton & Boyd 2003; Bolton 2005). Workers point to their ability to successfully manage their emotions within a work context as proof of their skills and abilities. Mears and Finlay found that models regularly enact emotional work as a means of gaining an edge over their competitors; this involves 'sell[ing] themselves to clients and agents, to create illusions for observers and the camera, and to find dignity in a job that [can be] degrading and humiliating' (2005: 318).

Viviana Zelizer's (2002, 2007) work allows for further nuance to be brought into this scholarship. She draws attention to the impact of the social context of care work – or what she calls 'intimate labour,' which she defines as work that entails bodily or emotional closeness or personal familiarity (intimacy), such as sexual intercourse and washing genitalia, or intimate observation and knowledge of personal information, such as child care or housekeeping. Zelizer argues that rather than being seen as socially reproductive work existing outside of production, such work can be found today in all sectors of high-income countries – in homes, bureaucratic institutions, community centres, and public service organizations, as well as other locations.

Our volume demonstrates the utility of examining care work, or intimate labour, in formal organizations and informal settings and at the same time we draw attention to the manner in which workers are rewarded and the comparative opportunities that they have to negotiate the terms and conditions of their work. We thus take up Zelizer's challenge to examine four types of care work or intimate labour: paid and unpaid health care work in economic organizations and paid and unpaid health care work in intimate settings – and at the same time demonstrate how these types of personal service work are inevitably shaped by broader welfare state developments, including recent neo-liberal policies, which we turn to next.

Care Work under Different Welfare State Regimes

What is the relationship between care workers and the welfare state? T.H. Marshall's concept of citizenship customarily serves as the starting point from which to map the historical changes in individual rights as industrial capitalism took hold in the nineteenth and twentieth centuries. According to Marshall (1965: 92), 'citizenship is a status bestowed on those who are full members of a community ... All who possess the status are equal with respect to the rights and duties with which the status is endowed.' Marshall (1965: 91) demarcated three categories of rights of citizenship – civil, political, and social – each classification, in his view, represents a site of struggle between individual actors and the state over how the boundary between inclusion and exclusion of citizenship is determined. In general terms, *civil citizenship* refers to individual rights before the law, and dates back to the eighteenth century with the development of the modern judicial system. *Political citizenship* refers to individual rights to enter into democratic processes, including the right to vote, and dates for men from the middle of the nineteenth century, and for women from the early decades of the twentieth century. *Social citizenship* is a development largely peculiar to the second half of the twentieth century and the early decades of the twenty-first century, and it refers to individual rights of economic welfare, universal education, and social security conferred by the state in order to minimize the negative effects of industrial capitalism. It is in regard to social citizenship that Marshall discussed the formation of the 'welfare state' and its important role in promoting social democracy. He argued that a comprehensive welfare state would make available to citizens a broad assortment of social rights. The outcome, according to Marshall (1992: 33), is a 'general enrichment of the concrete substance of civilized life, a general reduction of risk and insecurity [and] an equalization between the more and less unfortunate at all levels – between the healthy and the sick, the employed and the unemployed, the old and the active, the bachelor and the father of a large family.'

Marshall was especially concerned about citizens who were members of the working class, particularly wage earners, or breadwinners, who in the first half of the twentieth century were extremely vulnerable to exploitation by capitalist employers. Marshall was thus chiefly concerned with enlarging citizenship entitlements for working class *men* since women at the time were only marginally attached to the economy and tended to hold subordinate positions to their husbands in matters regarding law and politics (Benoit 2000).

Esping-Anderson and Korpi (1987) also place the economically independent citizen – that is, the gainfully employed worker – central to their analyses, and they have developed typologies or cross-national comparisons for welfare state regimes (see also Esping-Anderson 1990; Esping-Anderson, ed. 1996). These authors work within a power resource model and propose that the following three cardinal dimensions form the core of welfare states: (1) the state-market relationship, or 'the extent to which needs are to be satisfied through the labour market or, as an alternative, through political mechanisms'; (2) the impact of welfare states on economic stratification, that is, 'the status relations among citizens within the framework of social policy'; (3) the constitution of social rights, that is, 'the range, or domain, of human needs that are satisfied by social policy' (Esping-Anderson & Korpi 1987: 40–1). On the basis of these three dimensions of variation, three types of welfare state regimes are distinguished, each founded on very different underlying principles of stratification and social rights for citizens: the liberal market regime, the conservative corporatist regime, and the social democratic regime (Esping-Anderson 1989). Implicit in the mainstream perspectives on welfare states is the assumption of gender neutrality – that is, that social provision has a similar bearing on men and women. Feminist scholars claim that the wage earner or breadwinner or citizen discussed in mainstream perspectives, whether stated explicitly or implied, is almost always considered to be male (Hernes 1987; Pateman 1988). The assumption remains that economic independence is essential for full citizenship, and employment is the chief distinctive feature of the [male] worker. As Helga Hernes (1988: 190) states, 'the social-democratic citizen is the citizen worker, a male family provider, a working-class hero. His identities and participation patterns were determined by his ties to the labour market, and by the web of association and corporate structures which had grown around these ties.' Feminist scholars highlight sexuality, reproduction, and physical bodies when discussing gender differences that shape the concept of citizenship, arguing that women face unique hazards to their bodies in the private and public spheres of capitalist countries which have hampered their full participation as autonomous individuals in the economy and civil society (Jones 1990).

In short, the welfare state affects women and men differently (O'Connor 1996). Further, even when the welfare state decreases women's dependency on men, women remain dependent on the state for economic support (i.e., in the form of social assistance). Once women become dependent on the welfare state for income, the welfare state gains public control over women's lives (Pascal 1986). The welfare state can hardly be seen as gender neutral, then, but rather as reinforcing a deeply ingrained sexual division of labour based on gender inequality.

Cross-national scholarship on engendering welfare states, in attempting to advance the mainstream approach, argues that women's citizenship rights – civic, political, and social – are premised on correcting what are possibly women's two major obstacles in high-income countries: (1) inadequate wages and unequal access to jobs and (2) economic dependence on others (men, state officials) as a result of women's inordinate caring responsibility for children and dependent others. As Ann Orloff (1993: 309) contends, 'relations of domination based on control of women's bodies in the family, the workplace, and public spaces undermine women's abilities to participate as "independent individuals" – citizens – in the polity, which in turn affect their capabilities to demand and utilize social rights. The ways that states intervene – or refuse to – are critical to women's situation.' This perspective calls for extension of the mainstream welfare regime approach to take into account actual gender differences in employment and family life, so that social policies not only aid decommodification – that is, making possible for a person to 'maintain a livelihood without reliance on the market' (Esping-Anderson 1990: 21–2), but at the same time result in positive changes that promote women's economic independence, a prerequisite for their equality with men in working and family life. It follows, then, that focus needs to be placed on those welfare state social policies that enhance women's position in paid care work, and at the same time grant them recognition for their substantial non-paid caring work so that they are not forced into dependency on male partners or stigmatized for reliance upon social assistance (O'Connor 1993; White 2001; Daly & Rake 2003).

In brief, the more that welfare states base their social policies on the principle of caring, the closer they come to championing gender equality in all sectors of society, one where men's involvement in caring work is championed, where there is an equal balance between paid and unpaid work for both women and men, with both sharing opportunities and responsibilities (Pateman 1989; Sainsbury 1996). Important social policies to consider in this regard include universally accessible maternal and paternal leaves and benefits, quality public child care, elder care, and care for the physically and mentally disabled. The Nordic welfare states have been the countries where these social citizenship rights have been the strongest but many other European countries have also been active in this regard.

Social Citizenship Rights in the Era of Neoliberalism

Market economies around the world have been undergoing fundamental restructuring in the past few decades, marked by neoliberalism, challenging the social citizenship rights that are the cornerstone of advanced welfare states. In its widest meaning, neoliberalism 'denotes a politically guided intensification of market rule and commodification' (Brenner, Peck, & Theodore 2010: 3). Among other things, neoliberalism involved the change from a Fordist to a post-Fordist economy, that is, one characterized by flexible production designed to respond to diverse consumer demands and fragmented markets spread across the globe (Williams 1994; Harvey 2005).

Brenner, Peck, and Theodore (2010: 2) have argued for a more nuanced approach to neoliberalism and rethink it as a diverse *process* which they call 'neoliberalization,' in order to capture the many ways in which neoliberalism has heralded regulatory transformation. Further to this, they argue for research that pays attention to the variegated and path-dependent nature of the processes of neoliberalization, in other words, to contextually, temporally, and policy-domain specific forms and outcomes of neoliberalism (Brenner, Peck, & Theodore, in press).

Many scholars have argued that the neoliberalist economic reforms have meant that initiatives to ensure dignity in work and care, such as family-friendly maternity units and work-life balance programs for employees, child and elder care services, and so forth, have fallen out of vogue. Instead, in an effort to reduce budgets, public and private sector managers have shifted their focus away from dignified work and care as a fundamental human right to an emphasis on worker performance and efficiency of the delivery system (Armstrong & Armstrong 2003; Ehrenreich & Hochschild 2002; Zelizer 2002; Zimmerman, Litt, & Bose 2006; Armstrong & Laxer 2006). Paid care workers, including those working in the health care sector, have been seen as a major target group for restructuring, downsizing, and privatization. The ideology of *familialism* – a gendered care ideology that privileges the family as the best site for care – has been used to justify the shift of paid formal care in public institutions to informal care settings where 'clients' are forced to rely on non-familial home care workers or members of their immediate or extended families. This development has resulted in paid care work in formal organizations in the public and private sectors once again becoming economically invisible in the intimate setting of the home or in the voluntary sector, where in many cases health care providers find poorer working conditions and non-paid providers and volunteers, who tend to be women, face greater informal care burdens.

It is important to note that much of the theorizing about neoliberalization and its negative impact on care work across various sectors of society has largely been based on research in the United States and Great Britain where this process has had its greatest impact. Following the recommendations of Brenner et al. (2010), we must be concerned with how applicable these findings are to Canada or to other high-income countries that have different historical traditions and political structures (Benoit & Heitlinger 1998; De Vries et al. 2004; Gesler & Kearns 2002; McDaniel 2002a). This lack of a comparative perspective has important implications when it comes to understanding how global trends associated with neoliberalization are reshaping care work, as well as its social recognition. In particular, focusing only on the Anglo-American experience with neoliberal policy trends has led to a certain kind of teleology in this literature, in which neoliberalization is treated as an historical agent, rather than the policy makers themselves. Accompanying this premise are assumptions that neoliberal policy trends are inexorable and inevitable, that they are taken up in a uniform manner by all nations, and that they inevitably result in a convergence of policy trends among nations.

However, as has been shown in many studies of the Nordic welfare states, the institutional histories and philosophical underpinnings of welfare states are important mediators of how the assumptions of neoliberal ideologies are both interpreted and taken up as social policy (Coburn 2004). There are several contextual factors of import here. First, there are contemporary and historical differences in terms of the parameters of social citizenship (Marshall 1965). The U.S. welfare state, for example, has traditionally been premised on a rather narrow conception of social citizenship, in which the state is seen to be obligated only to provide a kind of minimal protection to citizens from the vagaries of the market. On the other hand, as noted above, many of the Nordic welfare states have been built on a much broader understanding of social citizenship that includes for citizens a right to *meaningful* participation in the marketplace. Second, the politics of social citizenship have been profoundly shaped by women's activism. In the Nordic countries, for example, women's strong political and social activism has helped to widen the claims of social citizenship to encompass rights to *care* as well as to work (Bock 1991). Third, different welfare states support different histories of professional configurations in the health care sector that are more or less democratic (Henriksson, Wrede, & Burau 2006).

All of these issues together suggest that we require contextually sensitive analyses of care work in neoliberal policy regimes. Such an approach would not only give us needed nuance in terms of understanding how the normative assumptions associated with neoliberalism shape social policy, but also give us historical and cross-national comparative cases from which we can examine the range of possibilities that are available across different generations in a given sociopolitical context (McDaniel 2002b).

Placing Canada in Social Context

Cross-national comparative research is a mainstay in the study of work, including care work. In recent years there has been a push for more multidisciplinary and multinational research. The value of a comparative approach is indisputable, but the quality of the research suffers to the extent that it often ignores variations in the social organization of caring practices and social experiences. This is particularly true in the comparison of high-income countries, where researchers often unthinkingly assume similarity and convergence in terms of economic development, social structure, and medical practice (Freeman 1999; Hantrais 1999). In the cases of paid and unpaid care work, differences among these countries are often ignored; instead, countries are depicted to be in different stages of development and those that 'lag behind' are assumed to eventually converge with the other more 'advanced' countries.

This volume makes the case for a *decentred* analysis of care work that pays close attentive to an historically informed social-economic and cultural context (Wrede et al. 2006). Cross-national research using context-sensitive approaches remains rare even today. Instead, international collaborations are usually limited to sharing insights and bringing together results from individual projects rather than genuine integration of scholarship to make a product that is more than the sum of the contributing parts. Such collaboration has the potential to challenge the ethnocentrism that limits ethically sound and methodologically rigorous comparative work (Benoit et al. 2005). This latter type of collaboration requires sustained scholarly exchanges around a common set of ideas and presupposes economic and other resources conducive to team interaction, including emotional investment and individual collaborative skills (Jeffrey 2003; Melin 2000). The team of researchers participating in this volume, comprising social and health scientists from three different countries, have come together based on these principles. In doing so, we have attempted to go beyond Zelizer's challenge to look also at the impact of the wider social-political context (local, national, and international) on care work for both the workers as well as the recipients of care. We believe that this historically informed multilevel contextualized approach provides a useful framework for conceptualizing care work, and we invite other scholars to embark on other empirical studies to test whether the preliminary findings of our authors hold firm or are in need of revision.

Organization of the Volume

These collaborative chapters grew out of an international workshop held at the University of Victoria, British Columbia, Canada, in the spring of 2006. This workshop brought together students, academics, and health care practitioners from Canada, the United States, and the Nordic countries who are interested in investigating the gendered underpinnings of paid and unpaid care work in formal and informal health care settings in Canada and selected other high-income countries. A particular focus of the workshop was to attempt to unpack the complex interrelationships between gender and *equity* and *dignity* in care work. To this end, workshop participants were asked, first, to provide a comparative framework to think through how gender intersects with other factors to shape the organization of care work and its delivery and, second, to investigate the extent to which the remuneration and recognition of care work, or intimate labour, is a co-requisite of high-quality care.

This volume builds upon these core ideas. In particular, the subsequent set of chapters explores dimensions of the following three central themes that are integral to advancing our understanding of how care work is performed across different settings: (1) the rules and practices that shape the performance of care work or intimate labour are crucial to understanding how care in both formal and informal settings is gendered; (2) the larger policy context in which care work and care delivery are organized is also gendered, and highlights how rural and urban contexts as well as national configurations of the welfare state shape the gendering of paid and unpaid care work; and (3) neoliberal policy debates, under way in Canada and other high-income countries, are focused on enhancing efficiency, and accountability of health and social care systems has taken needed attention away from other crucial policy agendas, in particular how to ensure dignity and equity for both those who receive and those who provide unpaid and paid care work.

The volume is organized into six parts, each dealing with a particular aspect of the complex relationships between gender, care work, and the welfare state. This first part, which includes this opening chapter, is devoted to outlining some of the fundamental conceptual and theoretical considerations that ground an engendered analysis of care work across different societal sectors. This first chapter has outlined the importance of a comparative approach as well as introduced the basic parameters of the central concepts that run throughout the volume. The following conceptual chapter, by Thien and Dolan, focuses more specifically on how different social settings create unique and gendered challenges for both caregivers and recipients of care. Although this chapter provides some general discussion on the role of geography in shaping the contexts in which care work, or intimate labour, is performed and delivered, the particular interest of the authors is on rurality. Specifically, Dolan and Thien focus on how various cultural factors, such as gender ideologies and expectations, converge with more structural factors such as distance, underfunded services, and poverty to create conditions of health disadvantage for rural women.

The second part of this volume deals with the issues surrounding care work in the formal health care sector, that is, paid intimate work in economic organizations. Chapter 3, by Benoit, Wrede, and Einarsdóttir, puts the spotlight squarely on the theme of gender equity in care and care work. Drawing on policy documents and other secondary data sources, the authors highlight recent reforms in health care in Canada, focusing on pregnancy and childbirth, and compare these with developments in two Nordic countries – Finland and Iceland. Their analysis draws attention to the importance of the division of labour in maternity care and the pivotal role played by non-medical, professional groups in meeting the needs of lower-income populations. Even though neoliberal reforms have been identified in Finland, and Iceland is currently facing discontentment among its general practitioners labour force, when investing in preventive primary care these Nordic governments have been prepared to hold on to a non-medical, more equitable vision of how to provide maternity services to their respective populations. The chapter concludes with the suggestion that the collaborative maternity care models recently established in Canada can learn from these developments elsewhere.

The next chapter in Part 2, Chapter 4, by Bourgeault and Wrede, examines the role of working conditions and dignity in understanding the migration patterns of nurses in Canada and Finland. The authors report both similarities and differences between the two countries in this regard, including Finland's greater success at keeping domestic nurse recruitment at a more optimal level across economic ups and downturns, thereby avoiding the kind of acute nursing labour supply crisis that Canada is prone to. The authors also note that internationally implemented neoliberal reforms that changed earlier terms under which nurses worked into a more flexible direction are intricately connected to the devaluing of their intimate labour.

Part 3 shifts the focus away from paid care in economic organizations towards the paid work that occurs in intimate care settings, in particular, the home. In Chapter 5, Purkis, Ceci, and Bjornsdóttir use case studies to compare nursing home care work in Canada and Iceland and demonstrate the strong link between equity and dignity in health care and in home care work. Interestingly, the flexible character of the organization of home care nurse work in Canada prior to the economic retrenchment of the early 1990s, and still the case in Iceland, reflects an organizational ethos more likely to meet the needs of fragile individuals who live at home. Chapter 6 by Martin-Matthews and Sims-Gould presents data on the other side of the relationship – that is, the experiences of recipients, examining the ways in which publicly funded paid labour is provided and negotiated within the private sphere of the home, from the perspectives of clients and families as agents in this process. This chapter draws on data collected as part of a multi-method study of 150 home support workers, seventy-five elderly home care clients and thirty-five family caregivers in British Columbia. Qualitative data are examined in an analysis of social, spatial, temporal, and organizational aspects of the home care experience. The verbatim accounts of the elderly clients are the key focus, with some select comparisons with home support workers and family members, as appropriate. Preliminary analyses of these data suggest some key themes, including the following: protecting vulnerabilities, competing expectations. and the influence of service history. The final chapter in this part, by Eni, presents the standpoint of peer support workers on different Aboriginal reserves in Manitoba. Drawing on original ethnographic research, the author presents a detailed description of the everyday lives of peer support workers and their *bifurcated consciousness,* caught as they are between what their grandmothers and other elders tell them about cultural traditions about how to care for women in their local communities and the federal bureaucratic framework of health care provision imposed by Indian and Northern Affairs Canada.

The fourth part of this volume shifts the focus to unpaid care work in intimate settings. Chapter 8, by Treloar and Funk, looks at the delivery of unpaid care work during a significant life-course event: separation and/or divorce. Funk and Kobayashi, in Chapter 9, move the focus to unpaid caregiving by examining the degree of choice enjoyed by adult children taking care of their aging parents. In Chapter 10, Mackenzie, Brown, Callahan, and Whittington investigate the same issue for grandparents who have primary responsibility for their grandchildren. A common theme running throughout all three of these chapters is that while the voluntary health care work that occurs in informal settings is a key piece of our health care system, the physical and mental health and well-being of family caregivers are negatively affected by the ways in which 'responsibilization,' making people responsible, and familialism in the sociopolitical Canadian context constrain the enactment of care work and the exercise of choice in this work.

Part 5 of the volume moves to examining unpaid care work within economic organizations. This part includes Chapter 11, by Mellow, on the important role of volunteer labour within formal health care organizations, including hospitals, and the significance that both gender, as well as the social undervaluation of such work, play in creating and filling these volunteer positions. The chapter concludes with a discussion of the underlying tension between volunteerism and paid health care providers' struggle for appropriate remuneration examined in earlier in the book. This part concludes with Phillips, Casey, and Leischner on the role of unpaid work in shaping the care available to members of vulnerable populations. The authors' particular interest is in understanding how caring for stigmatized populations, such as people who work in the sex industry, may result in the transfer of stigma to those who perform this kind of care work.

The final part of this volume considers the various implications for public policy that an engendered understanding of care work would entail. Hallgrímsdóttir, Teghtsoonian, Brown, and Benoit discuss the implications of a *gendered* understanding of health care policy as well as of the diverse locations in which the effects of health care policy take place. Chapter 13 highlights the following four current policy trends, each of which have important implications for understanding the gendered dimensions of health care policies and health care work: (1) the downloading of care work from relatively more generously compensated practitioners to those whose skills are less valued and who receive less, if any, financial compensation for their work; (2) deteriorating conditions of health and social care work and their problematic effects; (3) the increased prominence of practices of responsibilization and familialization in health and social care policy; and (4) the different ways that these processes, and the policies shaping them, play out when implemented in the context of populations already stratified in terms of their racialized identity, age, class, and spatial location. The chapter concludes that equity and dignity in access to health care are inseparable from equity and dignity in the economic, social, and organizational conditions under which that care is provided.

Policy Implications

The chapters presented below make a case for scholarship that compares the organization of care work, or intimate labour, in three understudied high-income countries – Canada, Finland, and Iceland. All three countries have hybrid welfare states that have been the subject of structural reforms in health and social care delivery in recent decades and all three are currently under economic duress because of the global economic crisis. However, there are also important differences between these three countries related to the institutional arrangements of the state, their public and social health care systems, and their capacity to weather financial difficulties. In particular, compared with Canada, neoliberal health and social care strategies in Finland and, to a lesser extent, Iceland, have been less intense and also shorter-lived. Continuous government support in Finland and Iceland for publicly funded health and social care and, at the same time, a stronger emphasis on primary care services and democratic professionalism among care professionals have resulted in more opportunities for dignity in health and social care and caregiving work than has been possible to date in Canada. At the same time, while all three countries are facing formidable challenges brought on by the recent global recession, Iceland has been especially hard hit and the future remains open as to how it will recover financially.

Our ultimate aim has been to use cross-national comparison in order to produce contextually sensitive analyses of social policy in neoliberal policy regimes. Such an approach is meant not only to add needed nuance in terms of understanding how the normative assumptions associated with neoliberalism shape social policy but also to give us comparative cases from which we can examine the range of policy possibilities that are available during any given time and in a given sociopolitical context. We discuss policy implications in more detail in the final chapter of the volume. Here we would like to point out that, to be effective in the short and longer term, social policies need to keep two truths in mind: (1) care work or intimate labour takes place in all sectors of society and tends to be undervalued, whether carried out for a wage or unpaid; and (2) the costs associated with providing care work are currently unequally distributed, with girls and women shouldering a greater burden in most domains and those girls, women, and men who are already disadvantaged because of social class, race, immigrant status, age, and/or disability are more likely to work for inadequate wages and without dignity and respect. Social policies that are 'women-friendly' and also sensitive to the intersecting inequalities (Benoit et al., 2009) include, as noted above, universal primary health care, child care, elder care, adequately funded maternal and paternal leaves, and publicly financed care for the physically and mentally disabled. All are of crucial importance to not only care workers and care recipients but arguably for the quality of life of all members of our society.

REFERENCES

Abbott, P., & C. Wallace. (1990). *The Sociology of the Caring Professions.* London: Falmer. Applebaum, H. (1992). *The Concept of Work: Ancient, Medieval, and Modern.* New York: State University of New York Press.

Armstrong, P., & H. Armstrong. (2003). *Wasting Away: The Undermining of Canadian Health Care*. Toronto: Oxford University Press.

Armstrong, P., & K. Laxer. (2006). Precarious work, privatization, and the health care industry: The case of ancillary workers. In L. Vosko, ed., *Precarious Employment: Understanding Labour Market Insecurity in Canada*, 115–40. Montreal and Kingston: McGill-Queen's University Press.

Benoit, C. (2000). *Women, Work and Social Rights: Canada in Historical and Comparative Perspective*. Scarborough: Prentice-Hall Canada.

Benoit, C., & A. Heitlinger. (1998). Women's health care work in comparative perspective: Canada, Sweden and Czechoslovakia/Czech Republic as case examples. *Social Science and Medicine* 47: 1101–11.

Benoit, C., S. Wrede, I. Sandall, J. Bourgeault, E. Van Teijlingen, & R. DeVries. (2005). Understanding the social organisation of maternity care systems: Midwifery as a touchstone. *Sociology of Health and Illness*. 27: 722–37.

Benoit, C., L. Shumka, R. Phillips, H. Hallgrímsdóttir, K. Kobayashi, O. Hankivsky, C. Reid, & E. Brief. (2009. Explaining the health gap between girls and women in Canada. *Sociological Research Online.*14 (5). Retrieved from http://www.socresonline.org.uk/14/5/9.html.

Bock, G. (1991). *Maternity and Gender Policies: Women and the Rise of the European Welfare States, 1880s–1950s*. London and New York: Routledge.

Bolton, S. (2005). Women's work, dirty work: The gynaecology nurse as 'Other.' *Gender, Work and Organization* 12: 169–86.

Bolton, S., & C. Boyd. (2003). Trolley Dolly or skilled emotion manager? Moving on from Hochschild's Managed Heart. *Work, Employment and Society* 17(2): 289–308.

Brenner, N., J. Peck, & N. Theodore. (2010). Variegated neoliberalization. *Global Networks, 10*, 1. Available on line from http://sociology.fas.nyu.edu/docs/IO/222/Brenner_Peck_Theodore_2010_Global_Networks. 10, 182–222.

Brenner, N., J. Peck, & N. Theodore. (In press). After neoliberalization? *Globalizations*. Available on line from http://sociology.fas.nyu.edu/docs/IO/222/Brenner.Peck.Theodore.2010a.pdf.

Coburn, D. (2004). Beyond the income inequality hypothesis: Class, neoliberalism, and health inequalities. *Social Science and Medicine* 58: 41–56.

Daly, M., & C. Rake. (2003). *Gender and the Welfare State: Care, Work and Welfare in Europe and the USA*. Cambridge: Polity.

De Vries, R., S. Wrede, E. van Teijlingen, C. Benoit, & E. Declercq. (2004). Making maternity care: The consequences of culture for health care systems.

In H. Vinken, J. Soeters, & P. Ester, eds., *Comparing Cultures: Dimensions of Culture in a Comparative Perspective,* 209–31. Leiden: Brill Academic.

Diamond, T. (1992). *Making Gray Gold: Narratives of Nursing Home Care.* Chicago: University of Chicago Press.

Durano, M. (2003). The marketisation of social reproduction in the new service-led economy. In *Social Watch Annual Report 2003,* 22–3. Montevideo: Social Watch.

Ehrenreich, B., & A. Hochschild. (2002). *Global Woman: Nannies, Maids and Sex Workers in the New Economy.* New York: Metropolitan Press.

England, P. (2005). Emerging theories of care work. *Annual Review of Sociology* 31: 381–99.

England, P., M. Budig, & N. Folbre. (2002). Wages of virtue: The relative pay of care work. *Social Problems* 49: 455–73.

Esping-Andersen, G. (1989). The three political economies of the welfare state. *Canadian Review of Sociology and Anthropology* 26: 10–36.

Esping-Andersen, G. (1990). *The Three Worlds of Welfare Capitalism.* Princeton: Princeton University Press.

Esping-Andersen, G. (Ed.). (1996). *Welfare States in Transition: National Global Economies.* London: Sage.

Esping-Andersen, G., & W. Kropi. (1987). From poor relief to institutional welfare states: The development of Scandinavian social policy. In R. Erikson, E. Jørgen Hansen, S. Ringen, & H. Uusitalo, eds., *The Scandinavian Model: Welfare States and Welfare Research,* 39–74. New York: M.E. Sharpe.

Folbre, N. (1994). *Who Pays for the Kids? Gender and the Structures of Constraint.* New York: Routledge.

Folbre, N. (1995). Holding hands at midnight: The paradox of caring labor. *Feminist Economics* 1: 73–92.

Folbre, N. (2001). *The Invisible Heart: Economics and Family Values.* New York: New Press.

Freeman, R. (1999). Institutions, states and cultures: Health policy and politics in Europe. In J. Clasen, ed., *Comparative Social Policy: Concepts, Theories and Methods,* 80–94. Oxford: Blackwell.

Gesler, W., & R. Kearns. (2002). *Culture/Place/Health.* London: Routledge.

Glenn, E.N. (1996). From servitude to service work: Historical continuities in the racial division of paid reproductive labor.

Hall, E. (1993). Smiling, deferring and flirting: Doing gender by giving 'good service.' *Work and Occupations* 20: 452–71.

Hantrais, L. (1999). Contextualization in cross-national comparative research. *International Journal of Social Research Methodology* 2: 93–108.

Harvey, D. (2005). *A Brief History of Neoliberalism*. Oxford: Oxford University Press.

Henriksson, L., S. Wrede, & V. Burau. (2006). Understanding professional projects in welfare service work: Revival of old professionalism? *Gender, Work and Organization* 14: 174–92.

Hernes, H. (1987). *Welfare State and Woman Power: Essays in State Feminism*. Oslo: Norwegian University Press.

Hernes, H. (1988). The welfare state citizenship of Scandinavian women. In K. Jones & A. Jonasdóttir, eds., *The Political Interests of Gender*, 187–213. Newbury Park: Sage.

Hochschild, A.R. (1983). *The Managed Heart: Commercialization of Human Feelings*. Berkeley and Los Angeles: University of California Press.

Hodson, R. (2001). *Dignity at Work*. Cambridge: Cambridge University Press.

Jeffrey, P. (2003). Smoothing the waters: Observations on the process of cross-disciplinary research collaboration. *Social Studies of Science* 33: 539–62.

Jones, K. (1990). Citizenship in a woman-friendly polity. *Signs* 15: 781–812.

Leidner, R. (1993). *Fast Food, Fast Talk*. Berkeley and Los Angeles: University of California Press.

Marshall, T.H. (1965). *Class, Citizenship, and Social Development*. New York: Anchor Books.

Marshall, T.H. (1992). Social rights in the twentieth century. In T.H. Marshall & T. Bottomore, eds., *Citizenship and Social Class*, 27–43. London: Pluto Press.

McDaniel, S. (2002a). Women's changing relations to the state and citizenship: Caring and intergenerational relations in globalizing Western democracies. *Canadian Review of Sociology and Anthropology* 39: 125–50.

McDaniel, S. (2002b). Intergenerational interlinkages: Public, family, and work. In D. Cheal, ed., *Aging and Demographic Change in Canadian Context*, 22–71. Toronto: University of Toronto Press.

Mears, A., & W. Finlay. (2005). Not just a paper doll: How models manage bodily capital and why they perform emotional labor. *Journal of Contemporary Ethnography* 34(3): 317–43.

Melin, G. (2000). Pragmatism and self-organization: Research collaboration on the individual level. *Research Policy* 29: 31–40.

Messing, K. (1998). *One Eyed Science: Occupational Health and Women Workers*. Philadelphia: Temple University Press.

O'Connor, J. (1993). Gender, class, and citizenship in the comparative analysis of welfare state regimes: Theoretical and methodological issues. *British Journal of Sociology* 44: 501–18.

O'Connor, J. (1996). From women in the welfare state to gendering welfare state regimes. *Current Sociology* 44: 1–125.

Orloff, A. (1993). Gender and the social rights of citizenship: The comparative analysis of gender relations and welfare states. *American Sociological Review* 58: 303–28.

Owings, A. (2002). *Hey Waitress!* Berkeley and Los Angeles: University of California Press.

Prentice, S., & E. Ferguson. (2000). Volunteerism, gender and the changing welfare state. In S. Neysmith, ed., *Restructuring Caring Labour: Discourse, State Practice, and Everyday Life,* 118–41. Don Mills: Oxford University Press.

Pascall, G. (1986). *Social Policy: A Feminist Analysis.* New York: Tavistock.

Pateman, C. (1988). *The Sexual Contract.* Stanford: Stanford University Press.

Pateman, C. (1989). *The Disorder of Women: Democracy, Feminism and Political Theory.* Cambridge: Polity Press.

Sainsbury, D. (1996). *Gender, Equality and Welfare States.* New York: Cambridge University Press.

Sharma, U., & P. Black. (2001). Look good, feel better: Beauty therapy as emotional labour. *Sociology* 35(4): 913–31.

Stacey, C. (2005). Finding dignity in dirty work: The constraints and rewards of low-wage home care labour. *Sociology of Health and Illness* 27: 831–54.

Wharton, A., & R. Erickson. (1993). Managing emotions on the job and at home: The consequences of multiple emotional roles. *Academy of Management Review* 18: 457–86.

White, L. (2001). Closing the care gap that welfare reform left behind. *Annals of the American Academy of Political and Social Science* 577: 131–43.

Wrede, S., C. Benoit, I. Bourgeault, E. Van Teijlingen, J. Sandall, & R. DeVries. (2006). Decentred comparative research: Context-sensitive analysis of maternal health care. *Social Science and Medicine* 63: 2986–97.

Zelizer, V.A. (2002). How care counts. *Contemporary Sociology* 31: 115–19.

Zelizer, V.A. (2007). Caring everywhere. Keynote Address, Conference on Intimate Labours, University of California, Santa Barbara, 4–6 Oct.

Zemke, R., & D. Schaaf. (1989). *The Service Edge.* New York: New American Library.

Zimmerman, M., J. Litt, & C. Bose. (2006). *Global Dimensions of Care work and Gender.* Stanford: Stanford University Press.

2 Emplacing Care: Understanding Care Work across Social and Spatial Contexts

DEBORAH THIEN AND HOLLY DOLAN

Health may be a 'highly individualised project' but it is also a gendered one.

— Doel and Segrott (2003)

Mainstream health and policy discourses now commonly acknowledge that where one lives affects how well one lives (Lalonde 1974; Romanow 2002). A recent Canadian study, *How Healthy Are Rural Canadians* (Canadian Institute for Health Information [CIHI] 2006), identified that as distance from an urban centre increases, health decreases, demonstrating that geography matters to health status and that geographical and socioeconomic disadvantages work together in complex ways to create negative health conditions for rural people. Rural women, in particular, are especially vulnerable to negative health conditions for they have been found to be less healthy compared with their urban counterparts as well as with rural men (CIHI 2006). In one Canadian study, mortality was more than 20% higher among rural women aged between 20 to 64 years than for urban women over a ten-year period (DesMeules et al. 2003). Accidental deaths and chronic diseases, such as diabetes and heart disease, contributed significantly to this rural/ urban health gradient. Although women in general still earn less than men, and are more likely to be poor and to be raising children alone in poverty (Lochhead 2000; Statistics Canada 2006), rural women have lower labour force participation rates, have higher fertility rates, experience more domestic violence, smoke more and are exposed to more second-hand smoke, have less postsecondary education, and tend to be poor compared with their urban counterparts (Leipert 2005; CIHI 2006). Among rural women, some are especially vulnerable, including

Aboriginal, elderly, and disabled women (Stout, Kipling, & Stout 2001; Adelson 2005). In Canada, Aboriginal women die younger, and suffer higher rates of violence, substance abuse, suicide, and chronic diseases (e.g., arthritis, hypertension, heart problems, diabetes) compared with non-Aboriginal women; this health gradient, to some degree, stems from the significant challenges of living in rural and northern communities (Stout, Kipling, & Stout 2001).

A determinants-of-health framework, widely accepted in Canadian health policy, asserts that a range of conditions and factors influence human health. In Canada, Lalonde (1974) first identified the broad categories of human biology, environment, lifestyle, and health care systems as the key factors in determining human health. Since then, these determinants have been expanded on and formally adopted by the Public Health Agency of Canada (PHAC), which endorses twelve health determinants – income and social status, social support networks, education and literacy, employment/working conditions, social environments, physical environments, personal health practices and coping skills, healthy child development, biology and genetic endowment, health services, gender, and culture – as part of a population health approach that informs the development of public policy in Canada (PHAC 2001). An understanding of the role of these determinants on health is not uncomplicated, and research activity continues to offer both compositional and contextual explanations for health inequalities across multiple scales, including more recent attention to the contribution of characteristics of place and space to health status at the local or neighbourhood level (e.g., Kawachi & Berkman 2003; Cummins et al. 2005; CIHI 2006; Wilson et al. 2009).

Evidence indicates that rural contexts pose distinct challenges that can limit rural women's access to some of the multiple health determinants to create significant differences between rural and urban women's health. However, research examining the interplay between women's health and place is still limited (Leipert 2005), and population health research tends to overemphasize socioeconomic determinants. Income, education, access to health care, and health behaviours are prioritized at the expense of other factors, such as the gendered nature of work (paid and unpaid) and working conditions; regulatory and institutional environments; and issues related to racism, discrimination, and stigmatization associated with gender, age, and class, among others; as well as the interconnections between these factors (Benoit & Shumka 2009). We argue that health research and policy would benefit from adopting ideas from geographical and feminist scholarship that link gender, geography, and health.

Feminist geographer Liz Bondi draws inspiration from psychotherapeutic and humanistic analyses of therapeutic relationships to argue that 'the crucial importance of relationships in all kinds of care is widely recognizsed but generally under-theorised' (2008: 251). Drawing from relational theories of *place* and *gender*, as articulated in feminist and geographical literature (e.g., Bondi 2003, 2008; Massey 1994, 2004, 2005; Thien 2005a; see also Conradson (2005) on conceptualizing the relational self and Berg's (2008) extension of this framework to an analysis of racialization), we offer a nuanced framework that builds on insights of health determinants as explanations while situating women as recipients and providers of intimate labour within a 'relations of care' context. In this chapter, we introduce a relational framework and discuss how this theoretical modality contributes to a better understanding of rural women's health and well-being in the context of neoliberalism and the subsequent reorganization of work, including the ubiquitously feminized spaces of intimate labour, in Canadian society. Although we position our framework within a neoliberalist Canadian context, it is applicable to other high-income countries addressed in this volume. Like Canada, Finland, Sweden, Norway, and the United Kingdom have experienced recent neoliberalist reforms and global market pressures that have exacerbated inequalities in health and care access, including geographical disparities (Vilhjalmsson 2005; Huber et al. 2008), with specific gender implications (Suominen-Taipale et al. 2006). The use of a relational framework ensures continued attention to the ways that contemporary political and ideological changes interact with the specificities of place and gender relations to affect conditions of dignity for women as recipients and providers of care, and provides direction for policy (Benoit & Hallgrímsdóttir, this volume).

Globalization, Restructuring, and Health

As noted in Chapter 1, globalization, which is at once a complex and substantive process with material outcomes, has generally involved the exposure of national markets to international competitive pressures. The response by industry has been to export jobs to low-wage countries and to intensify and cheapen the extraction of labour from workers, achieved through significant technological changes and efficiencies, the concentration of production to fewer centres, the introduction of new management strategies within industries, and industrial outsourcing and downsizing (Philips & Philips 2000).

Alongside its material manifestations, globalization is a neoliberal discourse adopted and deployed by governments and used as an imperative for restructuring (Neysmith & Chen 2002: 245). Neoliberal discourse dictates that markets are the best and most efficient allocators of resources in production and distribution, that societies are composed of autonomous individuals (producers and consumers) motivated primarily by material or economic considerations, and that competition is a major market vehicle for innovation. It essentially advocates an adherence to a market economy and market-oriented society (Rose & Miller 1992; Coburn 2001) and 'a retreat from the welfare states' publicly funded commitments to equality and social justice' and 'views citizenship as consumption and economic production' (Green 1996: 112). Restructuring is therefore a response by governments entrenched in neoliberal philosophy to globalization (including the threat of capital mobility), and the pressures of international institutions. In this chapter, we use 'restructuring' broadly to represent the material and symbolic outcomes of both globalization and government policy decisions (i.e., retrenchment of the welfare state) that embody a neoliberalist philosophy (Hallgrímsdóttir et al. this volume). Globalization and restructuring together have radically exacerbated international and national inequalities and reconfigured the social fabric of communities globally (Naples 1997).

In rural economies that are often dominated by a single industry, dependent on a natural resource, and in some cases, isolated, the impacts of these restructuring processes are manifest spatially and compounded. Over the past decade and more, Canadian rural communities have experienced significant job losses, particularly in manufacturing and primary industries. These jobs are often the best and perhaps the only 'good' jobs available in rural communities. When industries downsize or close altogether, 'good' replacement jobs are difficult to find, as often there are few employers and a large reserve of unemployed workers. This has led to high unemployment, underemployment, and 'occupational skidding,' a process whereby people are pushed into work that is lower paid, often part-time, and with limited fringe benefits (Leach & Winson 1995; Leach 2000; Neis et al. 2001; Dolan et al. 2005).

At the same time, rural communities have seen closures of federal services (e.g., post offices, employment insurance offices) and provincial services (e.g., child and family support services), a result of government withdrawal from social programs and the deliberate reduction in support payments under national debt reduction and efficiency ideologies (Hanlon & Halseth 2005). Also, since the mid-1990s the Canadian federal government and provinces through health care reforms began downsizing health care services, broadly characterized in rural communities by the centralization of services (e.g., maternity care, rural hospital, bed and clinic closures), the privatization of services (e.g., more fee-for-service models of care), and the shifting responsibility for services to the community level (e.g., deinstitutionalization of care) (Armstrong et al. 2001).

Although impacts of restructuring are not specific to rural populations, the characteristics of rural communities (such as limited job opportunities and lower population densities, together with problems of distance and access to good jobs and incomes, formal education, and child care) can significantly exacerbate problems and rural – urban disparities (Hanlon & Halseth 2005). Infrequent, irregular, and limited health services and lack of access to care services locally is a reality for most rural Canadians. For example, in 1993 Canadian rural residents lived on average approximately 10 km away from a physician compared with an estimated 2 km for residents in larger urban areas and over two-thirds of the population in northern and remote regions lived more than 100 km away from a physician (Ng et al. 1999). Nonetheless, health care reforms are further exacerbating significant rural distances to travel for care, which is costly, inconvenient, and even dangerous given precarious environmental conditions, especially in the north (Leipert & Reutter 2005a, 2005b; McBain & Morgan 2005; Simpson 2005).

Many believe that women bear the brunt of neoliberal restructuring, including health care reform, and that restructuring could not be possible without taking advantage of gender inequalities and women's paid and unpaid care work (Naples 1997; Neysmith & Chen 2002). Much like the larger neoliberalist agenda, which places responsibility for societal problems, such as poverty, in the hands of individuals, rather than as a consequence of political processes and policies pursued by federal and provincial governments (Neysmith & Chen 2002), such health care reforms reassign care onto individuals and families. Discourses such as 'closer to home' and 'home is best' reinforce a transfer of major responsibility for care from the state to the private domain (Anderson 2000) and rely on care policies that attempt to invoke a sense of familial responsibility for dependants (Milligan 2000). This often means a relocation of caregiving from institutional settings to the domestic sphere, 'blurring the boundaries' between public institutional spaces and domestic spaces, relying more heavily on an existing network of informal caring and support, and transferring or downloading intimate care work onto individuals and families (Milligan 2000; Botting et al. 2001; Funk & Kobayashi, this volume). For those families with limited social support networks, or inequitable labour divisions, this can result in 'compulsory altruism' a role more likely adopted by women (Armstrong & Armstrong 2001).

From a determinants-of-health perspective, restructuring impacts population health both through its effect on the social determinants of health, for example, effects on the distribution of wealth, and through its effect on the organization of the health care system, for example, reduced access to publicly funded health care (Coburn 2001). However, given pervasive gender ideologies, which place women at a socioeconomic disadvantage to men and perpetuate gender inequalities in terms of domestic and familial responsibilities, restructuring renders women more vulnerable to the impacts of restructuring, including worsening health status (Spitzer 2005). In rural communities, gender and geography intersect to have particular consequences for rural women, and these consequences are further exacerbated by restructuring. In the following section, we introduce a relations-of-care framework as a way to better understand and theorize intimate labour across social and spatial contexts; to understand the potential health implications of restructuring for women in rural places; and to develop a framework for actively improving health status.

Relations of Care: Replacing the Frame on Gender, Health, Care, and Rurality

Recent geographical research (e.g., Massey 2004, 2005; Conradson 2005; Valentine 2006) indicates that the experience of place is co-implicated with identity. A relational sense of place posits places as dynamic entities resulting from the multiple possible connections and disconnections, flows of people, ideas, and capital that extend within and outwards from any particular place. This understanding is linked to the relational nature of identities (such that identity is always constituted in relation to an 'other') – a theoretical perspective that has gained momentum through feminist scholars (Butler 1990, 1997; Probyn 2003). These insights underscore the importance of identities as produced in and by particular spaces, such as the home, church, community, landscape, or workplace. Paying attention to the way that identities emerge in relation to place begins to reveal the ways that power operates in and through particular spaces to systematically reproduce particular inequalities (Valentine 2006). Rather than attempting to explain health inequalities by adding up isolated, separate, and fixed forms of oppression such as gender, race, class, or place (e.g., rurality), we seek to understand these as always ongoing and dynamic relations that are interwoven, collectively constitutive, and that work in complex ways to give particular form to women's everyday life experiences (Ng 2000: 238; see also: Massey 2005; Bondi 2008).

Sex as a singular category is often used in population health research as a proxy for 'gender.' It is intended to represent more than simply 'biological (sex) differences' between women and men, identifying inequalities in access to health determinants between and among women and men. Such approaches fall short of further appreciating the ways in which gender is both materially and symbolically experienced and reproduced to shape women's health. Gender is more productively understood as a relationship (Haraway 1997) constituted by myriad ongoing 'processes whereby sex differences are made real or objectified as differences between men and women, and where these differences are valorized in differential ways' and 'in particular places' (Ng 2000: 237). These processes of differentiation and valorization lead to the creation of particular feminized subjectivities, wherein, for example, women's domestic or caring work is perceived as an extension of women's 'natural' abilities, and furthermore, to the devaluing of these 'reproductive' skills in contrast to the valuing of men's productive labour (Thien 2005b). In this way, caring work, whether paid (e.g., nursing, child care, home care) or unpaid (e.g., caring for dependent children, parents) is portrayed as 'women's work,' and as such is of less value, materially and symbolically, compared with 'men's work' (Benoit & Hallgrímsdóttir, this volume).

In a relational frame, rurality becomes more than a material determinant of health that distances women from accessing health determinants, but signals a series of specificities of power and oppression co-implicated with complex gender and other identities. Place (rurality) alters the meaning of gender, while gender makes meanings of place, a set of relations that affects women's health. For example, rural spaces are conceived of as 'natural,' 'peaceful,' and 'caring' places. The countryside is represented as an essentialized female space, in opposition to a 'man-made' city (Valentine 1997: 109), and as such is understood as a place of warmth and close association, a particularly gendered rendering. Rural inhabitants may live at a distance from neighbours, but are presumed to be socially more proximate than urban dwellers (Parr 2002). While the experience of distance may limit or restrict health care options, the experience of a feminized proximity is assumed to engender close and caring relations (Thien 2005b). Caring, embodied in material and symbolic ways by women, dictates we 'care first for, and have our first responsibilities towards, those nearest in' (Massey 2004: 9). Thus, women's care roles extend beyond the domestic and familial realm to include the reiteration of a feminized rural landscape contingent on the reproduction of neighbourliness and intergenerational stability (Thien 2005b). This rural idyll is 'instrumental in shaping and sustaining patriarchal gender relations and ... incorporates both consciously and unconsciously, strong expectations concerning aspects of household strategy and gender roles and consequently impacts on the nature of women's experience within the rural community' (Little & Austin 1996: 102). These gender relations are perpetuated and sustained by economic development based on powerful patriarchal values that place men as the full-time breadwinners, especially in rural resource-based economies in forestry, fishing, mining, and agriculture, and dominant discourses that simultaneously assign intimate labour as women's work and marginalize women's intimate labour in relation to men's productive work (Luxton 1980; Leipert 1998; Neis et al. 2001).

Because rural women carry out most of the unpaid and paid care work/intimate labour (Morris 2002), they have the most to lose under health care reforms (Armstrong et al. 2003). Any changes that reduce access to health care will disproportionately impact rural women who already access care less frequently, rarely seek health care services related to prevention, and are more likely to delay seeking care until they are very ill (Centres of Excellence for Women's Health 2004). Because women are more likely to be responsible for familial care, such as making arrangements for doctors, and taking children, elderly parents, and other dependants to appointments, they are more likely to travel long distances to access medical services and to seek necessary financial resources for these activities, adding to their stress of daily living and increasing their vulnerability to vehicle accidents and other health consequences (Leipert & Reutter 2005b). In addition, women are still more likely to lose time from their 'paid' work for personal and family responsibilities and to work part-time because of child care or other responsibilities compared with men (Statistics Canada 2006). In rural communities where job opportunities are increasingly precarious and insecure (as a result of restructuring), increased distances (and time) to access care services, and increasing burdens associated with family care can add additional stress to women's lives with potential negative health consequences (Skillen et al. 2001).

Not only is rural women's access to care constrained under reforms (e.g., diminishing access to medical services for themselves and their families for which they have primary responsibility), but they are increasingly called upon to meet the care needs left behind by formal health care restructuring. A relational framework challenges us to examine more closely the material and symbolic patterning of restructuring across rural landscapes and among rural populations. In rural communities, where traditional gender roles are more entrenched, an increasing reliance on 'familialism' by the health care sector translates to an increasing reliance on the unpaid intimate labour of women and, consequently, increasing risks to women's health and well-being (see Treloar & Funk, this volume). However, despite intimate care responsibilities assumed by women, women still often report encountering disrespect when dealing with health professionals (Anderson et al. 2000); attention to caring about and for health is too frequently devalued as 'women's work' within a society that devalues women (Robinson 1999). In rural contexts, the effects of restructuring are shaped by conditions and ideologies of place and mediated by gender relations. Rural restructuring has meant significant employment changes (e.g., job losses, increased part-time work and temporary contracts), particularly in male-dominated 'good' occupations (e.g., manufacturing, primary resource industries), and has expanded the low-wage and part-time service economy, which is overrepresented by women (Philips & Philips 2000). Women have lost jobs in manufacturing and primary industries; some argue that because of rural masculinist values that continue to position men as natural 'breadwinners,' women are particularly disadvantaged because they can be pushed out of these good jobs first or excluded altogether and left with few options but to work in the service sector (Halseth & Lo 1999; Winson & Leach 2002). Female-dominated 'good' jobs have also been affected by restructuring, particularly in social services and health care – an intentional target of neoliberalist reforms (Benoit & Hallgrímsdóttir 2008). Approximately 95% of Canadian rural registered nurses (RNs) are female (CIHI 2002), and their absolute numbers have decreased relative to absolute increases in rural populations (MacLead et al. 2004). Restructuring leaves both women and men with fewer options for good paid work, with reduced incomes and/or with deteriorating working conditions (Benoit & Hallgrímsdóttir 2008); however, for women, in a neoliberal-ist climate, this is matched with increased amounts and kinds of labour (including caring labour) as women's paid work is increasingly called upon to fill the income gap left behind by restructured male work. Recent research in restructured Canadian rural communities found that women experienced increased stress due to family income instabil-ity and changing gender roles as women assumed more responsibility for securing the household income while maintaining traditional care roles (Ommer 2007). Women's paid work has always been important to family and community economic and social development, but it was generally seen as supplementary to men's employment, of lower pay and quality; meanwhile, women maintained primary responsibility for unpaid domestic care (Naples 1997). Unfortunately, women's increased economic responsibility is not necessarily matched with an increase in the availability of good jobs and a reduction in unpaid care respon-sibilities. In 2001 adult women (15 years of age and older; rural and urban combined) still devoted more hours to unpaid household work and child care (21% and 16% respectively) compared with men (8% and 7% respectively) (Statistics Canada 2003). Furthermore, limited employment opportunities for rural women and extra domestic bur-dens together may restrict women from accessing good replacement jobs (Leach & Winson 1995) or may force some women to seek employ-ment further from home. Although evidence remains limited, women's paid workloads appear to be increasing under restructuring while they maintain primary domestic responsibilities, but in compressed time, with less support, greater stress, and less time for their own leisure activities and self-care.

A relational framework exposes the ways that contemporary politi-cal and ideological changes interact with place and gender relations to affect women as recipients and providers of care, and it also miti-gates against the uncritical use of essentialist theories of oppression; these too readily assume a base identity – arguably white, heterosex-ual, able-bodied, male – to which all other identities are added (Naples 1997; Valentine 2006). We cannot understand, for example, an Aborigi-nal woman's experience, by simply adding the experiences of being a (white) woman to the experiences of Aboriginality because 'the expe-rience of race alters the meaning of gender' (Valentine 2006: 13). In a relational framework, gender, race, class, age, and so on are not simply concrete social relations (although they may manifest in tangible ways) but are contingent on relations and enmeshed in each other such that they produce specific effects; thus, it is not only the material disadvantages of certain subjectivities, such as poverty or race, that are health limiting (e.g., poverty limits access to material health determinants) but also (as Phillips et al., illustrate elsewhere in this volume) the embodiment of the social labelling or stigmatization of 'being poor' or 'being Aboriginal' or 'being female' that adversely affects health experiences.

Clearly, then, women's experiences of distance in the context of health and care in non-urban places occur in relation to multiple other forms of marginality, and not all rural women will have the same experiences, of course. Health care privatization means that many services, such as physiotherapy, occupational therapy, ambulatory assistance, and maternity care, among others, are increasingly unavailable or pay-for-service. These additional costs may be especially problematic for women, because women more often live in poverty, raise children alone in poverty, and represent a greater proportion of the population living alone on fixed incomes, such as the elderly and disabled (Lochhead 2000; Statistics Canada 2006).

For women on social assistance, living in poverty, or in unequal power relationships, access to health care may be especially difficult and/or costly, for example, when public transportation is limited or non-existent, which is not uncommon in rural and remote communities (Milligan 2000; Simpson 2005). A relational framework pays attention to the ways that gender relations may render some rural women more vulnerable to isolation and exposes how the effects of restructuring can be mediated by gender relations that, for example, assign activities such as driving as men's responsibility, particularly in older generations, and potentially further isolate women within rural communities.

A relational framework, therefore, recognizes that identities are formed by and reproduced in specific spaces and that power operates within these spaces to systematically reinforce dominant discourses that can exclude certain socially recognizable groups such as women (Valentine 2006: 19). Such a framework pays attention to how decision and policy makers often do not recognize their power to define 'needs' in relation to their own needs, and therefore render invisible the ways that dominant discourses and practices subordinate marginalized groups, such as women, and especially poor and uneducated women and ethnic minorities, within communities and within the health care system. Dominant rural ideologies that assign familial work as women's domain and a relative lack of employment opportunities, place women as secondary actors in the labour force and in politics; they are marginalized in their own communities and distanced from the sites of political and economic power within the regional or national economy (Reed 2005). Women's marginalization is reinforced by gendered expectations and the material and spatial effects of power intersect to create women's health inequalities. Nevertheless, while all rural women may experience the challenges of geography – experiences that are shaped and reinforced by gendered ideologies that can marginalize women, materially and symbolically, and render them vulnerable to poor health – some are in 'greater peril' (Leipert 2005: 113). Complicating the analysis, rural women's identities and health experiences may in part be shaped by their consistency with rural and gender ideologies about women's domestic and care responsibilities (Little 1994; Little & Austin 1996). What is acceptable to women in terms of their behaviours, attitudes, and assumptions can often stem from powerful expectations of femininity, including motherhood and a 'womanly' identity within a rural community (Little & Austin 1996). Such expectations of family responsibility and intimate labour, however, may contradict the economic and social realities of rural women's lives (Thien 2005c). Women may find themselves emotionally conflicted as they feel pressured to take on full unpaid intimate domestic responsibilities, and at the same time increasingly contribute to the financial stability of their family. The consequences of this bind lead to increased stress and mental hardship without a corresponding respect for this 'intimate labour' (Benoit & Hallgrímsdóttir, this volume).

With mounting evidence that unpaid intimate labour increases the risk of mortality and morbidity (Lee et al. 2003), and because 'care' work remains central to personal and cultural gender identities (Thien 2005a), rural women are especially vulnerable to poor health under restructuring. A relational framework exposes how rural restructuring impacts are both reflected in gender divisions and, at the same time, determined by them (Leach 2000) and gives meaning to why some women are seemingly unable and/or unwilling to give up care responsibilities regardless of the emotional, physical, or financial costs (Spitzer 2005).

Summary and Conclusions

A relational framework is more than a theoretical positioning. It reflects how women's lives are embedded in places that are not only sites of economic production, but also are places of social relations (Massey 1994; Tigges et al. 1998), and it is not just paid work (primarily male work) that is restructured, but all forms of women's work (paid and unpaid), including 'relations of care' (Leach 2000). We have demonstrated how relational aspects of women's lives have material consequences for their health and well-being as recipients of care and as the overdetermined providers of care, and further, we have explored how globalization and restructuring can operate in relation to gender and rurality to further widen health inequalities in rural contexts (Neysmith & Chen 2002). The analysis highlights how other forms of marginality (e.g., class, race, age, ability) are not discrete experiences, but are instead nodes in networks of relations, which shape women's experiences of restructuring and render them especially vulnerable to deteriorating health in specific places.

However, the understandings that relational analysis provides must be brought to bear in the policy arena. Without contributing to concrete shifts in social and political contexts, the value of this framework is diminished. We identify two implications of this relational framework for health and care policy. First, a relational analysis demands a move away from conceptualizing intimate labour and its provision as simply 'women's issues.' To understand experiences of care as taking place within a set of relations is to understand 'women' not as a universal identity set against a universal 'man'; instead, these gendered identities are relational, a reconfiguring that underlines both the specificities of experience, and our diversity. The shift away from a universal 'woman' allows for the loosening of the overdetermined association of women with care. If understandings of care are broadened to encompass relationships within a global context (Massey 1994), care is no longer simply assigned to the province of women, but becomes a collective responsibility (Hallgrímsdóttir et al., this volume). This is not an attempt to depoliticize care (we suggest such depoliticizing is the consequence of a health determinants framework which presumes a neutral backdrop against which all health is measured) nor to devalue connectivity or caring relations; rather, it is an appeal for re-politicizing health and care policy, making explicit the ways that power and power relations, including relations of gender and care, reinforce and (re)produce material and symbolic spaces of power and oppression. Second, we suggest a relational framework invites renewed attention to participatory and/or collaborative policy-making models by directing attention towards the complexity of women's narratives and demonstrating how these are inextricable from wider discourses of gender, health, and place.

In conclusion, the relational model, by emphasising the complexities of identity, and underscoring the ways in which power is implicated in relations of health and place, makes explicit the multiple realities women experience. Not all women will have the same experiences of restructuring; nor will all women have the same experiences of gender. We suggest this shift to a relational analysis leads to a more accurate reflection of women's complex positions within a relations of care context, offers direction for future policy work, and ultimately provides a better understanding of, and more equitable access to, health and well-being for all women. These are critical steps towards ensuring conditions of dignity for those who work and care in rural areas.

ACKNOWLEDGMENT

Adapted, with permission from the Canadian Public Health Association, from the following article by H. Dolan and D. Thien (2008), 'Relations of Care: A Framework for Placing Women and Health in Rural Communities,' *Canadian Journal of Public Health* 99 (Supplement 2): S38–S42.

REFERENCES

Adelson, N. (2005). The embodiment of inequity: Health disparities in Aboriginal Canada. *Canadian Journal of Public Health* 96 (Suppl. 2): S45–S61.

Anderson, J. (2000). Gender, 'race,' poverty, health and discourses of health reform in the context of globalization: A postcolonial feminist perspective in policy research. *Nursing Inquiry* 7: 220–9.

Anderson, L., T. Healy, B. Herringer, B. Isaac, & T. Perry. (2000). *Out in the Cold: Barriers to Health Care for Lesbians in Northern Communities.* Prince George, B.C.: Centre of Excellence for Women's Health.

Armstrong, P., & H. Armstrong. (2001). Women, privatization and health care reform: The Ontario case. In P. Armstrong, C. Amaratunga, J. Bernier, K. Grant, A. Pederson, & K. Willson, eds., *Exposing Privatization: Women and Health Care Reform in Canada,* 163–215. Aurora: Garamond Press.

Armstrong, P., M. Boscoe, B. Clow, K. Grant, A.Pederson, & K. Willson. (2003). *Reading Romanow: The Implications of the Final Report of the Commission on the*

Future of Health Care in Canada for Women. Toronto: National Coordinating Group on Health Care Reform and Women.

Armstrong, P., C. Amaratunga, J. Bernier, K. Grant, A. Pederson, & K. Willson. (Eds.). (2001). *Exposing Privatization: Women and Health Care Reform in Canada.* Aurora: Garamond Press.

Benoit, C., & H. Hallgrímsdóttir. (2008). Engendering research on care and care work across different social contexts. *Canadian Journal of Public Health* 99 (Suppl. 2): S7–S10.

Benoit, C., & L. Shumka. (2009). *Gendering the Health Determinants Framework: Why Girls' and Women's Health Matters: A Primer on Women's Health.* Vancouver: Michael Smith Foundation for Health Research.

Berg, A.J. (2008). Silence and articulation, whiteness, racialization and feminist memory work. *NORA: Nordic Journal of Women's Studies* 16(4): 213–27.

Bondi, L. (2003). Empathy and identification: Conceptual resources for feminist fieldwork. *ACME* 2(1): 64–76.

Bondi, L. (2008). On the relational dynamics of caring: A psychotherapeutic approach to emotional and power dimensions of women's care work. *Gender Place and Culture* 15(3): 249–65.

Botting, I., B. Neis, L. Kealey, & S. Solberg, (2001). Health restructuring and privatization from women's perspective in Newfoundland and Labrador. In P. Armstrong, C. Amaratunga, J. Bernier, K. Grant, A. Pederson, & K. Willson, eds., *Exposing Privatization: Women and Health Care Reform in Canada*, 49–93. Aurora: Garamond Press.

Butler, J. (1990). *Gender, Trouble: Feminism and the Subversion of Identity.* New York: Routledge.

Butler, J. (1997). *The Psychic Life of Power: Theories in Subjection.* Stanford: Stanford University Press.

Canadian Institute for Health Information (CIHI). (2002). *Supply and Distribution of Registered Nurses in Rural and Small Town Canada 2000.* Ottawa: Author.

Canadian Institute for Health Information (CIHI). (2006). *How Healthy Are Rural Canadians? An Assessment of Their Health Status and Health Determinants.* Ottawa: Author.

Centres of Excellence for Women's Health. (2004). Canada's health system failing women in rural and remote regions. *Network* 7(2/3): 3–5.

Coburn, D. (2001). Health, health care and neoliberalism. In H. Armstrong, P. Armstrong, & D. Coburn, eds., *Unhealthy Times: Political Economy Perspectives on Health and Care in Canada*, 45–65. Don Mills: Oxford University Press.

Conradson, D. (2005). Landscape, care and the relational self: Therapeutic encounters in rural England. *Health and Place* 11(4): 337–48.

Cummins, S., M. Stafford, S. Macintyre, M. Marmot, & A. Ellaway. (2005). Neighbourhood environment and its association with self-rated health: Evidence from Scotland and England. *Journal of Epidemiology and Community Health* 59: 207–13.

DesMeules, M., D. Manual, & R. Cho. (2003). Mortality, life and health expectancy of Canadian women. In M. DesMeules & D. Stewart, eds., *Women's Health Surveillance Report: A Multidimensional Look at the Health of Canadian Women*, 17–18. Ottawa: CIHI.

Doel, M., & J. Segrott. (2003). Self, health and gender: Complementary and alternative medicine in the British mass media. *Gender, Place, and Culture* 10(2): 131–44.

Dolan, A., M. Taylor, B. Rosemary Ommer, J. Eyles, D. Schneider, & B. Montevecchi. (2005). Restructuring and health in Canadian coastal communities. *Ecohealth* 2: 1–15.

Green, J. (1996). Resistance is possible. *Canadian Journal of Woman Studies* 16(3): 112–15.

Halseth, G., & J. Lo. (1999). New voices in the debate: The Quesnel women's resource centre and sustainable community development. *Forestry Chronicle* 75: 799–804.

Hanlon, N., & G. Halseth. (2005). The greying of resource communities in northern British Columbia: Implications for health care delivery in already under-serviced communities. *Canadian Geographer* 49(1): 1–24.

Haraway, D. (1997). *Modest Witness @ Second Millennium. FemaleMan_Meets_ OncoMouse: Feminism and Technoscience.* New York and London: Routledge.

Huber, M., A. Staniciole, J. Bremner, & K. Wahlbeck. (2008). *Quality in and Equality of Access to Healthcare Services.* Brussels: Director General for Employment Social Affairs and Equal Opportunities, European Commission.

Kawachi, I., & L. Berkman. (2003). *Neighborhoods and Health.* Oxford: Oxford University Press.

Lalonde, M. (1974). *A New Perspective on the Health of Canadians.* Ottawa: Ministry of Supply and Services.

Leach, B. (2000). Transforming rural livelihoods: Gender work and restructuring in three Ontario communities. In S. Neysmith, ed., *Restructuring Caring Labour: Discourse, State Practice, and Everyday Life,* 209–25. Toronto: Oxford University Press.

Leach, B., & A. Winson. (1995). Bringing globalization down to earth: Restructuring and labour in rural communities. *Canadian Review of Sociology and Anthropology* 32(3): 342–64.

Lee, S., G. Colditz, L. Berkman, & I. Kawachi. (2003). Caregiving and risk of coronary heart disease in U.S. women: A prospective study. *American Journal of Preventative Medicine* 24(2): 113–19.

Leipert, B. (1998). *Northern Voices: Health, Community and Economic Perspectives in Northern British Columbia*. Prince George: University of Northern British Columbia.

Leipert, B. (2005). Rural women's health issues in Canada: An overview and implications for policy and research. *Canadian Woman Studies* 24(4): 109–16.

Leipert, B., & L. Reutter. (2005a). Developing resilience: How women maintain their health in northern geographically isolated settings. *Qualitative Health Research* 15(1): 45–65.

Leipert, B., & L. Reutter. (2005b). Women's health in northern British Columbia: The role of geography and gender. *Canadian Journal of Rural Medicine* 10(4): 241–53.

Little, J. (1994). Gender relations and the rural labor process. In T. Marsden, P. Lowe, & S. Whatmore, eds., *Gender and Rurality*, 335–42. London: David Fulton.

Little, J., & P. Austin. (1996). Women and the rural idyll. *Journal of Rural Studies* 12: 101–12.

Lochhead, C. (2000). *The Dynamics of Women's Poverty in Canada*. Ottawa: Status of Women Canada.

Luxton, M. (1980). *More than a Labour of Love: Three Generations of Women's Work in the Home*. Toronto: Women's Press.

MacLeod, M., J. Kulig, N. Stewart, J.R. Pitblado, & M. Knock. (2004).The nature of nursing practice in rural and remote Canada. *Canadian Nurse* 100(6): 27–31.

Massey, D. (1994). *Space, Place and Gender*. Minneapolis: University of Minnesota Press.

Massey, D. (2004). Geographies of responsibility. *Geografiska Annaler* Series B 86: 5–18.

Massey, D. (2005). *For Space*. London: Sage.

McBain, L., & D. Morgan. (2005). Telehealth, geography and jurisdiction: Issues of healthcare delivery in northern Saskatchewan. *Canadian Woman Studies* 24(4): 221–4.

Milligan, C. (2000). 'Bearing the burden': Towards a restructured geography of caring. *Area* 32(1): 49–58.

Morris, M. (2002). *Gender-Sensitive Home and Community Caregiving Research: Synthesis Paper*. Ottawa: Health Canada.

Naples, N. (1997). Contested needs: Shifting the standpoint on rural economic development. *Feminist Economics* 3(2): 63–98.

Neis, B., B. Grzetic, & M. Pigeon. (2001). *From Fish Plant to Nickel Smelter: Health Determinants and the Health of Newfoundland's Women Fish and Shellfish Producers in an Environment of Restructuring.* Toronto: National Network on Environments and Women's Health (NNEWH) and St John's: Centres of Excellence for Women's Health Program, Newfoundland.

Neysmith, S., & X. Chen. (2002). Understanding how globalization and restructuring affect women's lives: Implications for comparative policy analysis. *International Journal of Social Welfare* 11: 243–53.

Ng, E., R. Wilkins, J. Pole, & O. Adams. (1999). How far to the nearest physician? *Rural and Small Town Canada Analysis Bulletin* 1(5). Ottawa: Minister of Industry.

Ng, R. (2000). Restructuring gender, race, and class relations: The case of garment workers and labour adjustment. In S. Neysmith, ed., *Restructuring Caring Labour: Discourse, State, Practice, and Everyday Life,* 226–45. Toronto: Oxford University Press.

Ommer, R.E. (Ed.). (2007). *Coasts under Stress: Understanding Restructuring and the Social-Ecological Health of Coastal Communities.* Montreal and Kingston: McGill-Queen's University Press.

Parr, H. (2002). *Rural Madness: Culture, Society and Space in Rural Geographies of Mental Health.* Los Angeles: Association of American Geographers.

Philips, P., & E. Philips. (2000). *Women and Work: Inequality in the Canadian Labour Market.* Toronto: Lorimer.

Probyn, E. (2003). The spatial imperative of subjectivity. In K. Anderson, M. Domosh, N. Thrift, & S. Pile, eds., *Handbook of Cultural Geography,* 290–9. London: Sage.

Public Health Agency of Canada (PHAC). (2001). *What Determines Health?* Retrieved 15 Aug. 2009 from http://www.phacaspc.gc.ca/ph-sp/index-eng.php.

Reed, M. (2005). Learning about the place of women in forestry and land use debates on British Columbia's west coast. *Canadian Woman Studies* 24(4): 18–25.

Robinson, F. (1999). *Globalizing Care: Ethics, Feminist Theory, and International Relations.* Boulder: Westview Press.

Romanow, R. (2002). *Building on Values: The Future of Health Care in Canada – Final Report of the Commission on the Future of Health Care in Canada.* Ottawa: National Library of Canada.

Rose, N., & P. Miller. (1992). Political power beyond the state: Problematics of government. *British Journal of Sociology* 43: 173–205.

Simpson, P. (2005). Trials of transportation in the rapidly developing community of Georgina. *Canadian Woman Studies* 24(4): 147–52.

Skillen, D., B. Heather, & J. Young. (2001). *Reflections of Rural Alberta: Work, Health and Restructuring.* Toronto: National Network on Environments and

Women's Health (NNEWH) and Ottawa: Centres of Excellence for Women's Health Program,Women's Health Bureau, Health Canada, Ottawa.

Spitzer, D. (2005). Engendering health disparities. *Canadian Journal of Public Health* 96 (Suppl. 2): S78–S96.

Statistics Canada. (2003). *E-Book, 2003.* Retrieved 1 March 2006 from http://142.206.72.67/r000_e.htm.

Statistics Canada. (2006). *Women in Canada: A Gender-Based Statistical Report.* 5th ed. Ottawa: Minister of Industry, Statistics Canada.

Stout, M., G. Kipling, & R. Stout. (2001). *Aboriginal Women's Health Research: Synthesis Report.* Ottawa: Centres of Excellence for Women's Health, Women's Health Bureau, Health Canada.

Suominen-Taipale, A., L. Martelin, S. Koskinen, J. Holmen, & R. Johnson. (2006). Gender differences in health care use among the elderly population in areas of Norway and Finland: A cross-sectional analysis based on the HUNT study and the FINRISK Senior Survey. *BMC Health Services Research* 6: 110. Available at http://www.biomedcentral.com/1472-6963/6/110.

Thien, D. (2005a). *Intimate Distances: Geographies of Gender and Emotion in Shetland.* Doctoral dissertation, Department of Geography. Edinburgh, University of Edinburgh.

Thien, D. (2005b). Recasting the pattern: Critical relations in gender and rurality. In L. Little & C. Morris, eds., *Critical Studies in Rural Gender Issues,* 75–89. Ashgate: Aldershot.

Thien, D. (2005c). Intimate distances: Considering questions of 'us.' In J. Davidson, M. Smith, & L. Bondi, eds., *Emotional Geographies,* 191–204. Ashgate: Aldershot.

Tigges, L., A. Ziebarth, & J. Farnham. (1998). Social relationships in locality and livelihood: The embeddedness of rural economic restructuring. *Journal of Rural Studies* 14(2): 203–19.

Valentine, G. (1997). Making space: Lesbian separatist communities. In P. Cloke & J. Little, eds., *Contested Countryside Cultures: Otherness, Marginalisation and Rurality,* 109–22. London: Routledge.

Valentine, G. (2006). Theorizing and researching intersectionality: A challenge for feminist geography. *Professional Geographer* 59(1): 10–21.

Vilhjalmsson, R. (2005). Failure to seek needed medical care: Results from a national health survey of Icelanders. *Social Science and Medicine* 61: 1320–30.

Wilson, K., J. Eyles, S. Elliott, & S. Keller-Olaman. (2009). Health in Hamilton neighbourhoods: Exploring the determinants of health at the local level. *Health and Place* 15(1): 374–82.

Winson, A., & B. Leach. (2002). *Contingent Work, Disrupted Lives: Labour and Community in the New Rural Economy.* Toronto: University of Toronto Press.

PART TWO

Paid Care Work in Formal Organizations

3 In Search of Equity and Dignity in Maternity Care: Canada in Comparative Perspective

CECILIA BENOIT, SIRPA WREDE, AND
ÞORGERDUR EINARSDÓTTIR

Recent international economic policy has been focused on boosting exports and free trade, deregulating domestic economies, liberalizing capital markets, and promoting market-based pricing. These macroeconomic 'neoliberal' reforms have typically been accompanied by policies to reduce public expenditure, including public outlay for health. Evidence mounting from low- and middle-income countries points to increasing inequality, as the affluent few can afford to overuse health care, paying for the consumed services out of pocket, while the bulk of the population face a 'medical poverty trap,' unable to access health care for even basic conditions (Sen 2002; Armstrong et al. 2003).

A question remains as to the impact of neoliberal reforms on more developed welfare states with universal public health care systems. Although some scholars have argued that such reforms have enhanced the efficiency and effectiveness of public health care systems (Esmail & Walker 2005), other researchers maintain that the reforms have largely been negative. The result is poorer working conditions for health care providers (Denton et al. 2002a, 2002b), especially those delivering primary care services (Armstrong et al. 2003; Aronson & Sammon 2000; Bezanson & Luxton 2006), as well as a decline in the quality of health care available for lower-income populations (Mackintosh & Koivusalo 2005) and, of special relevance to maternity care, the medicalization of normal life events (Conrad & Leiter 2004; Van Teijlingen 2005).

The first section of this chapter focuses on Canada, highlighting the consequences of neoliberal reforms for the organization of maternity care. The chapter then examines recent changes in the maternity care systems of Finland and Iceland. We argue that a comparative study of maternity care organization that includes Canada, Finland, and

Iceland can contribute valuable knowledge about the variable impact of health care reforms on equitable health services for lower-income populations and on dignified working conditions for health care providers. Comparing and contrasting new cases helps the analysis to reach beyond partly outdated welfare state models. In particular, as noted by Benoit and Hallgrímsdóttir in the opening chapter of this volume, rather than treating the Nordic model as unitary, by focusing on the diversity and difference across the Nordic welfare regimes we can draw more comparative insights helpful to understanding the Canadian case and create an opportunity for positive policy development (DeVries et al. 2001; McDaniel 2002; Benoit et al. 2005; Wrede et al. 2006).

Health Care Reform in Canada

Although inequities in access to physician and hospital services in Canada had risen to the political agenda by the 1950s, universal health insurance did not arrive until the passage of the Medical Care Act of 1968 (implemented in 1972). The Act teamed national principles with provincial administration through an innovative program, eventually known as Medicare. Importantly, under this Act, Canadians for the first time had free access to hospital and physician services (Naylor 1986). Yet it is important to note that the Canadian system was never intended to be fully 'socialized' in the sense that the government is the principal employer of doctors and other health care providers, as is the case in Sweden (Olsen 2002). Rather, Canadian physicians work largely as private practitioners and are paid fees for the package of negotiated services they deliver to patients.

Since its enactment, Medicare has been funded by a mix of federal government cash payments to provinces, province-specific taxes, and federal government equalization payments to poorer provinces. Before 1996 federal government dollars towards health care and postsecondary education were made under the Established Programs Financing (EPF), while transfers for welfare and social assistance services were made under the Canada Assistance Plan (CAP). Federal government outlays to EPF and CAP were substantial during the initial period after Medicare was established. In 1996–97 the federal government decided to collapse these two programs into a single block transfer: the Canada Health and Social Transfer (CHST). One outcome was reduced federal financial outlay for health care (as well as other social programs), and less provincial accountability for federal dollars transferred. In 2003 the federal government attempted to deal with the ensuing problems caused by funding shortages by enacting Bill C-28, which divides the CHST into two distinct transfers: one for health care and one for other social programs, and increased the cash transfer to the provinces and territories. Although Bill C-28 resulted in real growth in cash transfers, it did not fully restore the federal cash funding that was provided prior to the creation of the CHST (Odette 2003; Canadian Institute for Health Information [CIHI] 2005).

Provincial/territorial governments embarked on a series of health care reforms throughout this period to meet the deficit caused by the federal government's withdrawal of core funding and the growing cost of funding Medicare services. These reforms, depending on the province, involved reduction in human resource training, especially for physicians and nurses, and the regionalization of health care governance, whereby smaller hospitals were closed down or consolidated with larger ones and regional health authorities were given the mandate to ration health care services in their local areas. At the same time, health care authorities also pressured hospitals to reduce their costs by closing down wards and opening outpatient facilities. Other reforms included contracting out of hospital services (such as food and cleaning) and the deployment of nurses and other health care providers to the home care services.

These reforms, plus the fact that non-hospital dental care, many drugs, ambulance transportation, and non-medical health professional services are not covered by many provincial health plans, have meant an increasing proportion of health care expenditures being shouldered by Canadians, either through privately financed employee benefit plans or paid for out of pocket. Total health care expenditures for the country were $97.6 billion in 2000–01, an increase of 7.2% from expenditures of $91 billion in 1999–2000. This means that, in 2001, $3,174 was spent on the health care of the average person in Canada.

Non-insured private health care costs made up 30% of total health care costs in Canada in 2006, in contrast to 20% in Finland and 16% in Iceland. In 2004 all other member countries of the Organisation for Economic Co-operation and Development (OECD), except for the United States, Switzerland, Greece, Portugal, and Mexico, had greater public financing for health care than did Canada (OECD 2008a).

Implications of Health Care Reforms for Maternity Care

As noted, Canada's Medicare system was initially conceived as a concerted effort by federal and provincial governments to address inequities in access to physician and hospital services around the country. Pregnant women, for the first time, had free access to physician and hospital services. For women facing obstetric complications and without the means to pay for hospital and physician fees, Medicare opened up access to core services that hitherto had been available only to the privileged. Table 3.1 shows the downward trend in maternal mortality rates by cause between 1979 and 1999, which can be attributed in part to increased availability of publicly funded maternity care services, as well as better access to education, food, housing, birth control, etc. Complications during the course of labour and delivery, hypertension, antepartum and postpartum hemorrhage, and pulmonary embolism were the most common causes of direct maternal death at the beginning of this period. With the exception of pulmonary embolism, the rates for these causes fluctuated but generally declined.

Medicare also had an underside, however. The new legislation consolidated the dominance of physicians – who were virtually all male at the time – in the maternity division of labour, granting them a virtual monopoly over the provision of the country's formal care of pregnant women. This monopoly was reinforced by the fact that public reimbursement was provided for services offered by physicians but not for those of other providers, such as midwives, a primarily female occupational group whose members were being established as essential primary care providers in public health care systems in most other high-income countries during this period (Wrede, Benoit, &

Table 3.1   Direct Maternal Deaths in Canada (Excluding Ontario) per 100,000, 1979–99

Cause	1979–81	1985–90	1991–96	1997–99
Complications labour/delivery	9.5	1.4	3.5	1.6
Hypertension	6.1	8.9	4.9	1.6
Interpartum hemorrhage	3.4	2.7	4.9	1.6
Postpartum hemorrhage	4.1	3.4	1.4	1.6
Pulmonary embolism	6.8	3.4	9.1	6.3

Source: Canadian Perinatal Service System (2003).

Sandall 2001). Additionally, Medicare allowed physicians to retain their right to remain private entrepreneurs and establish their practices wherever they deemed appropriate. Finally, Medicare established the hospital as the linchpin of the maternity care system. The result was the 'medicalization' of pregnancy and childbirth, which for most women are uncomplicated natural processes (Benoit & Heitlinger 1998; Eni, this volume).

As many observers have noted, the medicalization of childbirth and maternity care was also a kind of masculinization as it involved a largely male appropriation of the traditionally feminized work of childbirth support (midwives) as well as of the female body itself (Benoit & Shumka 2009). In addition, this historical phenomenon, coupled with the health care reforms described earlier, including cutbacks in physician training, hospital closures in rural communities, and the centralization of childbirth in large urban hospitals, also had the effect of furthering limiting access to primary maternity services for lower-income and other marginalized populations (O'Neil & Kaufert 1996; see Thien & Dolan, this volume). Thus, medicalization had gendered effects on both equity and dignity in maternity work and care.

Political pressure throughout the 1990s, and the complex mix of factors already outlined, resulted in gender-sensitive legislative changes that introduced certified midwives into the public health care systems of some provinces and territories and midwifery education programs in two provinces. Currently, Canadian women's access to public/private midwifery services is thus largely determined by availability and provincial coverage (Bourgeault, Benoit, & Davis-Floyd 2004). Results from recent surveys indicate that women across Canada are amenable to having greater choice of health care professionals – including certified midwives and nurse practitioners – as their primary care providers (Wen et al. 1999). Research shows that women value the care they receive from these primary care providers (Harvey et al. 2002). This has been confirmed in a study completed by the second author and colleagues (Benoit et al. 2007) assessing an assortment of personal characteristics as they relate to choice of maternity care provider and the level of satisfaction with the care received. Women who chose certified midwives as their primary care provider were comparatively not as well off economically and yet reported higher overall levels of satisfaction with the maternity care they received. The group of women with family physicians also rated highly the care they received. The respondents from both groups who said they were satisfied with their care gave largely the same reasons: good bedside manner, choices regarding birth plans and service details, and continuity of care. Apart from technical competence, women were less satisfied with the care they received from obstetricians, who were not rated highly on these other aspects.

Yet the small number of midwife-attended births in Canada hardly signifies a revolutionary change from earlier decades of medical dominance over maternity care. As shown in Table 3.2, the overall Canadian proportion of midwife-attended births in 2001 was less than 1%. Furthermore, as previously noted, the public funding of midwifery services has been accompanied by a reduction in the number of nurses and physicians trained to provide health care, including maternity care. The resulting physician and nursing shortage has had a twofold negative effect: on the one hand, it has left practising primary care providers overextended and dissatisfied with their working conditions, and at the same time, as also argued by Dolan and Thien (elsewhere in this volume), it has left members of many vulnerable groups, including Aboriginal women living on reserves, pregnant women in other rural communities, and inner city women, with poor access to prenatal, childbirth, and post-birth services. Moreover, the integration of other non-medical providers into maternity care provision, such as nurse practitioners, remains minimal, even though these providers are ideally suited to care for vulnerable pregnant women (Peterson et al. 2007).

Although family physicians are still the most common providers of prenatal care and the primary attendants at childbirth, their portion of service provision has declined over the decades. In addition, they are less likely to deliver multiple births or perform Caesarean sections. Instead, obstetricians, trained to take care of abnormal births, are increasingly under pressure to serve as women's primary attendants, providers who by training and outlook are ill-prepared for this role (CIHI 2007).

Table 3.2   Distribution of Maternity Care Provider Type at Birth, Canada 1996–2001 (in per cent)

Type of primary attendant at vaginal birth	1996	2000–01
Obstetricians/gynecologists	56	61
General practitioners/family physicians who practice obstetrics	44	39
Certified midwives	n/a	<1

Source: Canadian Institute for Health Information (2004).

These various changes in maternity human resources have resulted in the increased medicalization of childbirth. As shown in Table 3.3, the proportion of babies delivered by Caesarean section, for example, increased from just under 24% in 2000–01 to 26.3% in 2005 (CIHI 2007). Of those women delivering in 2005–06 who had had a previous C-section, 81.9% had a repeat C-section.

The data also show that the proportion of Canadian women who have a repeat C-section is increasing and, conversely, the rates of vaginal birth after C-section (VBAC) are on the decrease (CIHI 2007). The Caesarean and VBAC rates are, moreover, not uniform across social groups and geographical areas. There is a clear social gradient in Caesarean rates: age-adjusted rates are significantly higher among women in low-income neighbourhoods than among women in high-income neighbourhoods (Leeb et al. 2005), and the rates also vary among the country's various provinces and territories, and even among health authorities in the same province.

At the same time, nearly half of all vaginal deliveries in Canada in 2002–03 were accompanied by an epidural, and by 2005–06 the rate of epidural use among both vaginal and all deliveries increased again (see Table 3.3). Although the Canadian rate of epidural use is lower than the U.S. rate (59%), the Canadian rate was more than four times that of England (12%) (CIHI 2004). As with C-section and VBAC rates noted above, there is no objective science when it comes to epidural rates. In fact, in 2005–06, there was an eightfold difference in the rate of epidural use among vaginal deliveries across the country, with the highest provincial rates being in Quebec and Ontario.

On a positive note, there was a decrease in vacuum extractions and use of forceps between 2002–03 and 2005–06, as well as in the use of episiotomies. The latter procedure was performed in half of all vaginal

Table 3.3   Maternity Morbidity Data, Canada, 2002–03 and 2005–06 (in per cent)

	2002–03	2005–06
Total C-section	23.8	26.3
Epidurals (all types)	44.6	47.9
Vacuum exts	10.5	9.8
Forceps	4.5	3.7

Source: Canadian Institute for Health Information (2007).

births in 1991–92 but by 2000–01, the rate had dropped to less than a quarter of all births (CIHI 2004). The recent drop in episiotomy rate is attributed by some to changes in obstetric practice that are likely connected to scientific evidence that routine use of episiotomy increases maternal morbidity.

In summary, recent health care reforms in Canada appear to be worrisome for both primary care providers and pregnant women and their families. A shortage of physicians attending maternity clients has been accompanied by less-than-ideal working conditions and poor access to primary maternity care for lower-income populations in many urban areas, as well as for Aboriginal women on reserves and other rural women. Certified midwives have in a small way filled the void in some cities. However, their numbers are small, and less than half of the provincial/territorial health plans cover midwifery services. In other jurisdictions, families have to pay out of pocket. With regard to efficiency, it should be noted that pregnancy and childbirth remain the leading causes of hospitalization among Canadian women, accounting for 24% of acute care stays in 2001–02 (CIHI 2007). The recent increase in obstetricians providing primary care to pregnant women without obstetric complications, the continuously rising Caesarean section rates, and the increase in hospital readmission after Caesarean section all suggest that the reforms Canada has enacted to reorganize the maternity care system have not been successful in providing greater equity in health care for lower-income populations or attractive working conditions for primary care providers (Whitehead, Dahlgren, & McIntyre 2007). Finland and Iceland, like Canada, have adopted a number of measures to reform their respective maternity care systems recently, and their systems have features that are worth considering as Canada attempts to deal with the crisis it faces in maternity care provision.

Maternity Care Reform in Finland and Iceland

All Nordic countries provide their citizens with a comprehensive package of publicly funded health and social welfare services, including maternity care. State-regulated midwives, who in the twentieth century gradually became recast as nurse-midwives, have traditionally provided maternity care in the Nordic countries. The evolving modern welfare states have continued to endorse midwives and primary care nurses as core providers during normal pregnancy and childbirth, along with some variability in how prenatal and postnatal care is orga- nized (Wrede 2001).

As indicated in Table 3.4, Finland and Iceland, like the other Nordic countries, are countries with low income inequality, with a Gini index rate that is substantially lower than that for Canada. Both countries pro- vide mothers with free maternity care mainly by non-medical profes- sionals, covering virtually the entire pregnant population. This strategy has remained intact even during the recent periods of neoliberal health care reform. Though adopting somewhat different strategies, both Fin- land and Iceland report infant mortality rates that are among the lowest in the world and have been able to keep their C-section rates near those recommended by the World Health Organization (Table 3.4). Next we examine how these two systems work in practice.

Finland

Community-based midwives became the first point of contact for uni- versally available maternity care in the 1940s (Wrede 2001). With the 1972 Primary Health Care Act, separate maternity care centres and home birth services were withdrawn. Prenatal and postnatal care activities became incorporated into newly established municipal primary health care centres (PHCs). The first point of contact was no longer the mid- wife but still a female-dominated primary care professional – the public health nurse. Since that time, the revised maternity care program has included regular visits to the maternity care centre beginning at the early

Table 3.4 Comparative Data, Canada, Finland, and Iceland

	Income inequality Gini index	Infant mortality rate, deaths per 1,000 live births	% Babies with low birth weight (<2,500 g)	Total Caesarean section rate (%)
Canada	32.6	5.4[b]	6.1%[b]	26.3[b]
Finland	26.9	2.8[a]	4.5%[a]	16.3[a]
Iceland	26[b]	1.4[a]	n/a	17.5[a]

Sources: Canadian Institute for Health Information (2004, 2008); Organisation for Economic Co-operation and Development (2008); United Nations Development Programme (2008); Statistics Iceland (2008); Icelandic Birth Registration (2006); STAKES (2008).
[a] Data for 2006.
[b] Data for 2005–06.

stages of pregnancy. The majority of the visits include examinations by the public health nurse, but a minimum of three medical examinations are done by primary care doctors employed by the PHC. In addition to the regular health checks, pregnant women and their partners receive health information and preparation for the delivery is included. In 2007 the average number of prenatal visits was 16.5, with the first visit taking place between the ninth and tenth weeks of pregnancy. The average number of visits to hospital outpatient clinics during pregnancy was three (OSF Statistical Summary 2008, Table 3.1). If the pregnant woman is willing to pay a substantial part of the cost out of pocket, she can always choose to have additional medical examinations with a private gynecologist. While data show that a small of number of women make use of this option, most rely on the highly accessible public services as their primary form of maternity care. In a European comparison of disparity in prenatal care, Finland had the lowest proportion of pregnant women – just 3% – entering prenatal care late in the pregnancy (Delvaux 1999). The good outcomes of teenage pregnancies in Finland have also been attributed to the next-to complete coverage of prenatal care (Raatikainen et al. 2005).

The PHCs also liaise with hospital outpatient clinics to coordinate the care of women facing complicated pregnancies. Some researchers have been critical of the outpatient clinics, viewing the clinics as a stronghold for a medical model of childbirth, given the dominant position of the hospital in the larger health care division of labour (Kojo-Austin, Malin, & Hemminki 2003). Nevertheless, prenatal care provided by the PHC maternity centres continued throughout this period to be central for most pregnant women, where the focus continued to be on reducing social inequalities and placing the mother, child, and family unit at centre-stage.

In brief, the social democratic orientation underlying Finland's maternity care system during this period in the 1980s resonated with what Finnish scholars have identified as the 'social service professionalism' of the Nordic health care systems. The policies were premised on egalitarian relationships between medical and other health care professionals, gender equality between male and female health care providers, and partnership with knowledgeable clients (Henriksson, Wrede, & Burau 2006).

A series of health care reforms in Finland in the early 1990s under the so-called population-responsibility model fragmented the PHC prenatal care system by allowing the municipalities greater leeway in the organization of primary care (Gissler et al. 2003). This neoliberal reform prodded municipalities to compose more 'flexible' practice patterns for the primary care workforce, reflecting the attention to cost consciousness and effectiveness that were central values underlying the new health care policy. At the core of the decentralization of public management was the restructuring of public funding for welfare services. Municipalities with independent taxing power became the primary public funder of health care in Finland.

These measures created short-term efficiencies: the proportion of health care costs of the gross national product in Finland continued to be lower than the OECD average (OECD 2007). Yet efficiencies were not realized in maternity care services. Until 2002 PHC prenatal visits increased for all pregnant women, regardless of age and the number of previous pregnancies. At the same time, visits to hospital outpatient clinics increased even more rapidly for all categories of pregnant women. Criticism was focused particularly on the fragmented work pattern of public health nurses and the unnecessary medicalization of prenatal care (Finnish Ministry of Social Affairs and Health 2007). Working conditions and well-being among the personnel employed in Finnish social and health care has been repeatedly surveyed since the early 1990s, when the far-reaching reforms of the public sector were launched. A key finding is the constantly rising dissatisfaction with management style in these sectors; for example, in 2005 36% of public health nurses reported dissatisfaction with the management style of their unit. Among those surveyed, public health nurses were found among the groups least satisfied with their jobs and they felt unjustly treated by management (Laine et al. 2006: 61). Furthermore, one-third of public health nurses reported being stressed by constant organizational changes and an increasing number considered that the services offered were not adequate in relation to the demand (Laine et al. 2006: 26–7).

Partly because of these concerns over the quality of maternity care and the decline in working conditions for primary care providers, Finnish policy has recently shifted away from a focus on efficiency to a re-emphasis on dignity in working conditions and equity in primary health care provision. Since 2005 the government has required that detailed rules on the content and scope of prenatal care be developed. In 2007 a new policy instrument, a national action program for the promotion of sexual and reproductive health, was created. Maternity care has been reinforced as a core universal public health area and the service package is mandated to be unitary in character (Law on the

Changes of the Public Health Act 2005). This policy instrument is linked to a revised Health Care Act that aims to restructure the entire public provision of health care services (Finnish Ministry of Social Affairs and Health 2008).

In sum, the Finnish version of neoliberal reforms enacted in the 1990s entailed fragmentation of prenatal care and worsening working conditions for the female-dominated profession of primary care providers. However, these policy decisions have recently been reversed, and new models of service provision are being proposed to reduce unnecessary medicalization of maternity care, promote equity of care provision, and improve working conditions for primary care professionals. The reform even provides tools for integrating prenatal care and the maternity care provided at the hospital in a way that means that the primary level coordinates the program. The future will show whether these promises will be fulfilled.

Iceland

Iceland, similar to Finland, has a relatively universal and comprehensive health care system. Under the Icelandic Health Care Act of 1973, the public was given access to qualified health care practitioners, and primary health care services were emphasized. The country's health care system is primarily financed through the public purse, directly from the state budget or indirectly through the State Social Security Institute (Vilhjálmsson 2007: 198–9). Although Iceland delivers a relatively high-quality health service, it does so at a high cost – in fact, the most rapidly increasing cost of all the OECD countries (Halldórsson 2003).

Another underside of the Icelandic health care system has been its unclear legal framework – that is, it has a complicated ad hoc system, with fragmentation and diffuse definitions of responsibilities and jurisdictions, all of which makes long-term policy making very difficult (Halldórsson 2003; Sigurgeirsdóttir 2006). The responsibility for providing primary care lies with the municipalities, but during the past decade the responsibility has been moving back and forth from the state to the municipalities, and the financial costs have been divided between the two (see Purkis et al., this volume). The end result is that the health care system has become a playground where the tension between the state and the market are played out, with health care professions, and health care providers, especially, physicians, vying for power.

Iceland also has a long tradition of private health care, in particular that provided by physicians in private practice, but to an increasing degree also by other professionals. In 2007 approximately 83% of health care expenditures were financed by the state and the remaining 17% were direct household payments (Vilhjálmsson 2007: 199). Health care in Iceland, then, is to an increasing extent paid for by patients directly out of pocket, although, as noted above, less so than in Finland (20% in 2006) and substantially less so than the average Canadian householder has to bear (30% in 2006). The Icelandic government has time and again made attempts to introduce a referral system in order to reduce health care costs in the state budget, but under great protests from doctors (Vilhjálmsson 2007: 200).

Notwithstanding these structural constraints on the health care system, Iceland has managed to develop a relatively extensive publicly funded maternity care service that provides high-quality care to pregnant women. The Icelandic maternity care system dates back to 1943, when the Reykjavik Centre for Preventive Health Care was made the main centre of maternity care (Kristjánsdóttir 2004). Prenatal care is provided free of charge to all mothers/prospective parents (Health Service Act No. 40 2007; Regulation on Health Care Centres No. 787 2007). As in Finland, Icelandic expectant mothers visit their local PHC a variety of times throughout their pregnancy, with ten visits the recommended number for first-time mothers (as stated in the national guidelines issued in 2008 by the Directorate of Health (see Directorate of Health 2008). In uncomplicated cases the prospective mother is placed under the care of a nurse-midwife, sometimes in cooperation with a general practitioner or an obstetrician if complications should arise. She receives information on pregnancy, birth, and breastfeeding, and is offered prenatal classes.

For the past few decades, maternity care has been divided between the Reykjavik Centre for Preventive Health Care, the PHCs, the Landspitali University Hospital (previously the Icelandic State Hospital), and doctors in private practice. The bulk of deliveries take place at the University Hospital in Reykjavík, while the remainder occur in smaller maternity units around the country. Better transportation between rural and urban centers, as well as evolving preferences by women, have resulted in a decline of midwife- and physician-attended births in rural areas (Bjarnadóttir et al. 2006). Although nearly all pregnant women make ample use of the free prenatal care services offered, many women in Iceland choose to complement their prenatal care with the services of private gynecologists (Gottfredsdóttir 2009: 8).

On the other hand, and as in Finland, Icelandic nurse-midwives are the primary attendants at over 70% of all deliveries. Icelandic midwives have also been solidifying their professional knowledge base and identity in recent decades, contesting the medicalization and technologization of the birth process (Gottfredsdóttir, Karlsdóttir, & Lausnarsteinar 2009). They are strong advocates of vaginal deliveries and resist interventions unless medically necessary; they have also been questioning the variety of screening tests for fetal abnormalities that have become routine in prenatal care in recent years (Gottfredsdóttir 2006; Ólafsdóttir 1995).

However, despite the relatively strong professional status of Icelandic nurse-midwives and their focus on primary maternity care, medical dominance remains intact in some domains, including with regard to early fetal screening, in particular, nuchal translucency screening (NT), which has been offered as optional prenatal screening in Iceland since 1999, to be paid for privately. The number of women choosing NT screening has rapidly increased, so that by 2005 85% of pregnant women in the capital area, and 65% in the country overall, chose to take the NT screening test, even though no official public policy had been formulated on the issue at that time (Gottfredsdóttir 2009: 18, 121). In Iceland there is a consensus, clearly emphasized in the national guidelines from 2008, that the NT fetal screening should be the choice of the prospective parents, that is, a private issue. However, as reflected in the large uptake, it has more or less become routine and has been the subject of largely uncritical discussion in the media, hailed as a scientific achievement and representative of an expansion of choice in maternity care. The midwives' challenge of the NT test as unnecessary medical intervention has therefore not had a significant impact (Gottfredsdóttir 2009: 121, 167–9). Discussion of complex moral issues is rare, and those who choose NT are in line with prevailing norms within the society in general. Hence, while formally a free choice, researchers refer to this widespread acceptance of NT as 'voluntary compulsion' (Gottfredsdóttir 2009: 127).

But there are also countervailing trends: while C-section rates increased in Iceland between the late 1980s up to 2003, they have decreased more recently (Bjarnadóttir 2006) and are low, as in Finland, when compared with the Canadian rates, which continue to climb. The interest for home births among Icelandic families is increasing (currently they are 1% of all births), and the majority of them are in the capital area (Icelandic Birth Registration 2005: 6). Finally, home service by midwives after hospital delivery and early return home has enjoyed increasing popularity and is further indication of the strength of the primary maternity care system in Iceland and the pivotal role of midwives in Iceland (Icelandic Birth Registration, 2009: 15).

In short, financial cutbacks and increased market incentives in the Icelandic health care system throughout the 1990s have not reduced universal access to, or the quality of, basic maternity care, nor have they negatively affected the working conditions of primary care professionals to any notable extent. On the other hand, Iceland, like Canada, suffers from a persistent shortage of nurses, nurse-midwives, and practical nurses (Statistics Iceland 2008; Halldórsson 2003), which is partly related to wage dissatisfaction (Association of Icelandic Midwives 2008). In addition, neoliberal trends in Iceland have led to increased medical dominance, a stronger focus on technology, and interest in privatization. The universal service is considered a minimal service, and the majority of pregnant women make use of private services at their own cost.

The outcome of these problems of the health care system in Iceland for the future of maternity care equity and dignified working conditions for maternity care providers, especially in light of the current global economic recession, which has hit Iceland particularly hard, remains to be seen.

Summary and Conclusions

This chapter has argued that recent health care reforms in Canada have been accompanied by a serious maternity care crisis characterized by unnecessary medicalization, labour shortage, and discontent among maternity care providers. Our comparison with Finland and Iceland highlights the central role played by non-medical, women-dominated professional groups in Nordic maternity care systems. Even though neoliberal reforms have had an identified negative impact in both Finland and Iceland, and both countries are currently facing discontent among primary maternity providers because of staff shortages and low wages among its nurse-midwives (Association of Icelandic Midwives 2008), equitable access to primary maternity care for all families and dignified working conditions for nurses and midwives have remained core features of each country's health care system across the decades. When investing in primary health care, these nations have been able to hold on to a more equitable vision of how to provide maternity care services to their respective populations. From the point of view of the health care labour force, the important lesson is that the state can endorse non-hierarchical relationships among team members and take gender inequalities seriously, developing policies to reduce them. As Canada struggles with increased C-section rates and inadequate access to primary maternity care, it could look to these other systems for guidance. A long view of the Nordic experience provides evidence that social equality and justice policies foster dignified working conditions and service provision. Attention to the impact of neoliberal reforms indicates, however, that these values are easily threatened by measures that emphasize efficiency over dignity and equity.

ACKNOWLEDGMENT

Adapted, with permission from the Canadian Public Health Association, from the article by S. Wrede, C. Benoit, and T. Einarsdottir (2008), 'Equity and Dignity in Maternity Care Provision in Canada, Finland and Iceland: Finding Dignity in Health Care and Health Care Work,' *Canadian Journal of Public Health* 99 (Supplement 2): S16–S21.

REFERENCES

Armstrong P., H. Armstrong, I. Bourgeault, J. Choiniere, J. Lexchin, & E. Mykhalovskiy. (2003). Market principles, business practices and health care. *International Journal of Canadian Studies* 28: 13–38.

Aronson, J., & S. Sammon. (2000). Practice amid social service cuts and restructuring: Working with the contradictions of small victories. *Canadian Social Work Review* 17: 167.

Association of Icelandic Midwives. (2008). Retrieved 31 July 2008 from http://www.ljosmodir.is/Felag/.

Benoit, C., & A. Heitlinger. (1998). Women's health care work in comparative perspective. *Social Science and Medicine* 47: 1101–11.

Benoit, C., & L. Shumka. (2009). *Gendering the Health Determinants Framework: Why Girls' and Women's Health Matters – A Primer on Women's Health.* MSFHR. Vancouver: Women's Health Research Network.

Benoit, C., S. Wrede, I. Bourgeault, J. Sandall, E. Van Teijlingen, R. DeVries. (2005). Understanding the social organisation of maternity care systems. *Sociology of Health and Illness* 27: 722–37.

Benoit, C., R. Westfall, A. Treloar, R. Phillips, & M. Jansson. (2007). Social factors linked with postpartum depression. *Journal of Mental Health* 16: 719–30.

Bezanson, K., & M. Luxton. (Eds.). (2006). *Social Reproduction: Feminist Political Economy Challenges Neoliberalism.* Montreal and Kingston: McGill-Queen's University Press.

Bjarnadóttir, R. (2006). No correlation between rates of caesarean section and perinatal mortality in Iceland? *Laeknabladid (Icelandic Medical Journal)* 91: 191–5.

Bjarnadóttir, R.I., G. Gardarsdóttir, A. Smárason, & G. Pálsson. (2006). *Faedingarskráningunni* (Icelandic Birth Registration). Kvennadeild og Barnaspítali Hringsins. Landspítali – Háskólasjúkrahús (Landspitali University Hospital).

Bourgeault, I., C. Benoit, & R. Davis-Floyd. (Eds.). (2004). *Reconceiving Midwifery.* Montreal and Kingston: McGill-Queen's University Press.

Canadian Institute for Health Information (CIHI). (2004). *Giving Birth in Canada: A Regional Profile.* Ottawa: Author.

Canadian Institute for Health Information. (2005). *Health Care in Canada.* Ottawa: Author.

Canadian Institute for Health Information. (2007). *Giving Birth in Canada: Regional Trends from 2001–2002 to 2005–2006.* Ottawa: Author.

Canadian Institute for Health Information. (2008). *Health Indicators.* Ottawa: Author.

Canadian Perinatal Service System. (2003). *Canadian Perinatal Health Report.* Ottawa: Health Canada.

Canadian Perinatal Surveillance System. (2000). *Perinatal Health Indicators for Canada.* Ottawa: Health Canada.

Conrad, P., & V. Leiter. (2004). Medicalization, markets and consumers. *Journal of Health and Social Behavior* 45: 158–76.

Delvaux, T. (1999). Buekens and the Study Group on Barriers and Incentives to Prenatal Care in Europe: Disparity in prenatal care in Europe. *European Journal of Obstetrics and Gynecology and Reproductive Biology* 83: 185–90.

Denton, M., I. Zeytinoglu, & S. Davies. (2002a). Working in clients' homes: The impact on the mental health and well-being of visiting home care workers. *Home Health Care Service Quarterly* 21: 1–27.

Denton, M., I. Zeytinoglu, S. Davies, & J. Lian. (2002b). Job stress and job dissatisfaction of home care workers in the context of health care restructuring. *International Journal of Health Services* 32: 327–57.

DeVries, R., C. Benoit, E. Van Teijlingen, & S.Wrede. (Eds.). (2001). *Birth by Design.* London: Routledge.

Directorate of Health (2009). *Statistics on Birth 2007.* Retrieved 5 Sept. 2009 from http://landlaeknir.is/lisalib/getfile.aspx?itemid=3845.

Esmail, N., & M. Walker. (2005). *How Good Is Canadian Health Care? 2005 Report.* Vancouver: Fraser Institute.

Finnish Ministry of Social Affairs and Health. (2007). *Seksuaali – ja lisääntymis-terveyden edistäminen. Toimintaohjelma 2007–2011.* Promotion of Sexual and Reproductive Health Action Programme 2007–2011. Helsinki: Author.

Finnish Ministry of Social Affairs and Health. (2008). *The New Health Care Act.* Memorandum of the Working Group Preparing the Health Care Act. Helsinki.

Gissler, M., J. Meriläinen, E. Vuori, & E. Hemminki. (2003). Register-based monitoring shows decreasing socioeconomic differences in Finnish perinatal health. *Journal of Epidemiology and Community Health* 57: 433–9.

Gottfredsdóttir, H. (2006). Breyttar áherslur í medgonguvernd í ljósi nýrra adferda til fósturgreiningar og skimunar (Changes in maternal care in the light of new methods for prenatal screening). In H. Jónsdóttir, ed., *Frá innsaei til inngripa: Thekkingarthroun í hjúkrunar- og ljósmódurfraedi,* 145–63. Reykjavík: Hid íslenska Bókmenntfélag.

Gottfredsdóttir, H. (2009). *Fetal Screening: Prospective Parents and Decisions Concerning Nuchal Translucency Screening.* Reykjavík: University of Iceland, Faculty of Nursing.

Gottfredsdóttir, H., S. Karlsdóttir, & I. Lausnarsteinar. (2009). *Ljósmódurfraedi og Ljósmódurlist: Reykjavík, Hid íslenska bókmenntafélag.* Reykjavík: Ljósmaedrafélag Íslands.

Halldórsson, M. (2003). *Health Care Systems in Transition: Iceland.* European Observatory on Health Systems and Policies. Copenhagen: WHO.

Harvey, S., D. Rach, M. Stainston, J. Jarrell, & R. Brant. (2002). Evaluation of satisfaction with midwifery care. *Midwifery* 18: 260–7.

Health Service Act No. 40 (Log um heilbrigdisthjónustu). (2007). Reykjavík: Icelandic Ministry of Health.

Henriksson, L., S. Wrede, & V. Burau. (2006). Understanding professional projects in welfare service work. *Gender, Work and Organization* 14: 174–92.

Icelandic Birth Registration. (2005). Retrieved 10 Aug. 2008 from http://www4.landspitali.is/lsh_ytri.nsf/pages/kven_0114/$file/faedingarskraningarskyrsla_2006.pdf.

Jónsdóttir, G., R.I. Bjarnadóttir, R.T. Geirsson, & A.K. Smárason. (2006). No correlation between rates of caesarean section and perinatal mortality in Iceland? *Laeknabladid (Icelandic Medical Journal)* 92: 191–5.

Kojo-Austin, H., M. Malin, & E. Hemminki. (2003). Women's satisfaction with maternity health care services in Finland. *Social Science and Medicine* 37: 633–8.

Kristjánsdóttir, H., & Allt vegna fóstursins. (2004). Afleidingar ómskodunar (All for the unborn child: Consequences of screening). In Ó.P. Jónsson & A.Ó. Jónsdóttir, eds., *Sjúkdómsvaeding (Medicalisation)*. Reykjavík: Fraedslunet Sudurlands, Sidfraedistofnun, Háskólaútgáfan.

Laine, M., G. Wickström, J. Pentti, M. Elovainio, A. Kaarlela-Tuomaala, & K. Lindström. (2006). *Työolot ja hyvinvointi sosiaali- ja terveysalalla 2005 (Working Conditions and Well-Being in Social and Health Care 2005)*. Helsinki: Finnish Institute of Occupational Health.

Law on the Changes of the Public Health Act. (Laki kansanterveyslain muuttamisesta). (2005).

Mackintosh, M., & M. Koivusalo. (2005). *Commercialisation of Health Care*. Basingstoke: Palgrave Macmillan.

McDaniel, S.A. (2002). Women's changing relations to the state and citizenship: Caring and intergenerational relations in globalizing Western democracies. *Canadian Review of Sociology and Anthropology* 39(2): 125–50.

Naylor, N. (1986). *Private Practice, Public Payment: Canadian Medicine and the Politics of Health Insurance, 1911–1966*. Montreal and Kingston: McGill-Queen's University Press.

Odette, M. (2003). The Canada Health and Social Transfer: Operation and possible repercussions on the health care sector. *Current Issue Review* 95-2E. Ottawa: Parliamentary Research Branch, Library of Parliament.

Ólafsdóttir, Ó.A. (1995). Breytingar og thróun í námi í ljósmódurfraedi (Changes and development in the education of midwifery). *Ljósmaedrabladid (Journal of Midwives)* 73: 14–17, 20–9.

Olsen, G. (2002). *The Politics of the Welfare State: Canada, Sweden and the U.S.* Toronto: Oxford University Press.

O'Neil, J., & P. Kaufert. (1996). The politics of obstetric care: The Inuit experience. In W. Mitchinson, P. Bourne, A. Prentice, G. Cuthbert Brandt, B. Light, & N. Black, eds., *Canadian Women: A Reader*, 416–29. Toronto: Harcourt Brace.

Organisation for Economic Co-operation and Development (OECD). (2007). OECD Health Data 2007. Retrieved 7 Oct. 2007 from http://www.oecd.org/document/16/0,3343,en_2649_37407_2085200_1_1_1_37407,00.html.

Organisation for Economic Co-operation and Development. (2008a). *OECD Health Data*. Geneva: Author.

Organisation for Economic Co-operation and Development. (2008b). *OECD Health Data 2008. Frequently Requested Data. Infant Mortality Rate*. Retrieved 14 Aug. 2008 from http://www.oecd.org/dataoecd/ 35/19/35027658.xls.

Peterson, W., J. Medves, B. Davies, & I. Graham. (2007). Multidisciplinary collaborative maternity care in Canada: Easier said than done. *Journal of Obstetrics and Gynaecology* 29: 880–6.

Raatikainen, K., N. Heiskanen, P. Verkasalo, & S. Heinonen. (2005). Good outcome of teenage pregnancies in high-quality maternity care. *European Journal of Public Health* 16: 157–61.

Regulation on Health Care Centres, No. 787 (Reglugerd um heilsugaeslustodvar). (2007). Reykjavík: Icelandic Ministry of Health.

Sen, A. (2002). Health: Perception versus observation. *British Medical Journal* 324: 860–1.

Sigurdsson, J.A. (2003). The GP's role in maternity care. *Scandinavian Journal of Primary Care* 21: 65.

Sigurgeirsdóttir, S. (2006). *Health Policy and Hospital Mergers: How the Impossible Became Possible.* Reykjavík: Háskólaútgáfan.

STAKES. (2008). *Finnish Birth Register data.* Retrieved 5 Aug. 2008 from http://www.stakes.fi/FI/Tilastot/Aiheittain/Lisaantyminen/synnyttajat/index.htm.

Statistics Iceland. (2008). Wages, Income and Labour Market. *Statistical Series.* (11 April). Retrieved 10 Aug. 2008 from http://www.hagstofa.is/lisalib/getfile.aspx?ItemID=8012.

United Nations Development Programme (UNDP). (2008). *Human Development Programme Report, 2007/2008.* New York: Palgrave Macmillan.

Van Teijlingen, E. (2005). A critical analysis of the medical model as used in the study of pregnancy and childbirth. *Sociol Research Online* 10(2). Retrieved on 2 July 2006 from http://www.socresonline.org.uk/10/2/teijlingen.html.

Vilhjálmsson, R. (2007). Íslenska heilbrigdiskerfid á krossgötum. In G.T. Jóhannesson, (ed.), *Rannsóknir í félagsvísindum,* vol. VIII, 197–206. Reykjavík: Félagsvísindastofnun.

Wen, S.W., L.S. Mery, M. Kramer, V. Jimenez, K. Trouton, P. Herbert, & B. Chalmers. (1999). Attitudes of Canadian women toward birthing centres and midwifery care for childbirth. *Canadian Medical Association Journal* 161: 708–9.

Whitehead, M., G. Dahlgren, & D. McIntyre. (2007). Putting equity centre stage: Challenging evidence-free reforms. *International Journal of Health Services* 27: 353–61.

Wrede, S. (2001). *Decentering Care for Mothers.* Åbo: Åbo Akademi University Press.

Wrede, S., C. Benoit, & J. Sandall. (2001). The state and birth / the state of birth: Maternal health policy in three countries. In R. DeVries, C. Benoit, E. Van Teijlinge, S. Wrede, eds., *Birth by Design,* 28–50. London: Routledge.

Wrede, S., C. Benoit, I. Bourgeault, E. Van Teijlingen, J. Sandall, & R. DeVries. (2006). Decentred comparative research. *Social Science and Medicine* 63: 2986–97.

4 Caring beyond Borders: Comparing the Relationship between Nursing Work and Migration Patterns in Canada and Finland

IVY BOURGEAULT AND SIRPA WREDE

Despite the complexity of modern nursing and its position as an important health care profession, the paid care work or 'intimate labour' (Zelizer 2007) nurses perform for patients is often undervalued in many countries, resulting in comparatively low salaries and poor working conditions. The age-old dynamic of treating nursing as a homogeneous activity which requires 'a pair of hands,' and qualities such as dedication, sympathy, and altruism, are awarded less value than the scientific and rational expert-task of 'curing' associated with doctors, dentists, and other medical practitioners. This situation is worsened by neoliberal efficiency-driven policies that increasingly commodify and quantify health care, allowing for nurses to be treated as an easily replaceable workforce (see Benoit & Hallgrímsdóttir, this volume). At the height of neoliberal reforms aimed at making public management more efficient and cost effective, many nurses were either made to 'multi-task,' to work under temporary contracts, or were even laid off. This was particularly salient in the 1990s for nursing in Canada when unemployment peaked at 2.4%. At that time, one-third of nurses working part-time wished to be in a full-time position, 12% held multiple jobs, and another 12% worked in temporary jobs (Pyper 2004). Similarly, a recent survey of Finnish nurses, conducted in 2005, found that more than one-third had significant periods of unemployment in their work history, and more than one in ten had had temporary contracts because of a dearth of work opportunities (Santamäki et al. 2009: 27). This has resulted in an overall increase in workload for those nurses who remain, leading to burnout, and exit from the profession altogether for a substantial minority (Armstrong et al. 2000).

Celia Davies (1992) argues that the high turnover of nurses, the vast majority of whom are female in virtually all high-income countries, is one of the key areas where the 'gender question' in nursing is visible. Fewer and fewer women in high-income countries appear to be willing to choose the simultaneously valued and devalued occupation of nursing (Hardill & MacDonald 2000). In the Canadian province of Ontario, for example, enrolments declined to a low of 751 in 1997, which was half of that in 1992 (Meyer, Williams, & Murphy 2009). This has proven to be especially challenging in the case of long-term nursing care, where the aging population has placed consumer pressure to improve the quality and quantity of publicly funded nursing services (Sibbald 1999; Purkis, Ceci, & Bjornsdóttir, this volume). Reflecting the growing need to fill vacancies in these countries, the international migration of nurses has rapidly become one of the key issues in a global crisis of intimate labour within the paid health care sector. Nursing work thus constitutes a key target of governments that have explicitly created and reinforced the redistribution and internationalization of care work (Misra, Woodring, & Merz 2006).

In short, at a time when the need for nurses is rapidly increasing because of demographic changes, many high-income countries are experiencing difficulties in finding sufficient numbers of new recruits and in retaining nurses already in the workforce (Aiken et al. 2004). This is particularly the case in many of the European OECD countries where younger age cohorts in the population are expected to decline by about 25% over the next twenty years (OECD 2008: 19–21). The Association of Finnish Local and Regional Authorities (2008) estimates that by 2025 more than a half of the present social and health care municipal workforce will retire. By that same time, these two sectors are predicted to need approximately 10,000 new employees to respond to the growing labour demand. A rapidly growing demand for health care workers is also forecast for Canada: The Canadian Nurses Association's 2009 report on human resources details how the country will be short almost 60,000 full-time equivalent registered nurses (RNs) by 2022, assuming the labour force and population aging trends remain the same. These vacancies in the professional division of labour create a space for international nursing migrants. Indeed, some argue that nursing work/life issues (in particular, adequate remuneration and dignity in work and opportunity to balance paid work and family demands) have not been as effectively addressed because governments have the option to recruit foreign health care workers, thus avoiding having to meet the demands of their domestic labour forces (Bach 2003). As Bach (2003: ix) has argued, it is an indictment of governments and employers that they prefer to rely on the relatively straightforward panacea of international recruitment rather than focusing on underlying problems of pay and working conditions. Improvements in these areas would ensure increased recruitment and retention among the existing health sector workforce. The result is what some scholars have called 'global care chains' (Hochschild 2000; Yeates 2004) where (largely female) workers in low-income countries (or less economically advantaged countries) are recruited to help solve the 'care deficit' in high-income countries. These international gendered labour practices often come with a price, however. When high-income countries recruit nurses from less-advantaged regions, they tap these countries for human resources they can ill-afford to lose. Because of this, the recruitment of internationally trained nurses has rapidly become one of the key issues in a global crisis of health care labour, evidenced in part by the WHO devoting its 2006 *World Health Report* to this topic. Furthermore, research suggests that migrant nurses from low- to high-income countries commonly face poorer working conditions and deskilling as compared with domestic nurses (Bourgeault 2008; Calliste 1996). From this perspective, the issue of nurse migration needs to be considered in a broad context that takes the issue of 'dignity' into consideration, not only as a consideration towards care recipients but also to care providers. Its contradictory gendered dynamics, linked not merely to the provision of care but also to women's overall position in society, as well as care-blind neoliberal reforms and the international migration flows that result from them, make nursing a critical case to analyse.

This chapter briefly compares the *contexts* of nurse migration in Canada and Finland, drawing on documentary data from both primary and secondary sources. These data are analysed according to key themes that emerged from a review of the nurse migration literature. Our aim is to explore more subtle transnational linkages that shape the patterns of nurse migration to and from these two high-income countries that are similar in many respects but different enough to make comparison worthwhile. Other countries have nationalized health care systems but highly different histories in relation to migration patterns and social welfare policies. Canada is historically a destination country for immigrants, whereas Finland has only very recently seen an increase in immigration. In Finland, the proportion of the population who are foreign citizens and former foreign citizens was 6.4% in

2008 (Statistics Finland 2009), whereas in Canada, nearly a fifth of its population was born outside of Canada (Chui, Tran, & Maheux 2009). There are also important differences in their welfare states: like the other Nordic countries, Finland has invested heavily in social policies aimed at increasing equality between women and men, including public child care and other programs that support women's (and men's) gainful employment and family participation. In addition, compared with Finland, public child care and other gender-sensitive programs are not as readily available to Canadian families, especially outside of Quebec.

These two countries also have very different trajectories concerning the international migration of health care professionals, including nurses. Canada, along with the United States and Australia, constituted large-scale receiving regions in the period since the Second World War. All of these countries started to change their immigration policies in the 1960s and 1970s, in favour of skilled professions, a shift reflecting the shrinking demand for non-skilled workers. Since the time of these policy changes, these countries have implemented selective immigration policies in which education and skill have been the core criteria. Some argue that the result of these policies has been a 'brain drain' that concerns expert labour from low-income countries, following the patterning of traditional international migration that involves permanent moving (Kapur & McHale 2005). A similar trend has occurred in Western Europe only since the 1990s, with an increasing number of countries becoming receiving countries for professional migrants from low-income nations (Majava 2002).

In this age of global markets, the dynamics of traditional migration patterns have gained new relevance. Established transnational labour markets, linguistic compatibility, sociocultural affinity, professional equivalence, and visa policies are key factors channelling migration. Policy-related factors, including income, job satisfaction, career opportunity, governance and management, safety and risks, as well as social and family reasons, offer further explanation to country-specific migration patterns (Joint Learning Initiative 2004). Policies in these various domains influence each country's overall gender system and ultimately the situation of practising professional nurses. Furthermore, both countries provide interesting examples of how the cultural, political, and economic ties related to the specific regional location of a country shape migration flows. Below we explore how broader social rights available to Finnish nurses in recent decades have been accompanied by better working conditions and lower turnover and out-migration from the profession as compared with Canadian nurses. We focus in particular on long-term care nursing because it is here that some of the issues we explore are currently the most salient.

The Context of Nurse Immigration to Canada and Finland

In comparison with other high-income countries, such as Finland, the development of the Canadian welfare state has lagged behind. Although a public system of hospital insurance were implemented as early as 1947, it was not until the late 1960s, with the implementation of Medicare, that it was generally regarded that Canada had a public health care system (Benoit, Wrede, & Einarsdóttir, this volume). Immigration was critical in this rather drawn-out expansion of the Canadian health care system. For many years, Canada relied on internationally trained health care professionals to help address underserviced areas (Bourgeault 2008). British nurses, in particular, especially those with advanced training in midwifery, were recruited by Health Canada from the 1950s- to the mid-1960s to serve in northern outposts, providing care to the country's rural and Aboriginal populations (Mason 1988). Both tighter immigration policies and a change in Health and Welfare Canada policy in the late 1960s and early 1970s – requiring all pregnant women residing in isolated and underpopulated northern areas of Canada to travel to urban hospitals located in the south to deliver their babies – led to an overall reduction in the number of immigrant nurse-midwives practising in rural and remote areas of Canada (Bourgeault & Benoit 2004; Eni, this volume; Benoit et al., this volume). Other forms of 'out migration' from nursing did not involve moving but instead concerned an inability to retain graduate nurses, particularly after marriage and motherhood (Armstrong, Choiniere, & Day 1993). Unfortunately, we do not have readily available demographic data to describe these trends.

Although more recent public debates in Canada have increasingly focused on the aging population and the associated growing nursing care shortage, the number of internationally educated nurses (IENs) in Canada had remained surprisingly steady over the past twenty years. While the numbers declined during the 1990s (at the height of neoliberal reforms and peak nurse emigration), there has recently been an increase (see Figure 4.1). While Canadian IENs comprised over 10% of the registered nurse workforce in 1980, there was a slight decline in

Figure 4.1. Number of New Internationally Educated Registered Nurses in Canada, 1999–2002

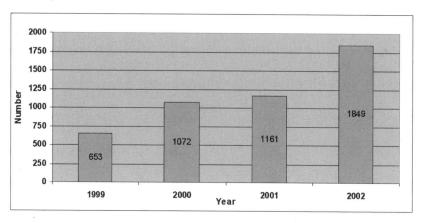

Source: A. Baumann, J. Blythe, C. Kolotylo, and J. Underwood, *Immigration and Emigration Trends: A Canadian Perspective* (Ottawa: Nursing Sector Study Corp., 2004).

the foreign RN population into the early 1990s, rising up to 8% of all nurses working in Canada in 2005 from 6.8% in 1999 (CIHI 2000). This puts Canada in comparable circumstances to other OECD countries in regard to IENs, except for Finland (see Table 4.1).

The proportion of IENs as per the population of active nurses may mask some of the recent changes that are best captured by statistics on new entrants. As illustrated in Figure 4.1, recent data suggest there has been a significant increase in the number of new IENs entering Canada each year. Since 1999, for example, the number of new IENs has more than doubled, and in the year 2002 there were reportedly 1,849 new internationally educated registered nurses entering Canada. Overall percentages may also differ by sector. Zeytinoglu et al. (2008) found a higher tendency for foreign-born workers to work in the home care sector. Visiting home care workers are a case in point: the authors reported 43% of them were born outside of Canada, whereas only 19% of office workers were immigrants.

In terms of source countries for IENs in Canada, the majority of internationally educated RNs in Canada graduated from schools in the Philippines (29.3%) or the United Kingdom (21.4%) (CIHI 2005). A significant portion of foreign-trained RNs also graduated in the United States (6.6%), as well as Hong Kong (5.3%), India (4.8%), Poland (3.3%),

Table 4.1   Nurses Trained Abroad
Working in Selected OECD Countries

	Number	% of Total
Canada	19,230	8
Finland	140	<1
Germany	26,284	3
Ireland	8,758	14
New Zealand	10,616	21
United Kingdom	65,000	10
United States	99,456	5

Sources: The World Health Report 2006:
   Working Together for Health (Geneva: World
   Health Organization, 2006); Canada's Health
   Care Providers (Ottawa: CIHI, 2007).

and Australia (3.3%), among other foreign source countries. These data, however, represent a cross-section of all IENs in Canada and thus may be less reflective of recent migrant nurses who are less likely to be from the United Kingdom than from the Philippines. The high proportion of IENs in Canada of Filipino origin reflects an explicit domestic policy of the Philippines towards the export of nurses (Palaganas 2008). Although the migration of such a large number of nurses from the Philippines has been argued to have had a positive effect on the country in terms of the substantial remittances Filipino nurses send home to their families, concern over how many domestic nursing posts remain unfilled and how there has been a rise in poor health outcomes that parallel this policy of 'nurses for export' have been raised. Sensitivity to these kinds of ethical issues is only beginning to become salient in Canada (McIntosh, Torgerson, & Klassen 2007).

Until the recent decade, the number of migrant health workers in Finland has been very small. This reflects not only a more protectionist welfare state tradition but also a situation where a sufficient domestic recruitment base has no only existed but at timesexceeded demand. Even as late as the 1970s, Finland was a relatively poor country. A sizable portion of the adult population moved abroad to find employment, and for many the move was permanent. Even when the Finnish economy expanded in recent decades, some level of emigration continued, reflecting a possible life choice for this segment of the Finnish population. In 2001 the number of first-generation Finnish citizens living permanently abroad was 305,000, corresponding to nearly 6% of the population (Korkiasaari 2004). The majority of these emigrants moved to Sweden, a wealthier neighbouring country where economic growth in the decades following the Second World War was very strong. Their move to Sweden was also likely facilitated by close cultural affinity and the many historical links they have to the country. Finland is officially a bilingual country and the Swedish language is taught in Finnish schools, so Finns moving to Sweden may have a familiarity with the official language.

Policies aimed at managing immigration of health care personnel to Finland have changed only slowly, as the state authority that licenses health care professionals continues to demand that IENs need to have good language skills, a requirement that is a major obstacle even for professionals of foreign origin already residing in the country. The entrance of IENs to the Finnish labour market is also hampered by the differences in nurse training and practice between Finland and most of the countries from where it would be possible to recruit nurses, primarily Russia and the Baltic states (i.e., nurses in these regions tend to be trained for less independent roles than in Finland and the other Nordic countries). The official policy, both concerning IENs already in the country and those recruited from abroad, is that nurses need complementary education in order to be able to practise in the Finnish context (Nieminen & Henriksson 2008). There are, however, also less visible obstacles to the integration of IENs in Finland. An analysis of policy documents conducted by Wrede (2008a) suggests that the Finnish nursing association upholds a protectionist strategy vis-à-vis IENs.

For all of these reasons, the number of IENs currently practising in Finland is comparatively small compared with other high-income countries, with only 2.8% of new nurse licences in 2006 awarded to IENs (Centre of Medico-Legal Affairs 2007). However, there are signs that the situation is changing. Finnish recruitment agencies are beginning to implement similar high-profile recruitment campaigns abroad that in earlier years irritated policy makers when nurses were recruited from Finland. Established sending countries like the Philippines have been among the first targets (*Helsingin Sanomat* 2008). The economic deregulation in the European Economic Area also enables and supports new forms of mobility for nurses and other health care professionals. One example is the difficult-to-regulate transnational temporary agency work, currently involving nurses from Estonia and the Philippines doing temporary work in Finland (Finnish Ministry of Employment and the Economy 2009). Although such new forms of work undermine potentially prejudiced protectionism, they also threaten efforts to secure equal access to employment-related social rights to internationally educated nurses that are commonplace among Nordic nurses. Currently, there are no reliable estimates of the numbers of this new type of frontier worker in Finnish health care.

In summary, there are important differences between Canada and Finland in regards to the immigration of nurses to these respective countries that help to explain the higher proportion of IENs practising in Canada. In turning to the situation of nurse emigration, we will see some interesting differences which are largely a result of the relative penetration and success of neoliberal policies.

Nurse Emigration from Canada and Finland

If wages and working conditions are critical features in the decision of nurses to immigrate to destination countries like Canada and Finland, it should come as no surprise that these are the very same structural reasons why Canadian and Finnish nurses emigrate. The neoliberal reforms of the 1990s restructured, downsized, and even privatized segments of Canada's public health care system. The resulting instability in the labour market at home encouraged more emigration of Canadian nurses: the number of Canadian nurses migrating to the United States, for example, increased from 330 per year in the late 1980s to 825 in 1996 and 1997 (Zhao, Drew, & Murray 2000). In 1995 this was equivalent to more than a quarter (i.e., 800 of the 3,000) of new Canadian RN graduates. Some estimates calculate that Canada has suffered a net loss of 5,000 to 16,000 registered nurses in total across all provinces in the 1990s (Little 2005). The Canadian Institute for Health Information (2004) reported that in 2003 over 5,000 nurses maintained their Canadian licence while working outside of the country, and over 80% of them were employed in the neighbouring United States (particularly in the border states). In fact, Canada was the second largest source country of IENs in the United States during this period (Buchan, Parkin, & Sochalski 2003). Many Canadian nurses were offered inducements by U.S. employers, including the expectation of rewarding jobs, higher salaries, and better working conditions (Baumann et al. 2004). A Registered Nurses Association of Ontario (RNAO 2001) study of Ontario RNs who left Canada between 1991 and 2000 found that nearly two-thirds of those surveyed said that job opportunities were the main reason they left Canada, especially the availability of full-time employment south of the border. The migration of Canadian nurses to the United States has also been eased by the North American Free Trade Agreement whereby Canadian trained nurses have special visa privileges. Other countries that attract Canadian nurses are Saudi Arabia, the United Kingdom, and Hong Kong where similar incentives are in place. These totals, however, only include nurses who maintained their Canadian licence while working abroad. These data may therefore underestimate the number of Canadian-trained nurses working abroad.

As noted at the outset, migration is intricately linked to working conditions. The 2005 National Survey of the Work and Health of Nurses suggests that nursing in Canada indeed is heavy work, if it is compared with other labour market sectors where women work. Nearly one-third of female nurses were classified as having high job strain and nearly half of nurses reported they were expected to work overtime; three in ten also worked regularly paid overtime (Statistics Canada 2006). Equally important, over one-quarter of nurses reported deterioration in care, while only 16% reported an improvement. Nursing in the long-term/home care sector in Canada – a sector in which the demand for care is increasing with the aging population – is particularly prone to high turnover. Some scholars have linked this outcome to the neoliberal reforms mentioned above. Denton et al. (2007), for example, found in their study of over 800 Ontario home care workers that restructuring towards a market-modelled approach to care – that is, managed care – led to decreased levels of job satisfaction among the nursing staff and a greater propensity for them to leave the home care sector.

As was the case in Canada, historically, nursing was a favoured career choice among Finnish women. After the end of the Second World War, much of Finnish public policy was centred on the building of a welfare state. This created professional opportunities for nurses and social recognition for their work. Growing social recognition did not change the fact, however, that in comparison with other Western European countries, nursing salaries in Finland remained low. As noted above, young professional workers, including nurses, were choosing to leave Finland in the 1960s and 1970s, some who were responding to active recruitment campaigns of those Western European countries that experienced great labour shortages in the postwar decades. The former West Germany and Switzerland, in particular, recruited nurses from abroad in the 1960s and 1970s when there were unique push factors for women to emigrate from Finland. The fact that the German language was commonly taught as the primary foreign language in Finnish schools offers one example of the factors facilitating the small-scale emigration of

Finns to both the former West Germany and Switzerland in this period (Björklund 1998). Even though the number of emigrating nurses in the 1960s and 1970s was relatively small and did not threaten the labour supply in the Finnish health care sector, it did establish a culture of international work in the profession. There were favourable conditions for this, as Finnish nursing education had been organized according to the dominant Anglo-American model since the 1920s and there was respect for foreign work experience as a professional resource.

Later emigration to the Nordic neighbouring countries was more sizable. Throughout the 1980s, Finnish nurses moved mainly to Sweden and, since the 1990s, to the United Kingdom and Norway. In 1999 4.7% of Finnish nurses were employed abroad. Although small in number compared with the entire population of Finnish nurses, when compared with other health care professionals, nurses tend to emigrate more often (Finnish Ministry of Health and Social Affairs 2001: 81).

The more recent emigration noted above occurred in a changed institutional context. Finland applied for membership in the European Union in March 1992, soon after the fall of Soviet Union in 1991. Upon becoming an EU member in 1995 Finland entered into a profoundly transformative process of economic, political, and social integration with Western Europe. These macro-political changes to the transnational links between Finland and its neighbours to the east and west also changed migration patterns in the region, thus shaping the opportunity structure for nurse migration. The emigration of nurses from Finland still continued but rather than simply reflecting poor conditions in Finland, the new opportunities created through European integration also played a role.

This is visible in the fact that the United Kingdom emerged as a new destination country, and the strong economic growth in neighbouring Norway also lured Finnish nurses (Finnish Ministry of Health and Social Affairs 2001: 80). Research evidence indicates that the nurses who left Finland tended to be young, newly graduated nurses who sought employment abroad in the context of an oversupply of nurses (Hardill & MacDonald 2000).

The large 'oversupply' of nurses in the 1990s was the result of state-led efforts to expand nursing training and fewer work opportunities resulting from health care cuts in practice settings. At the same time, nursing work was being reframed by managerialist reforms that increased the work pace of those employed (Wrede 2008b). Indeed, a survey of nurses in ten European countries showed that Finnish nurses reported comparatively high levels of feeling overstreched, and felt more often than nurses in other countries that they had but little influence at work (Hasselhorn et al. 2005). In a recent survey of registered nurses that was conducted in 2005, nearly 40% of Finnish nurses reported that they no longer would choose the occupation, and one-fifth said they were doubtful if they would still make the choice. Both groups reported similar reasons: bad salaries, working conditions, big responsibility under high pressure, and lack of recognition (Santamäki et al. 2009: 34). Registered nurses who graduated during the years 1987 to 1995 were especially likely to be discontented with their jobs (Santamäki et al. 2009: 36). It is during that time the shift to New Public Management occurred in the Finnish public sector (Julkunen 2001).

As noted above, neighbouring Nordic countries with more highly developed welfare states, especially Sweden and Norway, have been the most successful in recruiting Finnish nurses. These countries have been able to tempt nurses from Finland with higher salaries and better working conditions, especially during periods of economic decline in Finland, such as during the early to mid-1990s. Sweden and Norway, countries with less volatile public economies, have been able to maintain a more steady demand for nurses and pay them competitive salaries. Nurse migration from Finland to its Nordic neighbours has also been facilitated by a voluntary integration involving agreements made between the Nordic countries (Sweden, Norway, Denmark, Iceland, and Finland) that cover labour market regulation and the social rights of workers, not only during the recent neoliberal reform period but in fact since the 1950s. Since the early 1980s these agreements have included mutual recognition of professional qualifications for health care. Further, social entitlements, including compensation for parental leave, are at a higher level in Sweden and Norway than in Finland, constituting additional pull factors for Finnish nurses to seek employment in neighbouring countries when conditions at home are less attractive.

In short, the economic downturn of the early to mid-1990s as well as the integrated context offered by the Nordic region, where Nordic citizens can reside in any country with full access to welfare state rights, explains to a large extent why some Finnish nurses made the decision to migrate for employment in the 1990s, as well as during previous periods of economic uncertainty. Table 4.2 shows, however, that the number of nurses moving from Finland to countries outside of the Nordic region is still very small. The nurses who emigrate to the more distant destinations are scattered among a variety of countries, suggesting 'free'

Table 4.2 Circulatory Migration of Finnish Nurses (of Working Age) during the Peak Years, 2000–02

Working-age nurses	Returns by year			Departures by year			Total abroad by year		
State	2000	2001	2002	2000	2001	2002	2000	2001	2002
Norway	140	145	130	185	155	185	800	800	780
Sweden	65	95	115	205	190	205	1,650	1,720	1,790
U.K.	40	40	30	75	65	70	300	310	340
U.S.A.	5	5	15	20	25	20	150	170	200
Germany	15	15	15	20	25	20	280	280	280
Switzerland	5	10	5	25	20	25	320	330	340
Other states	25	25	55	65	75	80	530	580	651
Total	295	335	365	595	555	605	4,030	4,190	4,381

Source: Stakes, Statistics on Health Professionals Residing Abroad 31st of December, 2002 (provided by Reijo Ailasmaa, STAKES, 2 June 2003).

moving for individualistic reasons rather than forced migration result-ing from push factors (STAKES 2003). Table 4.2 also shows, against popular belief, that the number of nurses leaving Finland each year was relatively small (this was the case even during the peak years of nurse emigration), and each year a large number returned, thus contributing to a circulatory migration pattern. When nurse emigration was at its highest, only about 5% of Finnish nurses worked abroad and nearly 60% of them worked in neighbouring Sweden or Norway (Centre of Medico-Legal Affairs 2007).

Although both countries face problems in maintaining an adequate supply of locally trained nurses, our findings suggest Finland has been more successful than Canada in this respect. In part this has happened at the cost of nurses, some of whom have faced structural push factors. The emigration patterns of Finnish nurses suggest that structural reasons, such as a temporary oversupply of nurses, lack of employment oppor-tunities, and a comparatively low level of salaries do push nurses to migrate from Finland. Generally, however, even when moving for struc-tural reasons, Finnish nurses have been able to choose where they have moved to, and they have tended to choose the Nordic countries. There also are indications that a working holiday strategy is prominent among young Finnish nurses. Currently the large majority of the Finnish-trained nurses work in their own country and primarily in their own field (Ailas-maa 2007). This situation is no doubt tied to a relatively strong domestic economy (despite the 2008 global economic recession) and recent public reinvestment into the health care and other sectors. Yet, even though not at the crisis point found in countries such as Canada, an emergent shortage of nurses in Finland largely because of an population aging and growing demand has brought the issue of possible nurse immigration into the focus of national policy debates as discussed above.

Discussion and Conclusions

Developments in Canada and Finland occur in the broader context of international nurse mobility. Typically, the global flows of nurses and other health care workers migrating to high-income countries is argued to be caused in large part by three major push factors that are present in the majority of low-income countries: lack of investment in public health care, overburdened systems, and a globalized market for health care workers (Aiken et al. 2004). Others link nurse migration to Western impe-rialism and (neo)colonialism rather than simply to the structural forces within the national boundary of the receiving region (Choy 2003; Espiritu 2003). Choy (2003) argues in her analysis of the migration of nurses from the Philippines that it 'reflects [an] individual and collective desire for a unique form of social, cultural and economic success' which is seen as 'obtainable only outside the national borders of the Philippines.' In a similar vein, Ishi (1987) stresses the importance of demands of the service economy in high-income countries, and their cultural, political, military, and economic hegemony over low-income countries, as well as immigrants' experience of uncertainty over their futures in their homeland. This perspective not only emphasizes the historical legacy of deepening global inequality, but also the feminization of the migration process and the creation of a gendered labour force in the global system.

The examination of the Canadian and Finnish case examples of nurse migration reveals some key contextual factors that are both similar across both countries and unique to each country. Although Canada and Finland have different immigration and welfare state environments, the context of nursing work has come under similar pressures from neoliberal policies that tend to devalue the care work that nurses perform. These broader contextual factors have resulted in Finnish nursing being somewhat more resistant to these devaluing pressures. Further, despite having very different historical migratory trajectories, similar trends are revealed in terms of how language can be both an opportunity structure as well as a barrier to migration. English-language training influences the source countries for IENs in Canada (the Philippines, the United Kingdom, the United States, Hong Kong, and India), as well as the countries Canadian nursing graduates are destined for.

Similarly, German-language skills enabled Finnish nurses to migrate to the more lucrative environments in Germany and Switzerland. Conversely, the lack of English- or Finnish-language skills makes the integration of IENs into their respective systems more difficult. Both cases also reveal how the economic context of the health care system influences nurses' decision to migrate. Specifically, in times of economic downturn and cutbacks to the health care sector, there are added incentives to leave for countries that can offer better working conditions and remuneration. These are not unusual 'push' and 'pull' factors (Zeytinoglu et al. 2008; CIHI 2004), but a more informed analysis needs to look beyond these factors.

Differences between the two countries were also observed. Even though Finland has a longer history of nursing emigration, it has been more successful than Canada in keeping domestic nurse recruitment at a more optimal level across economic ups and downturns, thereby avoiding the kind of acute nursing labour crisis that Canada experiences from time to time. This seems to be at least in part related to the promotion of Finnish nursing through broader welfare state and gender equity policies and a reduced ability of neoliberal reforms to destabilize the public health care sector. For a long time, continued investment in publicly provided primary care, in particular, created dignified working conditions for many Finnish nurses (Benoit et al., this volume). In fact, the nurses who work in primary care tend to emigrate less often than nurses in other sectors (Finnish Ministry of Health and Social Affairs 2001: 81). A repeated survey of health care professionals suggests, however, that recent restructuring of the public sector has made these groups increasingly dissatisfied with the organization of their work (Laine et al. 2006). Nevertheless, the relatively high value of women's paid health care work in Finland, at least in the past, provides a contrast to the way the devaluing of women's care work in general, and nursing in particular, has been described in many other national contexts, including that of Canada (Armstrong et al. 2000). This devaluation of nursing has only started to turn around in Canada following years of organizational neglect. There is now a growing recognition of the need for a sustainable nursing workforce in the face of population aging in Canada, and dramatic changes to nursing enrolment and employment – including Ontario's guarantee of full-time employment for new nursing graduates – have been implemented to help address these concerns.

Our comparative analysis adds to the growing literature on health care workforce migration by tempering public debates about the recruitment of foreign care workers, including nurses, as a solution to the 'global care shortage' (Zimmerman, Litt, & Bose 2006). Our findings show, in fact, that there is as yet little evidence this is happening to a great extent on the ground. It is not clear how much immigration figures into the nursing care deficit in countries such as Canada and Finland. Our analysis does, however, highlight that internationally implemented neoliberal reforms that changed earlier terms under which nurses worked into a more flexible direction are intricately connected to the devaluing of their intimate labour. This is what pushes nurses from their country of training to other countries in search of better remuneration and working conditions. The national configuration of welfare states in source and destination countries also shaped the gendering of paid intimate labour and immigration patterns. As our case examples have shown, this is so whether movement be *to* or *from* Canada and Finland, even though we recognize that migrants from high-income countries, to a much greater extent, move by choice. There is also evidence to show that the emerging decentralized forms of labour market governance that challenge the regulating power of nation-states are becoming increasingly transnational. The rise of such new, largely market-based frames for decision making destabilizes the settlements that the welfare state offered to gendered social problems.

Our examination of the role of context in the nurse migration process offers a unique perspective on one important factor – the relevance and importance of the dignity and valuing of care work (Benoit & Hall-grímsdóttir, this volume). From the perspective of high-income, receiving countries, international migration of expert labour is changing the face of professions as nationally anchored groups (Allsop et al. 2009). At the same time, there are protectionist elements in national policies concerning the regulation of health care professions that condition the entry of migrants into the professions. Thus, complex stratification processes related to ethnic and cultural origin are to be expected within health care professions in high-income countries.

It is evident that immigrant nurses from high-income countries enjoy a privileged position when compared with immigrant nurses from low-income countries. It is also clear that nurses who migrate wish to have dignity as workers, but this recognition should not be considered separate from the overall recognition of health care workers, both in the 'receiving' and the 'sending' countries. In short, source and destination countries are not separate entities. They exist in changing networks of transnational connections in an increasingly globalized world.

ACKNOWLEDGMENT

Adapted, with permission from the Canadian Public Health Association, from the article by I. Bourgeault and S. Wrede (2008), 'Caring beyond Borders: Comparing the Relationship between Work and Migration Patterns in Canada and Finland: Finding Dignity in Health Care and Health Care Work,' *Canadian Journal of Public Health* 99 (Supplement 2): S22–S26.

REFERENCES

Aiken, L.H., J. Buchan, J. Sochalski, B. Nichols, & M. Powell. (2004). Trends in international nurse migration. *Health Affairs* 23(3): 69–77.
Ailasmaa, R. (2007). Sosiaali- ja terveysalan ammattilaiset ovat oman alansa töissä

(Professionals in social and health fields work in their own fields). *Kuntatyönantaja* 4: 15.

Allsop, J., I. Bourgeault, J. Evetts, K. Jones, T. Le Bianic, & S. Wrede. (2009). Encountering globalization: Professional groups in an international context. Special issue on Comparative Research on the Professions. *Current Sociology* 57: 487–510.

Armstrong, P., H. Armstrong, I.L. Bourgeault, J. Choiniere, E. Mykhalovskiy, & J. White. (2000). *Heal Thyself: Managing Health Care Reform.* Toronto: Garamond Press.

Armstrong, P., J. Choiniere, & E. Day. (1993). *Vital Signs: Nursing in Transition.* Toronto: Garamond Press.

Association of Finnish Local and Regional Authorities. (2008). Kuntatyö 2010 (Municipal Work 2010). Retrieved 15 Jan. 2009 from http://www.kunnat. net/k_perussivu.asp?path=1;55264;122868;75935.

Bach, S. (2003). *International Migration of Health Workers: Labour and Social Issues.* Geneva: International Labour Office.

Batata, A. (2005). International nurse recruitment and NHS vacancies: A cross-sectional analysis. *Globalization and Health* 1: 7.

Baumann, A., J. Blythe, C. Kolotylo, & J. Underwood. (2004). *Immigration and Emigration Trends: A Canadian Perspective.* Ottawa: Nursing Sector Study Corp.

Björklund, K. (1998). Suomalaiset Sveitsissä 1944–1996. *Siirtolaisuus-Migration* 3: 9–14.

Bourgeault, I.L. (2008) 'On the move: The migration of health care providers into and out of Canada. In B. Singh Bolaria & H. Dickenson, eds., *Health, Illness and Health Care in Canada,* 76–98. Toronto: Nelson Education.

Bourgeault, I.L., & C. Benoit. (2004). Introduction: Reconceiving midwifery in Canada. In I. Bourgeault, C. Benoit, & R. Davis Floyd, eds., *Reconceiving Midwifery,* 3–13. Montreal and Kingston: McGill-Queen's University Press.

Buchan, J., T. Parkin, & J. Sochalski. (2003). *International Nurse Mobility: Trends and Policy Implications.* Geneva: World Health Organization.

Calliste, A. (1996). Antiracism organizing and resistance in nursing: African Canadian women. *Canadian Review of Sociology and Anthropology* 33(3): 361–90.

Canadian Institute for Health Information (CIHI). (2000). *The Supply and Distribution of Registered Nurses in Canada, 1999.* Ottawa: Author.

Canadian Institute for Health Information (CIHI). (2004). *Supply and Distribution of Registered Nurses in Canada, 2003.* Ottawa: Author.

Canadian Institute for Health Information (CIHI). (2005). *Workforce Trends of Registered Nurses in Canada, 2004.* Ottawa: Author.

Canadian Nurses Association. (2009). *Testing Solutions for Eliminating Canada's Registered Nursing Shortage.* Retrieved 2 Oct. 2009 from http://www.cnaaiic. ca/CNA/documents/pdf/publications/RN_Highlights_e.pdf.

Centre of Medico-Legal Affairs. (2007). *Statistics on Licensure in 2006.* Retrieved 7 Feb. 2007 from http://www.teo.fi/uusi/tilastotiedot.pdf.

Choy, C. (2003). *Empire of Care: Nursing and Migration in Filipino American History.* Durham, NC: Duke University Press.

Chui, T., K. Tran, & H. Maheux. (2009). *2006 Census: Immigration in Canada – A Portrait of the Foreign-Born Population, 2006 Census: Findings.* Retrieved 10 Oct. 2009 from http://www12.statcan.ca/census-recensement/2006/as-sa/ 97-557/index-eng.cfm.

Davies, C. (1992). Gender, history and management style in nursing: Towards a theoretical synthesis. In M. Savage & A.Witz, eds., *Gender and Bureaucracy,* 229–52. Oxford: Blackwell Publishers / The Sociological Review.

Denton, M., I. Zeytinoglu, K. Kusch, & S. Davies. (2007). Market-modelled home care: Impact on job satisfaction and propensity to leave. *Canadian Public Policy* 23(Suppl.): 81–99.

Espiritu, Y. (2003). *Home Bound: Filipino American Lives across Cultures, Communities and Countries.* Berkeley: University of California Press.

Finnish Ministry of Employment and the Economy. (2009). Ulkomaalaisten tilapäinen työnteko Suomessa. Työ ja yrittäjyys 37/2009. Helsinki: Author.

Finnish Ministry of Health and Social Affairs. (2001). Sosiaali- ja terveydenhuollon työvoimatarpeen ennakointitoimikunnan mietintö. Komiteanmietintö 2001: 7. Helsinki: Author.

Folbre, N. (2006). Nursebots to the rescue? Immigration, automation, and care. *Globalizations* 3(3): 349–60.

Hardill, I., & S. MacDonald. (2000). Skilled international migration: The experience of nurses in the U.K. *Regional Studies* 34: 681–92.

Hasselhorn, H.M., P. Tackenberg, A. Buescher, M. Simon, A. Kuemmerling, & B.H. Mueller. (2005). *Work and Health of Nurses in Europe: Results from the NEXT Study.* Nurses Early Exit Study, University of Wuppertal. Retrieved 15 Jan. 2009 from http://www2.uniwuppertal.de/fb14/next/download/ NEXTnursieu071805.pdf.

Helsingin Sanomat, international ed. (2008). *Everyone who wants to go to Finland, raise your hands. Plans underway to bring tens of thousands of Filipinos to work in Finland.* Retrieved 12 Jan. 2009 from http://www.hs.fi/english/article/Every one+who+wants+to+go+to+Finland+raise+your+h ands/1135233465335.

Hochschild, A.R. (2000). Global care chains and emotional surplus value. In W. Hutton & A. Giddens, eds., *On the Edge: Living with Global Capitalism.* London: Jonathan Cape.

Ishi, T. (1987). Class conflict, the state, and linkage: Migration of nurses from the Philippines. *Berkeley Journal of Sociology* 37: 281–312.

Joint Learning Initiative. (2004). *Human Resources for Health. Overcoming the Crisis.* Harvard: Author.

Julkunen, R. (2001) *Suunnanmuutos.* Tampere: Vastapaino.

Kapur, D., & J. McHale. (2005). *Give Us Your Best and Brightest: The Global Hunt for Talent and the Impact on the Developing World.* Washington: Center for Global Development.

Korkiasaari, J. (2004). *Maastamuuttomaasta maahanmuuttomaaksi?* Institute of Migration, University of Turku. Retrieved 9 Feb. 2007 from http://www. migrationinstitute.fi/db/articles/art.php?artid=25.

Laine M., G. Wickström, J. Pentti, M. Elovainio, A. Kaarlela-Tuomaala, & K. Lindström. (2006). *Työolot ja hyvinvointi sosiaali- ja terveysalalla 2005* (Working Conditions and Well-Being in Social and Health Care 2005). Helsinki: Finnish Institute of Occupational Health.

Little, L. (2005). *The Canadian Case.* Presentation to Bellagio Institute Conference on the International Migration of Nurses. July. Retrieved 14 Jan. 2006 from http://www.academyhealth.org/international/nursemigration/ little.ppt.

Majava, A. (2002). Nykyajan kansainvaellukset: Siirtolaisuuden ja pakolaisuuden yleismaailmalliset näkymät. In K. Pitkänen, ed., *Artikkeleita Suomen väestön tutkimuksesta,* 220–32. Helsinki: University of Helsinki.

Mason, J. (1988). Midwifery in Canada. In S. Kitzinger, ed., *The Midwife Challenge,* 88–133. London: Pandora.

McIntosh, T., R. Torgerson, & N. Klassen. (2007). *The Ethical Recruitment of Internationally Educated Health Professionals: Lessons from Abroad and Options for Canada.* Canadian Policy Research Networks Research Report H11 Health Network. Retrieved 2 June 2009 from http://www.cprn.org/ documents/46781_en.pdf.

Meyer, R., W. Williams, & M. Murphy. (2009). *Review of the Nursing Education Data in Ontario 1990–2004.* NHSRU. Retrieved 15 Oct. 2009 from http:// www.nhsru.com/documents/Review%20of%20Nursing%20Education%20 Data%20in%20Ontario%201990%20-%202004.pdf.

Misra, J., J. Woodring, & S. Merz. (2006). The globalization of care work: Neoliberal economic restructuring and migration policy. *Globalizations* 3(3): 317–32.

Nieminen, S., & L. Henriksson. (2008). Immigrant nurses in Finland: Political negotiations on occupational membership. In S. Wrede, L. Henriksson, H. Høst, S. Johansson, & B. Dybbroe, eds., *Care Work in Crisis: Reclaiming the Nordic Ethos of Care,* 199–218. Lund: Studentlitteratur.

Organisation for Economic Co-operation and Dvelopment (OECD). (2008). *The Looming Crisis in the Health Workforce: How Can OECD Countries Respond?* OECD Health Policy Studies. Paris: Author.

Palaganas, E. (2008). *The Global Migration of Philippine-Trained Nurses: Causes, Impacts and Future Prospects.* Presentation to the University of Ottawa Global Health Equity Group. Retrieved 14 Oct. 2009 from http://www. globalhealthequity.ca/projects/proj_migration_work/pubweb.shtml.

Pyper, W. (2004). Employment Trends in Nursing. *Perspectives on Labour and Income.* 5(11): 5–17. Retrieved 14 Oct. 2009 from http://www.statcan.gc.ca/ pub/75-001-x/11104/7611-eng.htm.

Registered Nurses Association of Ontario (RNAO). (2001). *Earning Their Return – When & Why Ontario RN's Left Canada, and What Will Bring Them Back.*

Santamäki, K., T. Kankaanranta, L. Henriksson, & P. Rissanen. (2009). Sairaanhoitaja 2005. Perusraportti. *83/2009 Working papers.* Yhteiskuntatutkimuksen instituutti & Työelämän tutkimuskeskus, Tampereen yliopisto.

Sibbald, B. (1999). Nurses rally to fight staff shortages, deteriorating morale. *Canadian Medical Association Journal* 161: 67–8.

STAKES. (2003). *Statistics on Health Professionals abroad 31st of December, 2002.* Provided by Reijo Ailasmaa, STAKES, 2 June 2003.

Statistics Canada. (2006). Findings of The National Survey of the Work and Health of Nurses. Available at http://www.statcan.gc.ca/bsolc/olc-cel/olc-cel?catno=83-003-X&lang=eng. Statistics Finland. (2009). Väestö. Suomen kansalaisuuden saamiset 2008. Retrieved 18 Sept. 2009 from http://www. stat.fi/til/kans/2008/kans_2008_2009-05-27_fi.pdf.

Wrede, S. (2008a). Miten globalisaatio haastaa terveydenhuollon protektionismin? Ammattilaisten kansainvälinen liikkuvuus ja ammattijärjestöjen strategiat. In M. Helander, ed., *Going global – ayliikkeen menestysresepti globaalissa ajassa?* 249–82. Jyväskylä: SoPhi.

Wrede, S. (2008b). Educating generalists: The flexibilisation of Finnish auxiliary nursingand the dilemma of professional identity. In E. Kuhlmann & M. Saks, eds., *Rethinking Governance, Remaking Professions: International Directions in Health Care,* 127–40. Cambridge: Polity Press.

Yeates, N. (2004). Global care chains: Critical reflections and lines of enquiry. *International Feminist Journal of Politics* 6: 369–91.

Zeytinoglu, I., M. Denton, S. Davies, B. Seaton, B., & J. Millen. (2008). *Visiting and Office Home Care Workers' Occupational Health: An Analysis of Workplace Flexibility and Worker Insecurity Measures Associated with Emotional and Physical Health.* SEDAP II Research Paper. Hamilton: McMaster University.

Zhao, J., D. Drew, & S. Murray. (2000). Brain drain and brain gain: The migration of knowledge workers from and to Canada. *Education Quarterly Review* 6(3): 8–35.

Zelizer, V.A. 2007. Caring everywhere. Keynote Address, Conference on Intimate Labors, University of California, Santa Barbara, 4–6 Oct.

Zimmerman, M., J. Litt, & C. Bose. (2006). *Global Dimensions of Care work and Gender.* Stanford: Stanford University Press.

PART THREE

Paid Care Work In Intimate and
Community Settings

5 Patching Up the Holes: Analysing Paid Care Work in Homes

MARY ELLEN PURKIS, CHRISTINE CECI,
AND KRISTIN BJORNSDÓTTIR

Health care provided in the community, within people's homes, is variably viewed as a key component of a fully functioning public health care system (NACA 2000; Romanow 2002), as an unwelcome intrusion into a living space full of private decisions about how to live a life (Angus et al. 2005), and as a form of underpaid, undervalued work, or intimate labour, that has become a gendered ghetto for marginalized women (Armstrong & Armstrong 1996; Aronson & Neysmith 2006; Benoit & Hallgrímsdóttir, this volume).

In confronting the significant challenges posed by home-based care we hope to encourage critical reflection on the sorts of strategies that we have observed being incorporated into home care practice (Björnsdóttir 2002; Ceci 2006a, 2006b; Purkis 2001; Purkis & Björnsdóttir 2006). Through our various individual and joint field studies of home care practice in Canada (Ceci & Purkis) and in Iceland (Bjornsdóttir), we have observed relentless pressure being applied on nurses and allied health care workers to increase the 'efficiency' of their practices by making use of standardizing processes. These standardizing processes incorporate a task orientation into the work of caring for older people that shifts responsibility for work previously understood as professional to non-professional staff and to clients and family members themselves. We show below that such practices tend to work against supports and structures that would 'hold' the dignity of the work in place by undermining the worth of the work, the workers, and those in need of assistance (see Eni, this volume).

In this chapter we investigate the ways in which neoliberal efficiency strategies serve to *distract* managers and policy makers from formulating and addressing core questions that we believe *precede* those of how to ensure efficiency of service delivery. The questions we refer to here are ones that address the goals of a contemporary home care service, questions such as: what sort of effective and respectful partnerships could be built between state-supported health service delivery and the care provided by private citizens such as family members and/or neighbours to support the care of older adults now and into the long-term future? How can an effective service be developed when the needs of the older adult population are not regulated by times of the day but rather by circumstances that can change at a moment's notice? What kind of system supports the dignity of this sort of health care work, work currently performed largely by women? Sites in Canada and Iceland have been chosen to explore these questions because these are two countries that have travelled along a similar path, though at different speeds. Both have historical roots as welfare states, committed to using political power to mitigate socially produced dangers to individual and collective existence (Bauman 2004). Their respective health care systems are one example of this. Recent decades, however, have witnessed the withdrawal of the state from areas of collective concern, including home care. For Canadians, consideration of the Icelandic context reveals what has been altered and lost in Canada, at a very practical level, through globalization and the implementation of a neoliberal agenda. For Icelanders, the comparison offers a glimpse of future possibilities, one especially poignant as the recent (2008) economic collapse in Iceland has already resulted in significant retrenchment in health care spending. We begin with a brief overview of the policy contexts within which home care service delivery is currently emerging in both countries. We then present two case examples from separate field studies undertaken in Canada and Iceland that offer access to the everyday worlds of home care practice in these two countries. Our aim is to demonstrate, through a close reading of home care practice, how gendered political and organizational contexts influence the ways in which practitioners assess and respond to the situations that older adults live in.

Caring for People in Their Homes: The Policy Context of Canada and Iceland

The Canadian Context

Most high-income countries have developed systems for providing home-making and health-related supports to people – often seniors or those with chronic illness and/or disability – who require such assistance to continue to live in their own homes. In Canada the majority of older people (93%) live in their own homes, with the remaining 7% residing in collective dwellings such as nursing homes or hospitals (Turcotte & Schellenberg 2007). The rate of institutionalization has, in fact, been decreasing since the 1980s, especially among Canadians aged 85 and over. About one-third of Canadians aged 85 or older live alone in a private dwelling, compared with 22% of those between ages 65 and 74 years. Almost twice as many older women live alone than older men. Turcotte and Schellenberg note that the acceptability, or not, of living arrangements is mostly related to financial well-being and the presence of social support.

Although home has always been the principal site of care of the sick or frail by family members and other informal caregivers, home has over the past two decades become an increasingly important location for the delivery of professional health care services (Baranek, Deber, & Williams 2004; Coyte & McKeever 2001; Romanow 2002). As more people are either being treated or are recovering at home, the acuity traditionally associated with institutions is transferred to these home settings. At the same time, changing demographics, including an aging population means that the numbers of traditional clients of home health care, the frail elderly and the chronically ill, are also increasing.

This shift in location of care from institutional to home settings must also be recognized as a cost shift. As Baranek, Deber, and Williams (2004:4) observe, more than simply a change in the *site* of care, the move out of hospitals and other institutions 'results in an increasing proportion of care moving beyond the collective logic and institutionalized boundaries of the "Medicare" mainstream.' Unprotected by the auspices of the Canada Health Act of 1984, home care is governed neither by federal legislation nor national standards. Although most provinces fund some components of home care, local policy makers have been preoccupied with questions of cost-sharing and base levels of services. In general, the further one moves from traditionally conceived health care or medical services, and from professional to non-professional services, the more attenuated are arguments for the public provision of services. And, as Duncan and Reutter (2006) have observed, with an increasing neoliberal policy preoccupation with the acute or substitution (for institutional care) functions of home care, those who have benefited from longer-term maintenance and preventive services become further disadvantaged in the competition for what have come to be seen as scarce resources.

The Icelandic Context

Compared with many neighbouring countries, the Icelandic nation is relatively young. In 2002 only 11.7% of its population was 65 years or older, compared with 14.8% in Denmark and 17.3% in Sweden (Halldorsson 2003). Until recently institutionally based services for the elderly were the norm in Iceland. In their calls for reform in services, lobby groups and politicians have traditionally focused on the need for more institutional capacity, although that has changed in recent years. Therefore, the number of nursing home placements available in the country has been comparatively high (Halldorsson 2003). These statistics reflect what has been and still is among many people the expectation that when their health starts to fail and the ability to care for oneself declines, a transfer to a nursing home is the logical next step.

In spite of these realities, policies in Iceland have for some time stressed the right to live at home for as long as possible, even with decreased functional ability resulting from chronic illnesses or advanced age. This policy emphasis is reflected in the 1983 Act on the Affairs of the Elderly, revised in 1999. The health and well-being of the elderly was also a main focus in the 'Health for All' document entitled, *The Icelandic National Health Plan to the Year 2010,* which was passed by parliament in 2001. One objective of this report was to ensure that at least 75% of people 80 years of age or older would be able, with appropriate help, to live in their own homes (Ministry of Health and Social Security 2004). In the summer of 2006 the minister of health and social security issued another policy statement, *A New Vision – New Emphasis,* in which numerous improvements in services for the elderly were promised (Ministry of Health and Social Security 2006). Home care services, such as nursing and social services, were identified as being of central importance.

In the past several years years considerable attempts have been made to make home care services widely available to the nation. One of the main obstacles to the development of comprehensive home care services has been an undeveloped organizational structure and unclear responsibility for the provision of services. Another major complaint has been the poor coordination between health care and social services. Health care services are organized and administered at the federal level, while social services are the responsibility of the municipalities. Recent policy documents have suggested restructuring health and social services to enhance integration (Bjartmarz et al. 2006).

In short, the idea that everyone should be helped to live in his or her home as long as possible despite, even *in spite of* serious limitations in functional ability and complex health problems, is currently well established in Canada and in the process of being developed in Iceland. The successful accomplishment of such a policy goal would seem to require significant investment in supportive social-organizational capacities. Our intention in considering these two home care situations has been to clarify the extent to which dignity in health care encounters must not rely only on the well-intentioned desires of the participants, providers, and clients, but also on the systems that support them.

Methods

Two separate studies provided the data for this analysis. Both were ethnographic, involving an analysis of the context of health care as represented in policy documents and organizational structures; interviews with practitioners, patients, and family members; and observations of nursing practice in the home environment, and they were all similarly analysed using a constant comparison method (Glaser 1965). Following Yin's (2003) method of explanatory, single-case study, this chapter draws out the specifics of the constraints and possibilities of the work done by nurses in Canada and Iceland as they visit a typical client of home care service. Rather than arguing for the generalizability of the cases we aim to *illustrate* what nurses treat as necessary to find out during a home visit and how they use that knowledge to create a network with family and wider community resources in the provision of care. This ethnomethodological approach (Garfinkel 1967) allows us to offer an analysis of the work that always links back to an instance of typical practice.

The actual fieldwork for the Canadian study took place over approximately nine months in 2004. Seven case managers, all women, all experienced nurses with baccalaureate preparation, were the central participants in the study, allowing observation of their practices of screening clients, determining eligibility, making referrals, monitoring clients' status, and re-evaluating over time. These practices were both the entry point and centre of the analysis of this study, offering access to the field of care and the dilemmas currently shaping it. The study received ethical approval from the University of Victoria and the Vancouver Island Health Authority.

The Icelandic study involved thirty households where one individual was assessed to be in need of considerable assistance with daily activities and/or specialized treatment. This assistance was provided by registered nurses,[1] most of whom had diploma education, as well as lesser trained auxiliary nurses and relatives, when available. All the nurses were female, but the relatives were both men and women. The data collection took place in Reykjavik and neighbouring municipalities from 2001 until 2004. The project involved semi-structured interviews with patients, caregivers, and nurses, in addition to field observation written by the researcher during visits made by the nurse to the patients' homes. The study was approved by the National Bioethics Committee for Iceland.

Results

The Canadian case study is developed in some detail in order to illustrate what health care work looks like when circumscribed by discursive practices that emphasize efficiency and an imperative to enroll family members in its conduct. The Icelandic data suggest an alternative way to conceptualize the work, with practice organized around an idea of 'flexibility' that contrasts with the Canadian example.

We begin with the Canadian case study and a typical case manager activity – the assessment-oriented home visit. The case manager explains her task to the researcher:

> I have to go and see Mrs Watson, […] I am going to go in and do a review with the daughter at 0930 … the last time this woman has seen a doctor was sixty-nine years ago. She's 94 or 5 years old now … the family's really rallied, lots of help going in there. I think I am going to reassess her because she needs more hours … [T]he family's asking for 3 hours in the evening, I have to go and justify it … I can't at her current assessment level. She lived for a time in Brookside House, a [faith-based] assisted living place …

---

1 The term for a nurse in Icelandic is reserved for Registered Nurses. A different term is used for Auxiliary Nurses – *sjúkraliðar*. When we talk about 'nurses' in this chapter, we are referring to Registered Nurses (i.e., those with university degree preparation). It should be noted however, that Registered Nurses and Auxiliary Nurses worked very closely together and the boundaries between their work was flexible.

[T]hey said they couldn't keep her because she was too sick. (Ceci, Field-notes, 2004; names have been changed to ensure anonymity)

The information provided in this account points to a variety of policy structures that shape the work of this case manager. She identifies her main purpose in making the visit to be determining whether there is a 'justification' for additional home support hours for Mrs Watson in the evening. The information contained in Mrs Watson's file would not currently permit the case manager to approve additional time for evening support. However, if she can 'reassess' Mrs Watson, there is a sense of expectation that such reassessment will generate sufficient additional information to enable her to alter the level of support (measured in hours) that Mrs Watson is eligible for.

The case manager knows that Mrs Watson did try living in a more supportive environment: an assisted living facility run by her church. However, Mrs Watson required too much from that facility. She was deemed by them 'too sick' to remain there and so was sent back home again. The situation described by the case manager seems incongruous: Mrs Watson is 'too sick' for an assisted living placement and so she is returned home, where, except for the fact that her family has 'rallied,' there would be little support for her beyond the two hours of paid home support she receives each day. If we juxtapose this situation against the scope of the solution that's being considered by the case manager, that is, the addition of one more hour of paid support, it is hard to comprehend how this solution might actually be considered helpful and how a highly paid, intelligent professional could engage in this as legitimate and rewarding work, that is, as 'good' work. However, this is not the case manager's work. Instead, as we will see, she understands her work as a form of 'professional coordination.'

When the case manager gets to Mrs Watson's home, a woman who appears to be in her early 70s greets her at the door. This is Mrs Watson's daughter. The implications of elderly children being the 'family that rallies' to the aid of an even older parent are effectively hidden in the earlier discussion with the researcher. And, of course, at closer proximity, much more is revealed:

The smell of urine is very strong on entering the house and [the daughter] says, 'I left everything as I found it this morning when I arrived.' Aside from the smell of urine the home appears clean and tidy. Mrs Watson is seated at the dining room table. She is very small woman, appears well groomed, alert but frail. She greets the case manager cheerfully. The case manager sits at the table with Mrs Watson and [the daughter] sits in the living room. (Ceci, fieldnotes 2004)

The case manager begins the process of 'reassessment.' The case manager asks a series of questions, such as whether Mrs Watson has pain, what time she arises in the morning and goes to bed at night, and whether she wakes up during the night. Mrs Watson responds to each question in a way that suggests her hearing is very good and that she clearly understands the questions. It is only when her daughter, who is some distance away, contradicts nearly every response that a more complex picture begins to take shape.

Mrs Watson claims that she has no pain, arises each morning at approximately 7:00 a.m., goes to bed at approximately 9:30 p.m., and does not awaken at all through the night. Her daughter directly contradicts the claim regarding pain telling the case manager, 'that's not true.' She also reiterates her central concern that has been behind getting the case manager to visit today; apparently, Mrs Watson has been waking regularly at 4:00 or 5:00 a.m. and phoning members of the family complaining about being cold. When they come to check on her, she has most often been incontinent of urine in the bed or while trying to get to the commode that is kept near her bedside.

A walk down the hallway to determine how steady Mrs Watson is reveals precisely what the daughter meant when she said she had 'left everything as I found it this morning when I arrived.' In addition to urine, there were also small amounts of stool on the floor between Mrs Watson's bed and the commode. In this moment, the case manager sees both front stage and back stage (Goffman 1959) regions of this home. Mrs Watson provides a version of the 'front stage' of her life; her daughter directs the case manager to see the 'back stage' areas of her mother's life and, at the same time, her own life. At this moment we can see the precise 'rigid polarities between the economic and personal spheres with rationality on one side and sentiment on the other' proposed by Zelizer (2002: 116). Benoit and Hallgrímsdóttir (2008) describe this polarity as being materialized as a false binary between sentiment and caring, on the one hand, and in contrast to rational economic activity, on the other. In the particular situation we highlight here, the dichotomy between caring and economics is demonstrated to be much more complex than such a simple and false binary would suggest. Although Mrs Watson's capacity to live independently remains unresolved by the rationalities imposed on this situation by the case manager, Mrs Watson's daughter is being called upon to bolster a perception that Mrs Watson is living independently. The longer this situation persists, the more likely it is that ultimately the case manager will have two clients to provide for rather than just one, as the daughter's health deteriorates as she seeks to meet the increasing dependencies that her mother has on her. If this were a 'purely' rational process, one might expect that a more 'efficient' response (e.g., supportive housing) might be advanced by the case manager in order to avoid further deleterious impacts on both Mrs Watson and her daughter. This does not occur.

As the visit of an hour and a half in length draws to a close, Mrs Watson has visibly faded. The conversation has turned away from Mrs Watson and is more actively being conducted between the case manager and the daughter. Sensing that the discussion has shifted focus, Mrs Watson tries to reassert herself:

> I've never been so disgusted in my life ... people making such a fuss, making it a big reality that it's hard to rise above. (Ceci, fieldnotes 2004)

The 'Reality' of Home Care

The case manager now talks about having a 'picture' of Mrs Watson's life. The case manager reminds Mrs Watson and her daughter that:

> they [the home support workers] are doing laundry, cleaning, emptying the commode ... [T]here's no personal care being done ... so we'll be doing personal care ... [W]e have a lot happening here; we just have to coordinate it.

Referring to Mrs Watson, she says to the daughter:

> it's just not there, her memory is like swiss cheese, there's gaps ... [S]he's always been someone to direct traffic, your family can't leave her anymore to direct you ... [Y]ou are going to have to step in.

It is significant that this statement is made at this stage in the visit. Prior to the visit, the case manager described the family's contribution in quite positive ways. They had rallied to provide care for Mrs Watson and there was, apparently, 'lots of help going in there.' Now that the formal reassessment had been conducted, the case manager underlines that the rallying is not going to be just for a short time. The efforts currently being made by the family may not be sufficient. *Increased* involvement by the family is now recognized as part of the formal coordination of services.

Against this emerging picture of how things are according to the case manager, the daughter resists. According to her, Mrs Watson has *not* been the organizer in the family: 'She couldn't even organize herself to wash the dishes every day.' The case manager brings the conversation back to what, for her, is a more relevant place in relation to the coordinating work that she's there to accomplish:

> well she's slipping and it's harder and harder for her to hold on ... [Y]ou've stepped in and now it's a matter of coordinating things.

It appears that it does not matter who takes on the organizational work. By 'stepping in,' the daughter has signalled that she is available to be enrolled (Callon & Law 1982) as part of the gendered network of coordination that the case manager is making explicit.

Individualizing Practices

There are some key pieces of information that have been created through this home visit. Most noticeable in this last exchange between the case manager and the daughter is that, as much as the daughter is looking for relief from this situation, she has 'stepped in' and now the case manager needs her to remain 'in.' Despite the many clues offered by the daughter that the relationship between mother and daughter may not be positive, she must play a part in the coordination. The daughter is the person to whom the coordinated services are going to be attached. The case manager does not ask about other responsibilities the daughter may also carry. In not asking, the daughter is positioned as the most efficient rational response to this situation. There will be no collective option, such as supportive housing, offered. Instead, the case manager proposes to 'coordinate' family members to serve the interests of a rationalized, neoliberal health care system.

The 'Old' Way of Providing Home Care

The early data (2001–02) collected for the Icelandic study offer a clear contrast to the current Canadian situation. This situation is referred to as 'old' because it has not yet been infiltrated by a neoliberal economic discourse demanding a clear differentiation of the kind of work each worker is allowed to do – the sort of differentiation that is clearly embedded in the Canadian case study where the case manager will engage the services of a range of different workers, each of whom will only be able to come for specified periods of time and to undertake very particular aspects of the caring work. By contrast, the main characteristic of home care work in Iceland at the time of the fieldwork was flexibility. The nurses could decide upon the services to be provided based on their assessment of the patients' needs and their wishes related to how the assistance was to be provided. If a patient's condition deteriorated, they increased services with visits up to eight or nine times a day. In many cases, they also turned to the family for more participation, similar to what was done by the case manager above, but with an awareness of how, as one nurse said: 'families differ as to how much they are willing to or can offer' (Björnsdóttir, interview transcript 2001).

At the time of the study, home care nursing in Iceland was organized by neighbourhood community health care centres (for parallels in maternity care, see Benoit et al., this volume). The care provided by the nurses involved personal care such as bathing, assistance with mobility, and getting dressed; assistance with taking medications, symptom monitoring and management, wound care, incontinence care, and various psychological supports. Many of the responsibilities described above for case managers in Canada, such as coordinating services and applying for additional services, were also part of the Icelandic nurse's work. This organization of the work meant that, rather than many workers coming in to the home for different tasks, the work was mainly shared by home care nurses and people from the social services.

In the interviews, both patients and their relatives expressed satisfaction with the services provided through home care. The nurses were seen as knowledgeable and resourceful. Many of the patients, particularly those who were living alone and did not have much contact with friends or family, said that it was nice to have someone come to visit who was leading an active life, raising children, travelling, and going to the theatre or the movies. Relationships between nurses, patients, and caregivers were casual and relaxed. The nurse would sit at the kitchen table and talk when filling the medicine boxes for the week or have a cup of coffee and chat after completing a bath or wound dressing. They asked questions about how things had been going and usually had a pretty good overview of people's situations.

In informal conversations between visits and in interviews the nurses said that they liked their work. They felt that they were of considerable help to the patients and that their services made it possible for their clients to stay living at home. Most days they could easily manage the workload and give the patients the time they needed. Many of them even saw it as the role of public services to help the people with personal matters such as washing, getting dressed, and performing treatments in order for the patient and relatives to spend quality time together.

Although the flexibility of the services seemed to be highly beneficial, it was noticed that the informal organization and lack of coordination between systems could easily arouse frustrations among relatives. In that way, home care in Iceland was similar to Canada. Family caregivers were often overwhelmed by the responsibilities involved in their role. Many described how they had no time for themselves; they were always on call and felt that it was very difficult to get out of the house. They also described how difficult it had been to get access to home care services. They said that in the initial phases, when it was becoming apparent that the patient was beginning to need more help than they could provide, no one seemed to know where to turn for assistance.

A good example of this was Anna and her husband Bjorn who lived in an apartment building for the elderly. They had been married for sixty years and their marriage had been a happy one. Their four children visited frequently. Bjorn's cognitive function had become seriously impaired due to transient ischemic attacks (TIAs). He needed assistance with dressing and bathing and had suffered from incontinence for many years.

An auxiliary nurse came in the morning to help him get dressed and also in the evening to prepare him for bed. Bjorn spent the day at a day centre for the elderly. In between these times, Anna tried to manage the incontinence, supervising him constantly, assisting him to the bathroom, cleaning him, and changing his clothing. Anna's capacity to continue this unpaid care work, however, was a significant concern:

> At the interview Anna seemed confused and told me that she had nothing to tell me. I asked her if she wanted me to leave, but she told me that her daughter would be coming to talk to me. A few minutes later three of her children arrived ... She [the daughter] told me that 'something had to be done.' Her mother could not go on like this any longer. 'She spends all of

her waking hours cleaning and washing and she is about to break. It is just too much for her.' (Björnsdóttir, fieldnotes 2002)

Anna's daughter felt that her mother was entitled to more formal help, which in this case would mean a permanent placement for Bjorn in a nursing home. She said that the home care nurses were very helpful and she was happy with their services, but she now felt that the time had come for her father to go into a nursing home. In many ways her views reflected the expectations among Icelanders that moving into a nursing home is to be expected along with declining ability.

When the nurse in charge of Bjorn's care was interviewed, she said that she was surprised to hear that Anna's daughter had been trying to get her father into a nursing home 'behind the curtains':

the relatives have a very difficult time understanding that there are no easy solutions. Respite care and permanent nursing home placements are so few and you have to wait for a long time until your turn comes. (Björnsdóttir, interview transcript 2002).

She described her efforts to organize respite time for Bjorn, without success as yet, so that Anna could have an eye operation she required.

Summary and Conclusions

The intimate labour of home care work involves the sort of activities that are very often identified as 'domestic' – non-intellectual, task-oriented, to do with bodies and other private or personal matters. Even the 'professional' roles associated with home care, the work of case managers illustrated in this chapter remains primarily identified with ideas of women's work, focused as case managers tend to be, on (merely) coordinating the caring activities of others. The supportive care of older people is often thought of and treated as though it is work that is naturally and straightforwardly accomplished, particularly since most such work continues to be undertaken, for free, by family members.

Both of the case examples present in this chapter refute this assumption. The case studies exemplify how challenging and complex this work – figuring out what to do for people who have become frail – actually is. In both cases the 'family' does not know what to do anymore or no longer has the capacity or desire to cope. It turns to the 'safety net' of a publically funded health care system for assistance.

That system, in turn, redirects them to continue to provide the same sort of assistance they have been providing and from which they are now exhausted.

The market-based vocabulary of neoliberalism – efficiency, choice, competition – and associated ideals of individual autonomy, self-help, and personal responsibility (Knijn & Verhagen 2007) seem to have little to do with what is going on in these situations but policy and practices shaped by these values will certainly have effects – and these will often be *gendered* effects. When the care of frail elders is expected to be taken up by the family, there is ample evidence that it is female family members who experience increased responsibilities for caregiving, yet many families are simply no longer organized in ways that support women in easily taking on this additional work. It can no longer be assumed that women are 'at home' and able to provide care (Bjórnsdóttir 2002; Flood 1999; Gregor 1997).

The situation in the Canadian example underlines the dilemmas of home-based care for those who are frail and elderly, including aging family caregivers and care needs beyond the capacities of these informal carers. The Canadian case study illustrates that it is women, and increasingly elderly women, who are actually doing the work of caring in highly individualized situations, largely unsupported by the heavy, rationalized system of modern health care. In acknowledging this, we can trace the normative assumptions that are being made in these everyday practices about gender, social class, and increasingly, ethnicity (Knijn & Verhagen 2007) and demonstrate that neoliberal family policies have effects that tend towards undermining the equality of all women (Borchorst & Siim 2002). Thus, care work, public policy, and family are interdependent concepts and shaped by the larger gender system (McDaniel 2002). Who takes care of aging members of a society at any point in time depends on gendered intergenerational relations and the shape of the economy and welfare state. In the recent neoliberal period, public policy has emphasized social cohesion between the generations and has expected family members to pick up the slack for market failures: 'The principles on which our society has built so-called social safety nets are laced with holes and far from shockproof. This means that when shocks occur such as the economic restructuring Canada has experienced over the past decade, or various recent recessionary periods which has seen intractable high unemployment particularly among youth, families in multiple generations become the shock absorbers. As public transfers shrink even more, families may huddle ever more closely, for good or bad, to share resources and to maximize opportunities' (McDaniel 1998: 38).

The Icelandic study, on the other hand, provides an example of home care that in most ways meets the needs of individuals who need assistance. And although there are similarities in the organization of home care in Canada and Iceland, there are also important differences that seem to stem from each system's underlying philosophy. In Canada, home care at the present time is a highly structured and scarce commodity, shaped by an increasingly acute client base because of policies that enable the discharge of people from acute care hospitals ('sicker and quicker'), that narrow eligibility requirements for services, and that reduce the absolute number of long-term care beds available. Responding to these constraints has meant ensuring a formal kind of equity in the system – service maximums, time-task management strategies, strict eligibility requirements. Within a system that institutes scarcity in this way *and* also encourages people to remain in their own homes rather than moving to institutionalized care facilities, interventions are aimed at rationing care so that everyone has more or less equivalent access to the limited resources available. Yet the fairness of a care system that demands, indeed relies on, the efforts of a 70-year-old daughter who holds historical frustrations and anger towards her 94-year-old mother while providing one additional hour of support per day in response to this client's declining status is questionable. If every social situation can be understood as an encounter between public and private interests (Mouffe 2006), then this unhelpful response moves us in the direction of 'privatizing' the complicated and important care needs of older adults.

In Iceland, though the 'content' of the work, the people and their life concerns are similar, how the work occurs makes a difference that is worth paying attention to. Without valourizing the Icelandic context, we suggest that the *flexibility* that has been characteristic here, and in Canada prior to the economic retrenchment of the early 1990s (Duncan & Reutter 2006), reflects an organizational ethos more likely to meet the needs of fragile individuals who live at home. In Iceland, in 2002, there were no service maximums. The work was organized around a nurse-family relationship supplemented by other workers. Time for casual discussion and personal exchange was considered important, and though family members were expected to participate in care, if they were not available, the health care system stepped in. Although under this system there were people who could not obtain the assistance they needed, the system worked well once you had a nurse who would come to look after you. The practice of care was satisfactory, leaving Icelanders with other important political discussions, including how to ensure adequate amounts of it. But the care itself was conducted with a certain dignity, with the sense that this was indeed, work worth doing.

The central insight this comparison offers, then, is that in terms of ensuring the 'dignity' of this sort of health care work, time and resources are necessary precedents. That is, providers of all stripes may be endlessly caring and compassionate, but dignity, if it is not to be merely an abstraction, requires a framework integrating institutional structures and social legitimacy to make it real.

ACKNOWLEDGMENT

Adapted, with permission from the Canadian Public Health Association, from the article by M.E. Purkis, C. Ceci, and K. Bjornsdottir (2008), 'Patching Up the Holes: Analysing the Work of Home Care,' *Canadian Journal of Public Health* 99 (Supplement 2): S27–S32.

REFERENCES

Act on the Affairs of the Elderly. (1999). No. 125. Retrieved 31 Jan. 2007 from http://eng.heilbrigdisraduneyti.is/laws-and-regulations/.

Angus, J., P. Kontos, I. Dyck, P. McKeever, & B. Poland. (2005). The personal significance of home: Habitus and the experience of receiving long-term home care. *Sociology of Health and Illness* 27(2): 161–87.

Armstrong, P., & H. Armstrong. (1996). *Wasting Away: The Undermining of Canadian Health Care*. New York: Oxford University Press.

Aronson, J., & S. Neysmith. (2006). Obscuring the costs of home care: Restructuring at work. *Work, Employment and Society* 20: 27–45.

Baranek, P., R. Deber, & A. William. (2004). *Almost Home: Reforming Home and Community Care in Ontario*. Toronto: University of Toronto Press.

Bauman, Z. (2004). *Wasted Lives: Modernity and Its Outcasts*. Cambridge: Polity.

Benoit, C., & H. Hallgrímsdóttir. (2009). Engendering research on care and care work across different social contexts. *Canadian Journal of Public Health* 99 (Suppl. 2): S7–S10.

Bjartmarz, J., D. Hjartardóttir, E.B. Friðfinnsdóttir, G. Garðarsson, H. Jónsson, M. Pétursson, M., Frímannsdóttir, S. Sveinsson, & S.S. Sigurðsson. (2006). *Hver geri hvað í heilbrigðisþjónustunni (Who Does What in Health Care)*.

Skýrsla og tillögur nefndar heilbrigðis- og tryggingamálaráðherra um endurskilgreiningu verksviða innan heilbrigðisþjónustunnar. Reykjavík: Heilbrigðis- og tryggingamálaráðuneytið.

Björnsdóttir, K. (2002). From the state to the family: Reconfiguring the responsibility for long-term nursing care at home. *Nursing Inquiry* 9(1): 3–11.

Borchorst, A., & B. Siim. (2002). The women-friendly welfare states revisited. *NORA: Nordic Journal of Feminist and Gender Research* 2: 90–8.

Callon, M., & J. Law. (1982). On interests and their transformation: Enrolment and counter-enrolment. *Social Studies of Science* 12: 615–25.

Ceci, C. (2006a). 'What she says she needs doesn't make a lot of sense': Seeing and knowing in case management practice. *Nursing Philosophy* 7: 90–9.

Ceci, C. (2006b). Impoverishment of practice: Effects of economic discourses in home care case management. *Canadian Journal of Nursing Leadership* 19: 73–85.

Coyte, P.C., & P. McKeever. (2001). Home care in Canada: Passing the buck. *Canadian Journal of Nursing Research* 33(2): 11–25.

Duncan, S., & L. Reutter. (2006). A critical policy analysis of an emerging agenda for home care in one Canadian province. *Health and Social Care in the Community* 14(3): 242–53.

Flood, C. (1999). *Unpacking the Shift to Home Care*. Halifax: Maritime Centre of Excellence for Women's Health.

Garfinkel, H. (1967). *Studies in Ethnomethodology*. Englewood Cliffs: Prentice-Hall.

Glaser, B. (1965). The constant comparative method of qualitative analysis. *Social Problems* 12: 436–45.

Goffman, E. (1959). *The Presentation of Self in Everyday Life*. Garden City: Doubleday.

Gregor, F. (1997). From women to women: Nurses, informal caregivers and the gender dimension to health care reforms in Canada. *Health and Social Care in the Community* 5: 30–6.

Halldorsson, M. (2003). *Health Care Systems in Transition: Iceland*. Copenhagen: WHO, Regional Office for Europe on behalf of the European Observatory on Health Systems Policies.

Knijn, T., & S. Verhagen. (2007). Contested professionalism: Payments for care and quality of home care. *Administration and Society* 39: 451–75.

McDaniel, S. (1998). Public policy, demographic aging and families. *Policy Options* 20(7): 36–8.

McDaniel, S. (2002). Intergenerational interlinkages: Public, family, and work. In D. Cheal, ed., *Aging and Demographic Change in Canadian Context*, 22–71. Toronto: University of Toronto Press.

Ministry of Health and Social Security. (2004). *Icelandic National Health Plan to the Year 2010*. Reykjavik: Author.

Ministry of Health and Social Security (Heilbrigðis- og tryggingamálaráðuneytið). (2006). *Ný sý – ýjar leiðir: Áherslur heilbrigðis- og tryggingamálaráðherra í öldrunarmálum*. Reykjavík: Heilbrigðis- og tryggingamálaráðuneytið.

Mouffe, C. (2006). *On the Political*. London: Routledge.

National Advisory Council on Aging (NACA). (2000). *The NACA Position on Home Care*. Ottawa: Minister of Public Works and Government Services.

Purkis, M.E. (2001). Managing home nursing care: Visibility, accountability and exclusion. *Nursing Inquiry* 8: 141–50.

Purkis, M.E., & K. Björnsdóttir. (2006). Intelligent nursing: Accounting for knowledge as action in context of practice. *Nursing Philosophy* 7: 247–56.

Romanow, R. (2002). *Discussion Paper: Homecare in Canada*. Ottawa: Comission of the Future of Health Care in Canada and Canadian Health Services Research Foundation.

Turcotte, M., & G. Schellenberg. (2007). *A Portrait of Seniors in Canada, 2006*. Ottawa: Statistics Canada.

Yin, R.K. (2003). *Case Study Research: Design and Methods*, vol. 3. Thousand Oaks: Sage.

Zelizer, V.A. (2002). How care counts. *Contemporary Sociology* 31: 115–19.

6 My Home, Your Work, Our Relationship: Elderly Clients' Experiences of Home Care Services

ANNE MARTIN-MATTHEWS AND JOANIE SIMS-GOULD

Bridget

Bridget is 87 years old, and she receives home care twice a week for two hours each visit. She has lived alone since her husband died nine years ago. She has a stepson whom she seldom sees, and a foster son who lives on the other side of the province. Bridget goes to the seniors' centre regularly where she plays cards and other games. She does not want to move to a facility and is determined to stay in her own home as long as she can.

Bridget indicated that her health is 'pretty poor' as she suffers from physical ailments including arthritis and a hernia. The hernia is quite serious, and when combined with her arthritis, it limits her mobility and prevents her from lifting heavy objects. Bridget would rather not have home care services at all, but acknowledges that she really does need the help. She requires assistance from her home care workers with bathing, meal preparation, washing dishes, accompanying her to appointments, grocery shopping, vacuuming, and mopping the kitchen floor. Bridget complains, however, that there is too much dust in her home, and she emphasizes repeatedly that she wants her home care workers to wash the windows, vacuum behind the furniture, polish the furniture, and wash the curtains. When discussing her home care workers, Bridget says that 'there's nothing wrong with the girls,' but she knows that if they do something extra for her that they are not allowed to do, it 'jeopardizes their jobs.' She understands that there are limitations to what types of services the home care workers can provide, but what upsets her more than anything is the restriction on personal interaction. She is unhappy that her home care workers are not allowed to take her out for coffee or sit and chat with her. Bridget explains: 'you don't get much chance to get too attached.'

Introduction

In the opening chapter of this edited book, Benoit and Hallgrímsdóttir note that the rules and practices that shape the performance of care work/intimate labour are crucial to understanding such work is gendered in both formal and informal settings. Paid care work provided within the setting of a care-receiver's home is particularly challenging to examine in this context, for the interpretation of the rules and the conduct of the practices are undertaken largely in a context without direct supervision and oversight, a public service delivered in a private place. Paid intimate labour in the home setting uniquely occurs at the intersection of the public and the private spheres (Martin-Matthews 2007; Martin-Matthews & Phillips 2008). Although providers of paid intimate care may envision working in a home setting as an opportunity to have more independence, autonomy, and challenge in their work, for others working in private homes can be a source of stress, involving unsatisfactory conditions and without close professional supports (Canadian Home Care Association (CHCA) 2008). As Benoit and Hallgrímsdóttir (2008: 5) further observe, the requisites for dignity in work, such as good working conditions, respectful colleagues and managers, job security, and being valued both economically and socially, are important factors contributing to the recruitment and retention of health care workers. But, as they appropriately note, not only care providers, but also care recipients have rights to respect, privacy, autonomy, self-worth, and self-respect: dignity for care recipients is closely tied to dignity for the provider.

This chapter moves the lens to focus specifically on the experiences of elderly women who receive paid intimate care in their homes. Although certainly the providers of this paid labour, and the family members who complement and supplement it with their unpaid labour, are explicit and prominent in this discussion, they are not the focus. In introducing this chapter with a vignette to describe the home care situation of Bridget, we firmly establish her perspective and her voice as central to our focus.

In her pioneering work on the intimate labour of care Zelizer (2007: 10–11) has noted:

> People who give and receive personal care in intimate settings are actually negotiating definitions of their social relations in a rapidly changing

world. Everywhere and always, intimates create forms of economic interchange that simultaneously accomplish shared tasks, reproduce their relations, and distinguish those relations from others with which they might become confused: are you my mother, my sister, my daughter, my nurse, my maid, my best friend? Each has its own distinctive array of economic interchanges. In each case, people draw on available cultural models and they use power and persuasion to negotiate unequal social relations. Paid care in intimate settings raises the fundamental question: who are we, and what do we owe each other?

This chapter begins to address these issues, through a focus on elderly clients' experiences of receiving home care services. The vignette that opens this chapter illustrates relevant organizational, social, spatial, and temporal issues in Bridget's experience of home care; these issues are central themes in this discussion.

Contexts of Paid Intimate Labour Provision in Canada

Home care – the delivery of health and social services to individuals living in the community – stands at the forefront of current debates on health care in Canada. Home care costs have doubled over the past decade, from $1.6 billion to $3.4 billion (Canadian Institute for Health Information 2007). In this same period, the number of home care recipients has increased by 24% (Statistics Canada 2006). It is estimated that just under one million people in Canada use home care services annually (Shapiro 2002; CHCA 2008), and an 80% increase in home care expenditures is expected by 2026 (Coyte & McKeever 2001).

Health human resource projections suggest that Canada will need to double the number of home care workers (currently estimated at approximately 32,000) in order to meet demands by the end of the decade (Home Care Sector Study Corporation 2003). Each province has its own home care program, with no national standards in place (Shapiro 2002). Under provincial jurisdictions, the nature of service provision is determined more by where one lives in Canada than by need (Shapiro 2002; Martin-Matthews & Phillips 2003).

Home care involves a wide variety of workers with different levels of training and qualifications. They include nurses, care managers, social workers, physiotherapists, occupational therapists, and home support workers. Most home care workers are employed in home support, and are often 'unregulated' workers who provide non-professional services in the form of personal assistance with daily activities, such as bathing, dressing, grooming, and light household tasks. They are known across Canada as home support workers, personal support workers, community health workers, community health care aides, home helpers, and homemakers (Martin-Matthews 2007; Mahmood & Martin-Matthews 2008). In 2001 home support workers provided 70%–80 % of the home care needs for Canadian home care recipients. This included both personal care (bathing, toileting, grooming, etc., and work related to instrumental needs, including food preparation, cleaning, and laundry (Home Care Sector Study Corporation 2003).

Despite the desire to age in place and the demonstrated cost-effectiveness of home care, in British Columbia, and throughout much of Canada, there have been neoliberal developments in the opposite direction, including substantial reductions in the public provision of home support services coinciding with a shift from a provincial system of care to regionalization (Konkin, Howe, & Soles 2004). Although these shifts have had significant consequences, such as a 24% drop in individuals receiving home supports between 2000–01 and 2004–05 and a 12% drop in hours (Cohen et al. 2006), there have been few attempts to discern the key issues and concerns of home care employers, workers, clients, and their families.

Approaches to Studying Paid Intimate Labour

The data reported in this chapter were collected as part of a larger study (see http://nexushomecare.arts.ubc.ca) that examines the working relationships between home support workers and their elderly clients, family members of clients, and employer agencies (see Martin-Matthews & Sims-Gould 2008; Sims-Gould & Martin-Matthews 2010). The Nexus Home Care Project 2010 focuses on three intersecting sets of issues in the provision of paid intimate care to elderly people. The first set of issues is the intersection of the public and the private spheres, and the mechanisms by which home support workers negotiate the private sphere of clients' homes and families versus the public world of health services. The second set of issues is the intersection of professional and non-professional labour, and the associated issues facing home support workers in relation to perceptions of professional and non-professional roles and relationships with employers and co-workers, as well as elderly clients and their unpaid caregivers. The final set of issues is the intersection of paid and unpaid labour, including the balance of the emotional versus contractual nature of the 'care' relationship between paid workers and elderly clients, the prevalence of the use of unpaid time (by paid workers) to meet client needs, and the ways in which the unpaid labour of family and friends intersect with these arrangements.

Most studies of paid intimate labour provided in private homes (often referred to as domiciliary care) focus on the organizational aspects of home care service delivery, emphasizing working conditions and the associated stress and strain involved in providing care. Central to this focus is the premise that intimate paid labour is undertaken at the nexus of the public sphere of work and employment and the private sphere of home and personal life (Martin-Matthews 2007). Providers of this care operate within the framework of organizational and bureaucratic structures and regulations, but they also interpret (and interact with) the rules and resources of the sociospatial and temporal context of the client's care environment, settings that are embedded within larger socioeconomic, cultural, and political contexts. Thus, the rules and resources of the larger sociospatial environment also influence the types of activities that can take place within the home when health and social care is provided there (Giddens 1990; Mahmood 2002).

Mahmood and Martin-Matthews (2008) posit that the interactions and negotiations central to paid intimate labour (defined here as home care and home support work) are framed by organizational, social, spatial, and temporal domains. Although these domains are not explicitly developed in their conceptual model, the extant literature on home care suggests a number of ways in which these domains may be characterized. Elsewhere, we have defined these domains from the perspectives of the paid providers of intimate care (Sims-Gould & Martin-Matthews 2008). However, the experiences of elderly clients who receive these services remain largely unexplored.

The organizational domain frames much of the 'work' of home care. Home care workers are guided by the practices and procedures, and rules and regulations of home care agencies operating in the public sphere (themselves informed by municipal, provincial, and federal national policies and practices). When workers, guided by these procedures and policies enter the spheres of private homes and interact with clients, the negotiation of boundary management between *home* and *work*, between the formalized client 'care plan' and the observed needs of clients, is often required.

The social domain is highly relevant to the clients' experiences of intimate labour in a number of ways. Home care agency policies typically prescribe strong boundaries between paid work and home life. Analysis of the social domain enables the consideration of the strategies used by clients in managing these interfaces and interactions with workers, agency personnel, other resident family members, and other relatives and helpers.

The spatial domain is important because space is not a neutral backdrop. Bounded spaces actively influence the behaviour of people within them (Ardener 1993). In the provision of home care, health care activities from the public sector move into private residential space. The home is then not just a place of residence; it is also a work setting for staff providing care. Particular characteristics of the space of the home may potentially impact the service provided (and received) and aspects of the worker-client relationship. The role of gender and space is essential to this enquiry. Russell (2007), among others, has examined the role of gender in the 'lived experience' of aging, emphasizing the importance of the home as 'a woman's place,' with implications for our understanding women's and men's experiences of home as the site of care. One of the unique aspects of home care is the fact that the workplace of the care provider is the home of the care recipient. Nonetheless, most of the writing about home care has been crafted as if the word 'home' is merely a four-letter substitute for the words 'hospital' or 'institution.' However, as Rubenstein (1990: 37) observes, 'an important and neglected aspect of the home care experience is the experience of *home* ... with all the attendant developmental, psychological, and socio-cultural meanings embodied in the home environment.' Clients' perspectives on the receipt of a paid intimate labour being provided as a public service in their private space are important to this understanding. The temporal domain is reflected in the way in which service is delivered (and received by the client) in the form of time-bound tasks provided at regular or irregular intervals. In an earlier study of home support workers in Ontario, Martin-Matthews (2007) also found that temporal issues arise in home care service provision outside of 'paid' hours.

Client Perspectives on Intimate Labour of Care in the Home

The verbatim accounts of eighty-three elderly home care clients in British Columbia form the focus of our analyses in this chapter. Gender is relevant to these analyses in a number of ways that are both implicit and explicit. It is more implicit in terms of the context of home support services delivery. All of the case managers and agency personnel participating in our study are women; all but eight of the 119 home support workers interviewed in British Columbia are women (94%). Gender is therefore difficult to interrogate in this context largely because it is so overwhelmingly *assumed* that women deliver these services and gendered expectations of care differ for women and for men (Campbell & Martin-Matthews 2003).

In the accounts of the clients, gender is relevant because, as Twigg notes, 'deep old age is predominantly female' (2004: 65). Reflecting this, 67% of the eighty-three clients whom we interviewed, are women. Most of these women (75%) were widowed, separated, divorced, or ever single. Among the twenty-seven male clients, 41% were married and co-resided with their wives, who also interacted with the home support workers.

In the vignettes and verbatim accounts cited in this chapter, the gender of the elderly client is noted throughout. For many issues involving home as the site of care there were no apparent gender comparisons in terms of how issues were described. However, gender was frequently implicit in the use of language, a language frequently reflective of the 'stigma associated with being a direct care worker, particularly a home care aide or personal care attendant, such that one is frequently referred to as a "girl" or viewed as simply a domestic worker – "the maid"' (Paraprofessional Healthcare Institute 2003). In the vignette describing Bridget, she too uses the terminology of 'girls' to describe the women providing paid intimate care labour in her home. Elsewhere in the interviews, the language distinguishing 'girls' from 'men' implies further understandings of gendered care; in the words of one client:

... all the girls and – and the – the men that used to come and – for nights, eh, very nice, yeah. (85-year-old woman receiving home support)

Bridget, as do other elderly clients, implies a connection between women's traditional domestic roles in families and their capacity for, and ability in relation to, the more 'domestic' aspects of home support work:

To me, I think that all women, if they're old enough, they all know how to clean a house. I think, you know, ... it just goes with the territory. That I mean nobody has to teach nobody how to clean a house. They – most of them all have families of their own and ... things like that.

Throughout this chapter, gender is also implicit in the discussion in terms of our lenses as female researchers.

Organizational Domain

In our examination of home support work to elderly clients, we have cast a lens on an organizational setting in which workers deliver bureaucratically determined services through direct contact with clients, an environment described by Dill (1990: 248) wherein 'work is oriented toward maximizing the amount of autonomy and individual discretion they exercise. It is grounded as well in the competing demands of concerns for clients and organizational objectives.' Our data emphasize two aspects of the organizational domain: the prominence of 'care plans' in defining the tasks to be completed for the client (and within what time frame) and the changing nature of these plans over time, especially with the far-ranging reorganization of home care services within British Columbia in recent years (Hollander & Prince 2002; Sharman et al. 2008). But the lack of fit between what elderly home care users want and what home care workers provide is well demonstrated (Dalley 1991), and this lack is frequently 'managed' by workers (Sims-Gould & Martin-Matthews 2008) and acknowledged by clients. In the clients' accounts, a number of intersecting organizational issues were identified: these include the rotation of workers and associated uncertainty of schedules, and the role of the care plan in framing the rigidity of the intimate care provided and tasks completed. Many clients' accounts refer to 'the list' and the implications of whether a particular care 'task' is 'on the list or not.'

> I manage on my own but ... she's supposed to be doing it ... when she makes the report, I think she does say that she helps with the bath. Like I don't know where the damn list is. There's a list. They – they gave me the things that you're allowed – they're allowed to do. It's supposed to be on top of the fridge. I don't know where it is. (73-year-old woman receiving home support)

In Bridget's comments, clear distinctions are made between the attributes and personalities of 'the girls' and the rules and regulations that frame the care relationship. Bridget understands and acknowledges the predominant role of agency policies that, if violated, could jeopardize a worker's job. The organizational framing of personal interaction is more problematic for her, a framing that limits the extent of personal attachment between worker and client. This is a theme that recurs in the accounts of clients, as will be shown below.

Social Domain

A number of issues were identified by elderly clients in relation to the social domain, or were illustrated in the reports of their circumstances. In many cases, the complementarity of the paid and unpaid/ informal intimate labour provided to clients was quite striking. The circumstances of Helena, as presented in the vignette below, illustrate this well: the 'social domain' reflected in a social network of paid and unpaid care wherein, in the words of the Canadian Home Care Association, paid services 'complement and supplement, but not replace, the efforts of individuals to care for themselves with the assistance of family, friends and community. Home care programs encourage and support the care provided by the family and/or community' (2008: x). Even with the presence of other family members actively engaged in her care, however, Helena's case also illustrates the importance of other social aspects of intimate paid labour, such as companionate activities, covert 'friendships,' and contingent relationships.

Helena

Helena enjoys reading, loves spending time in her garden on sunny days, and takes pleasure in caring for her flowers. She is 82 years old and has been divorced for over forty years. Helena's family is very supportive, and she currently lives with Joyce, her 50-year-old daughter, and Ken, her 28-year-old grandson. Joyce works as a registered nurse, and Ken left his job in another province to help out at home. Helena has not walked for nearly seven years, and she describes her own health as being 'the pits.' She suffers from a variety of health concerns including post-polio syndrome, rheumatoid arthritis, heart problems, breathing problems, and seizures. She explains that her difficulty breathing was likely caused by her time spent in an iron lung during her youth. Helena has been hospitalized several times in the past year, and requires the use of an electric wheelchair. Her grandson Ken helps her with transferring and lifting, and she explains that she would not be able to manage at home without him. Helena currently receives home care services four times a day, for one hour each visit. Her home care workers prepare meals for her, as she can only swallow pureed food because of difficulties with her esophagus. Helena's home care workers also help her with the laundry, taking out the garbage, going to the bathroom, and personal care. Despite her physical limitations, Helena keeps a positive attitude and enjoys having conversations with her home care workers. She is pleased with her home care; however, she feels that the workers should not have to follow such rigid care guidelines. She finds it strange that the home care workers are not allowed to water her plants or feed the dog, even if they have enough time. Helena firmly believes that home care workers should be allowed to do whatever they can, within reason, to make their client's life more meaningful.

> Home care isn't just washing and dressing and feeding. If that's all it is, it shouldn't be called home care, I don't think. Because the highlight of your day, and of mine, isn't getting dressed, getting washed, and eating. There is much more to a life than that, there has to be ... If you've got time in that hour, do what makes the client's life meaningful instead of the rules you've decided that they have to do.

Helena's comments illustrate the important distinction between the 'instumentality' of the workers' care plan and list (reflective of agency policy) and the affectual importance of the workers' presence and companionship. Although direct care workers serve as the 'eyes and ears' of the care system (Paraprofessional Healthcare Institute 2003), in the execution of their assigned duties and by their presence and monitoring of the private domain of the household, these workers 'also provide the "high touch" that is essential to quality of life, as well as quality of care, for elders and chronically disabled individuals' (Stone & Dawson 2008: 5). Clearly, both Helena and Bridget call for more emphasis on the 'high touch' that is the essence of the social domain and less on the instrumentality of the task list in the provision of paid intimate labour.

Many of the elderly clients whom we interviewed noted the importance of this social domain in the receipt of care, and they spoke openly of their ignoring agency policies as they introduced reciprocity and a 'furtive' friendship tie into the paid relationship. For example, as one client noted:

> Oh, well, yeah ... [*laughs*] ... I've given them little gifts and that. You're not supposed to but you do when you like them and I've got gifts – got cards from them, too. (89-year-old woman receiving home support)

And, as another also noted:

> Evidently they're not supposed to associate with you other than when they take you out which is stupid ... you're good friends. (88-year-old woman receiving home support)

Spatial Domain

Space is not a neutral backdrop to the labour of paid intimate care. In the accounts of many home support workers, reference is frequently made to issues of managing their intrusion into the private space of a client's home and respecting that space (Martin-Matthews 2007). Similarly for elderly clients, the presence of a succession of strangers in one's home is also to be 'managed':

> At first, it was really hard on me. For the first bit, it was really hard, right? Because it was an invasion into my privacy, because I am a very private person. But, then it just became normal. And particularly the ones that keep, that are the return ones, the constant return ones ... they know where everything is in my house ... And ... when they come into my home, they, they take pride in – in – in like my kitchen, for instance, they take pride in having it neat looking. They take pride in what they do to make my life as comfortable as possible. It's almost as if, in some cases, especially with the two [workers], right, that it's like their second home. When they're in here you can tell it's what they would do if I was in their home kind of a thing. (66-year-old woman receiving home support)

The interviews with clients also firmly indicate that elderly clients are by no means merely passive recipients of the care they receive; the observations of many clients reflect an 'asserting' of space. In the words of one client:

> We're closer and she probably feels she can be more familiar with me ... if she did something I wouldn't be afraid to say, 'No, I – I don't – I don't like that' and she would understand. (89-year-old woman receiving home support)

This observation was not uncommon among the clients we interviewed, and well reflected Dannefer et al.'s observation that 'care is thus a mutually generative, interactive and hence truly dialectical process' (2008: 106).

And finally, the accounts of the clients illustrate how clients use the space of their home differently because of the presence of the workers. The situation of Flora depicts this.

Flora

Flora is 72 years old and she lives alone. Her husband passed away eleven years ago, and her four children do not live nearby. Flora has one good friend whom she seldom sees, and occasionally she attends Bible study and craft making at her church. Flora is in very poor health. She has heart disease, chronic obstructive pulmonary disorder, vasculitis in her legs which prevents her from walking, very bad esophagus reflexes, and cataracts. Flora uses a scooter to move around and wears compression stockings. Her doctor helped arrange home care services for her, which she now receives seven days a week, with five 30-minute visits and two one-hour visits. She has been receiving home care services for eleven years, and primarily requires assistance with putting on the compression stockings, making the bed, and bathing. Flora complains, however, that the constant changing of workers and inconsistency is 'the pits.' On some days she must teach the home care workers how to put on her stockings for her. Despite these complaints regarding the service, Flora is very pleased and grateful that the home care workers are available to help her. She explains that her children are also pleased that she is receiving home care services. Flora really appreciates the companionship aspect of her home care, and enjoys the opportunity to 'chitchat' with her home care workers. The home care also benefits Flora as it motivates her to get up in the mornings, something that she is reluctant to do because of her depression.

> I think they keep me sane. I have a problem with depression and ... I get depressed a lot. And if you have someone coming in every day and – you gotta get up and you gotta get moving and you gotta get on with your life. Where otherwise I would never get dressed unless I had to go out.

Temporal Domain

Here we are referring to allocations of time when services are brought into the private sphere of the home. This includes such structural features of time as the scheduling (amount of time, frequency, and regularity of visits), as well as the use of time in terms of task allocation, freedom to make decisions about time, and the meaning and experience of time and timing. The temporal nature of the provision of paid intimate labour in the home has already been implied in several of the vignettes, for example, Bridget's comments about the balance of priorities (as when workers have time 'left over' and yet cannot complete certain tasks not prescribed in the care plan). Another perspective, as demonstrated in the following verbatim account, emphasizes both the pacing of tasks and the difference of opinion between worker and client regarding task priorities and the allotment of time:

She sort of stays when she hasn't made the whole hour up. She sits and has a little conversation. I used to think, you know, it's a wonderful thing to do for people, how it was nice for some old ladies to have some visitors sometimes. But now I think, I don't want you sitting here ... if you're going to be here on my pay, I want you to wash the dishes. (88-year-old woman receiving home support)

A frequent observation made by clients, however, also focused on the ways in which the temporal order of the bureaucracy of care affected the natural tempo and rhythm of their days, as they strove to adapt to agency timing and scheduling of service. Silvia's comment illustrates this concern:

[I don't like] ... the whole business of adjusting my schedule to hers. She has to tell me when she's going to bring me my breakfast so I sleep in till then. Some people tell me they're going to bring my breakfast at 7–7:30 so then I put the alarm on. So you have to sort of roll with the punches. (87-year-old woman receiving home support)

Workers and clients alike refer to the 'tyranny of time,' although workers usually frame this discourse in terms of how they strive to avoid the perception of it, while clients indicate that they are well aware of workers' efforts in this regard.

Well, they try not to show they're rushed, you know ... some of them, I'll say, 'Well, sit down, have a cup of tea,' or something like that. And they're not supposed to do any of these things. (83-year-old woman receiving home support)

Summary and Conclusions

The delivery and receipt of home support occurs at the intersection of private space (my home), public places (your work), and at its core involves social interaction (our relationship). The model developed by Mahmood and Martin-Matthews (2008), which has framed the discussion in terms of the organizational, social, spatial, and temporal aspects of the receipt of paid intimate care in the home, has been of utility in advancing our understanding of clients' experiences of such care.

In situating home at the nexus of the private and the public spheres, this chapter has also considered the contingent nature of home support work and of the provider-client interaction within the private sphere of the home. Framed within the context of governmental home care policies and agency guidelines, for elderly clients 'the worker embodies both what the system can and cannot do for them' (Bowdie & Turwoski 1986: 44). Gender both implicitly and explicitly contributes to this framing in differing contexts: with female workers assisting female or male clients; female workers assisting female or male clients with co-resident spouses; and female workers assisting male or female clients with sons and daughters.

In this chapter we have also demonstrated that the elderly clients who are the recipients of home support services, while among the most vulnerable and voiceless in society (in that they are predominantly older women), nevertheless have agency. The clients of home care have opinions, ideas, and preferences, developed over the course of long lives and complex personal histories. They are individuals who require both instrumental care to assist with their most basic and intimate needs and also require companionship, validation, and respect. We have shown that while the driving policies and procedures (i.e., care plans) behind service delivery can fail to fully meet individual needs and consider preferences, workers (who are also predominantly women) often work hard to navigate the chasm between what they have been assigned to do versus what needs to be done or is preferred by the older client. A focus on the perspectives of those older clients on the receiving end of service emphasizes that care is a dynamic, complex, (sometimes) negotiated, and interactive process, not simply a service to be actively delivered and passively received.

With the exception of some aspects of the organizational structure of home care services, the issues indentified by clients in this chapter are not the issues in the public discourse on home care as it sits on the agenda of national policy conferences in Canada and elsewhere. But these are issues of relevance to elderly men and women who live with the day-to-day reality of how their lives have been changed, not only by unexpected and debilitating illness in later life, but also by the delivery of services into the most intimate, private, and personal spheres of those lives. These are the issues of relevance to elderly people when paid intimate care is, in the words of Armstrong and Armstrong (2004: 24), brought 'closer to home.'

As the elderly clients with whom we spoke have illustrated, and Zelizer (2007: 12) has noted, 'both care providers ... and ... clients ... negotiate ... definitions of their social relations. In the cases of ... paid care within intimate settings, we have plenty more to learn about how people create viable relations, and for that matter how and why things go wrong in the delicate mingling of intimacy and labor.' Current neoliberal policies with an emphasis on cost containment and a focus on short-term, task-based post-acute care services as opposed to preventive and needs-based home care, create a climate for failure within the care delivery system. Home care policy must be informed by the perspectives of those who work within the system and of those who receive service. A model that truly puts the clients at the centre of the care system, with emphasis and value placed on the relationships between workers and clients working together to address unmet needs, is the only way to ensure both the viability and quality of home support. Examining home support from a perspective that animates its organizational, social, spatial, and temporal aspects is a first step in identifying the salient issues in home care delivery.

REFERENCES

Ardener, S. (1993). Ground rules and social maps for women: An introduction. In S. Ardener, ed., *Women and Space: Ground Rules and Social Maps*, 1–29. New York: St Martin's.

Armstrong, P., & H. Armstrong. (2004). Thinking it through: Women, work and caring in the new millennium. In K.R. Grant, C. Amaratunga, P. Armstrong, M. Boscoe, A. Pederson, & K. Willson, eds., *Caring for / Caring about: Women, Home Care and Unpaid Caregiving*, 5–43. Aurora: Garamond Press.

Benoit, C., & H.K. Hallgrímsdóttir. (2008). Engendering research on care and care work across different social contexts. *Canadian Journal of Public Health* 99 (Suppl. 2): S7–S13.

Bowdie, R., & A. Turwoski. (1986). The problems of providing services to the elderly in their own homes. In A.O. Pelham & W.F. Clark, eds., *Managing Home Care for the Elderly,* 31–46. New York: Springer.

Campbell, L.D., & A. Martin-Matthews. (2003). The gendered nature of men's filial care. *Journal of Gerontology: Social Sciences* 58B(6): S350–S358.

Canadian Home Care Association (CHCA). (2008). *Portraits of Home Care in Canada 2008.* Ottawa: Author.

Canadian Institute for Health Information. (2007). *The Yukon: Pioneers in Home Care Information.* Retrieved 3 Sept. 2008 from http://secure.cihi.ca/cihiweb/ en/downloads/HCRS_Yukon_AiB_ENG.pdf.

Cohen, M., A. McLaren, Z. Sharman, S. Murray, M. Hughes, & A. Ostry. (2006). *From Support to Isolation: The High Cost of B.C.'s Declining Home Support Services.*Vancouver: Canadian Centre for Policy Research. Retrieved 15 Feb. 2008 from http://www.policyalternatives.ca/Reports/2006/06/ ReportsStudies1380/index.cfm?pa=BB73645.

Coyte, P., & P. McKeever. (2001). Determinants of home care utilization: Who uses home care in Ontario? *Canadian Journal on Aging* 20(2): 175–92.

Dalley, G. (1991). Beliefs and behaviour: Professionals and the policy process. *Journal of Aging Studies* 5(2): 163–80.

Dannefer, D., P. Stein, R. Siders, & R.S. Patterson. (2008). Is that all there is? The concept of care and the dialectic of critique. *Journal of Aging Studies* 22(2): 101–8.

Dill, A.E.P. (1990). Transformations of home: The formal and informal process of home care planning. In J.F. Gubrium & A. Sankar, eds., *The Home Care Experience: Ethnography and Policy,* 227–51. Newbury Park: Sage.

Giddens, A. (1990). *The Consequences of Modernity.* Cambridge: Polity Press.

Hollander, M.J., & M.J. Prince. (2002). *The Third Way: A Framework for Organizing Health Related Services for Individuals with Ongoing Care Needs and Their Families.* Victoria: Hollander Analytical Services. Retrieved 6 Sept. 2008 from http://www.hollanderanalytical.com/downloads/continuum-final.pdf.

Home Care Sector Study Corporation. (2003). *Canadian Home Care Resources Study: Synthesis Report.* Retrieved 3 Aug. 2007 from http://www. homecarestudy.com/.

Konkin, J., D. Howe, & T.L. Soles. (2004). Society of Rural Physicians of Canada policy paper on regionalization. *Canadian Journal of Rural Medicine* 9(4): 257–9.

Mahmood, A. (2002). Managing the blurring of boundaries: A conceptual framework for social, spatial and temporal analysis of live-work settings. Gerontology Research Centre, Simon Fraser University. *Seniors Housing Update* 11(2): 1–3.

Mahmood, A., & A. Martin-Matthews. (2008). Dynamics of care work: Boundary management and relationship issues for home support workers and elderly clients. In A. Martin-Matthews & J. Phillips, eds., *Aging and Caring at the Intersection of Work and Home Life: Blurring the Boundaries*, 21–42. New York: Taylor and Francis.

Martin-Matthews, A. (2007). Situating 'home' at the nexus of the public and private spheres: Ageing, gender and home support work in Canada. *Current Sociology* (Monograph Series: Gender, Ageing and Power: Changing Dynamics in Western Societies) 55(2): 229–49.

Martin-Matthews, A., & J.E. Phillips. (2003). Home care work in Canada and England: Comparative perspectives of home care workers on relationship issues in the provision of home-based services to elderly persons. Paper presented at the annual conference of the Gerontological Society of America, San Diego, 21–25 Nov.

Martin-Matthews, A., & J. Sims-Gould. (2008). Employers, home support workers, and elderly clients: Identifying key issues in delivery and receipt of home support. *Health Care Quarterly* 11(4): 71–7.

Nexus Home Care Research. (N.d.) *Home Care in Canada: Working at the Nexus of the Public and Private Spheres.* Retrieved 22 Aug. 2008, from http://nexushomecare.arts.ubc.ca.

Paraprofessional Healthcare Institute. (2003). *Long-term Care Financing and the Long-Term Care Workforce Crisis: Causes and Solutions.* Washington: Author.

Phillips, J.E., & A. Martin-Matthews. (2008). Blurring the boundaries: Aging and caring at the intersection of work and home life. In A. Martin-Matthews & J.E. Phillips, eds., *Aging and Caring at the Intersection of Work and Home Life: Blurring the Boundaries*, 245–54. New York: Taylor and Francis.

Rubenstein, R.L. (1990). Culture and disorder in the home care experience: The home as sickroom. In J.F. Gubrium & A. Sankar, eds., *The Home Care Experience: Ethnography and Policy*, 37–57. Newbury Park: Sage.

Russell, C. (2007). What do older women and men want? Gender differences in the 'lived experience' of ageing. *Current Sociology* 55(2): 173–92.

Shapiro, E. (2002). *The Health Care Transition Fund.* Synthesis series: Home Care. Cat. J13-6/2002-2. Ottawa: Minister of Public Works and Government Services Canada. Retrieved 24 Aug. 2008 from http://www.hc-sc.gc.ca/hcssss/pubs/home-domicile/2002-htf-fass-home-domicile/index_e.html.

Sharman, Z., A.T. McLaren, M. Cohen, & A. Ostry. (2008). We only own the hours: Discontinuity of care in the British Columbia home support system. *Canadian Journal on Aging* 27(1): 89–100.

Sims-Gould, J., & A. Martin-Matthews. (2008). Employers, home support workers and elderly clients: Identifying key issues in delivery and receipt of home support. *Healthcare Quarterly* 11(4): 69–75.

Sims-Gould, J., & A. Martin-Matthews. (2010). Strategies used by home support workers in the delivery of care to elderly clients. *Canadian Journal on Aging* 29 (Special Issue 1): 97–107.

Statistics Canada. (2006). Government subsidized home care. *Health Reports* 17(4): 39–42.

Stone, R.I., & S.L. Dawson. (2008). The origins of better jobs better care. *Gerontologist* 48(1): 5–13.

Twigg, J. (2004). The body, gender, and age: Feminist insights in social gerontology. *Journal of Aging Studies* 18(1): 59–73.

Zelizer, V.A. (2007). Caring everywhere. Keynote Address, Conference on Intimate Labors, University of California, Santa Barbara, 4–6 Oct.

7 Bifurcated Conscience: Aboriginal Care Workers in Community Settings

RACHEL ENI

This chapter explores the role of Aboriginal prenatal peer support workers in carrying out their everyday work in community-based prenatal, postnatal, and mother and infant health care services. These peer support workers are representative of a unique group of women who are at the same time First Nations community members, mothers, daughters, granddaughters, intimate partners, advocates for maternal and infant health and wellness and for cultural reclamation, and trained individuals responsible for the local delivery of primary health care services. The work that they do is challenged by several factors, including current imbalances in Canadian power relations relating to gender, race, and class that impact the everyday work and intimate lives of Aboriginal women employed to carry out health care in their communities. Additionally, the institutional relations within which everyday work is encased affect recognition (including time and resources allotted to this type of work), respect, and value (including monetary) awarded to the women by others at different levels (from peripheral to most intimate relationships), as well as women's feeling of personal self-efficacy.

In the end, their contribution to the delivery of health care in Canada and to the goal of improving the overall health of Canadian mothers and infants (specifically those belonging to a segment of the Canadian population with significant health disadvantages) is undermined within a system that privileges *medicalized*, Eurocentric, and as often described, 'paternalistic' approaches to health care (Benoit, Wrede, & Einarsdóttir, this volume). This chapter describes the role and contribution to maternal and infant health of peer support workers utilizing a 'different' perspective based on the standpoints of Aboriginal female peer support workers implementing health care services in Manitoba First Nations communities. The ultimate aim of the chapter is to highlight how the workers, as a result of their complex positioning as care workers providing intimate labour while charged with bringing national health care policy imperatives down to the level of community, experience a phenomenon known as 'bifurcated consciousness.'

Understanding Bifurcated Consciousness

The underlying problematic and intent of the current analysis was the explication of existing tensions between the human condition, as it is discursively formulated by institutions of a ruling apparatus, and one that is experienced by a subjective individual herself. In the context of prenatal care, these sorts of conflicts abound. For instance, the notion of 'pregnancy' itself may be perceived as anything ranging from a medical condition requiring more or less intrusive measures to a natural, healthy biological process (Gjerdingen & Fontaine 1991; Miles 1991).

In an Aboriginal context, tensions arise with regards to what are culturally appropriate and effective practices in pregnancy and childbirth and whether or not and to what degree men ought to be included within this 'feminine' experiential realm (Anderson 2000; Eni 2005). Health governance issues presently contested at community and regional levels are also points of added tension. Within such infrastructures and depending upon specific community dynamics, women either abstain from or vie for power and recognition regarding childbearing matters.

These are the tensions that cause a 'disjuncture,' 'bifurcation of consciousness,' 'line of fault,' or 'rupture' between subjective experience and the world as it is generally known and idealized among dominant understandings. Conceiving a bifurcated consciousness makes tangible the struggle for meaning that may at times overwhelm a single individual who is at once caught up in multiple, different, and often, opposing, realities. This forking of one's consciousness, left unacknowledged, results in an alienation from one's own experiences. For example, alienation may stem from confusion or disconnection between how women experience, understand, and think about their worlds and the paternalistic concepts and terms imposed upon them. It is an alienation that inhibits language and deprives one of the authority to speak (Brooks 2003).

This chapter is based on original ethnographic research conducted in three Manitoba First Nations regions. Analysis was conducted utilizing a standpoint and ethnographic approach in order to allow for an investigation of the everyday work perceptions and experiences of women employed inside local environments of the home community to administer prenatal and postnatal health care services and within the context of a broader and institutional framework of First Nations health care delivery. In other words, to understand the potential of the intimate labour force and the losses incurred within a governing framework that undermines its contributions, the current analysis allowed for an articulation of 'what exactly happens in the realm of practices and relations through which societies and people are governed' (Mykhalovskiy & McCoy 2002: 20).

I first came across the concept of a *bifurcated consciousness* in my research, trying to understand the everyday meanings that women attributed to their work. This concept lies at the heart of a standpoint and institutional ethnography, within the space of the body, and in this case, a body that is feminine and Aboriginal: that sensual location wherein the plays of powerfully imbalanced and ideologically incompatible worlds collide. Within a multiplicity of directions, expectations, regulations, accusations, and judgments, a united self strives to develop, to be recognized, and to live in the world. The essence of the dilemma results in difficulties for women in developing integrated perspectives of self and other in a world that is defined beyond them, oftentimes contradicting their intimate experiences with it, and tending, consequentially, for the Aboriginal women working on the ground to evaluate themselves and the impact of their work from the eyes of the dominant perspective, which is generally in a negative or inconsequential light. As an example, rather than being seen as custodians of health, the women are regarded as handmaidens assisting in the implementation of institutional health care initiatives at provincial and federal levels. The consequence of bifurcated consciousness is that it leads to division wherein the true self is undermined: a life unfolding with 'two souls, two thoughts, two unreconciled strivings; two warring ideals in one dark body, whose dogged strength alone keeps it from being torn asunder' (Du Bois 2007).

The ethnographic data collected in the communities evinced an inveterate entanglement of dissimilar discourses from distinct and unequal universes as women articulated and tried to make sense of the meaning of their everyday care work. Perceptions of self and of other Aboriginal women were described based on ideals represented in the stories told by the grandmothers and tainted by a marginalizing political socioeconomic superstructure that sees no reasonable alternative to mainstream health provision, goals, and values. The intention of this chapter is to raise awareness of the value and potential impact of the work of the peer support workers to enhance the health of First Nations mothers, infants, and whole communities. Aboriginal women, and their unique traditions and health practices, can become lost in contemporary definitions of health and health care and in the measurements used to derive such concepts. The strengths of Aboriginal women are lost in a patriarchal model that values immediate results, individuality, intervention, competition, quantitative justification, and professionalization of intimate spaces and relations. Geographical remoteness and a Canadian constitution that retains authority over the use of land and natural resources also hamper political and programmatic involvement of Aboriginal women at the more central levels of government (Frideres 1986; Lake 1996). Within the currently dominant worldview, Couchie and Nabigon wrote, 'Aboriginal women work hard to protect, define and strengthen cultural ideology that is often articulated on a much more universal theme' (1997: 44). Bifurcated consciousness, as the struggle that manifests within a marginalized individual striving to belong and to earn a respectful living inside a neoliberal world that values other principles far removed from the intimate location of the sensual, sexual body and heart is a powerful entry point into the potential benefits of the development of an inclusive and diverse political economy.

The Study and Method

This ethnographic study was carried out in Manitoba First Nations communities between 2001 and 2005. Research activities included program participant observations wherein the researcher actively participated in assisting in the delivery of the peer support programs, coming along on home visits, and acting as a support, where needed, to pregnant and new moms. In-depth interviews were also held in homes and in program centres with nineteen peer support workers from three Manitoba First Nations regions. Most of the women were between 25 and 28 years of age. The youngest was 17 years old and the oldest was in her mid-fifties. Interviews lasted 1.5 to 2 hours in duration and focused on the experiences of peer helpers when carrying out their work responsibilities and the meanings they attached to these experiences. The endeavour included a search for tensions between personal identities, meanings, and perceived responsibilities of the workers towards self, community, and the greater institutional framework. Additionally, at least one focus group was held in each region wherein most of the interviewees and some additional workers attended. The average size of the focus groups was eight to ten people. In each case, Elders attended as supports to the peer workers and to the ensuring of cultural relevance of the research process. Qualitative analysis and interpretation was co-developed with the research participants to ensure that the knowledge generated reflected accurately the voices, perspectives, and opinions of these women.

The rationale supporting peer support programs is that peers will better understand the unique needs of a target population than, for example, professionals hired to work inside communities within which they have not lived and interacted. During times of need, people often turn to individuals from their social network(s) to help augment the formal care provided to them by the health care and social services systems. However well intentioned these individuals may be, they may not have the knowledge, specific experiences, appropriate strategies, time, or resources to adequately support the people in need. Peer support workers provide a unique type of intimate caring and support. They have had experiences and emotions tied to the program's focus and are willing to use them to support others in similar situations, for example, to support childbearing women living on-reserve in having healthy prenatal and birthing outcomes. A Cochrane review defines peer support workers as 'any health worker carrying out functions related to health care delivery, trained in some way in the context of the intervention; having no formal professional or paraprofessional certificated or degree tertiary education' (quoted in Paul et al. 2007: 4).

Following Dennis et al. (2002: 22), staff in the prenatal programs typically defined peer support as a particular style of social support that incorporates informational appraisal (feedback) and emotional assistance. Often it is lay assistance provided by volunteers who are not part of the participants' families or immediate social networks. In the First Nations communities studied here, however, peer support is typically provided by staff who may or may not be related to the participants, but who possess experiential knowledge of the behaviours of interest to the program (e.g., successful breastfeeding skills and determinants associated with healthy pregnancy) and have similar characteristics (e.g., age, socioeconomic status, cultural background, and location of residence).

Peer support is not a recent concept. Anthropologist Dana Raphael used the term *doula,* a term with Greek origins meaning 'a friend from across the street' (Lawrence 2002: 42) to describe the work of a peer support worker during childbirth. The peer support worker is someone who is not a health care professional but a true friend of the pregnant woman or new mother and is available to support the woman throughout the childbearing time (Lawrence 2002). Essentially the peer support worker is perfectly situated to articulate the challenges, strengths, and interests of women in her community and has, in the course of her everyday work, multiple opportunities to experience women's stories as they are played out over time. However, the naturalness of this very feminine work, when encased within a medicalized approach to pregnancy care, contributes to its devaluing. Instead, as with much other intimate labour (see Benoit & Hallgrímsdóttir, this volume), this work becomes part of the invisible background of expectations of the mainstream medical system. In the case of prenatal peer support workers, this work is incorporated into the system as unpaid intimate labour that they will perform in order to prepare pregnant women and women in labour for the 'real work' of the medical practitioners. This systemic expectation is played within the psyches of the women when they opt out of peer support programming claiming, as one peer support worker said,

> there is a feeling that 'why should I go to the program when the doctor is just going to go over the same kinds of questions and really that's where it really matters.'

Peer support work is embedded inside a fairly recently expanded conception of prenatal care; an expansion that brings governing incentives into the local proximity of women's work and women's bodies. The past decade and a half has seen an overwhelming amount of research calling for increased investment in prenatal care and support programs (Conway & Partha 2003; Conway & Kutinova 2003; Heaman 2001). The bulk of the research focuses on the benefits of physician-oriented prenatal care and risk reduction to maternal and infant physical health (see Benoit et al., this volume). Some of the research delves into matters of quality, including content and specific types of program utilization styles. Research in First Nations communities includes questions such as program governance and community/cultural applicability as central programming issues with possible health and self-determination effects.

Although prenatal care has recently been reconceptualized from being a strictly medical (obstetrical) visit to a public health intervention, this has occurred while remaining within the boundaries of 'business as usual'; in other words, the system of prenatal care is still controlled by physician experts measuring, examining, assessing, and controlling women's bodies. Although greater opportunities for women's participation exist, the meaningfulness and impact of their work is judged within the paradigmatic confines of that external system. For example, while carrying out their daily routines, the peer support workers engage in administrative imperatives upon which their jobs depend and have less to do with providing the kind of care that they are uniquely positioned to provide. As one worker explained,

> we have multiple forms to complete for every visit. Sometimes just filling out the forms takes up most of the time we have with the moms.

In other words, rather than delivering essential services, workers are seen as preparing prenatal women for their obstetric visits.

Current prenatal programming devalues the intimate labour of peer support workers while simultaneously relying on it quite heavily. The 'high-risk prevention' discourse, for example, places the brunt of the responsibility for the disease burden in the hands of individual Aboriginal women, while crediting the medical system with the technology to amend the situation. This fact is not unnoticed by critics of the current medicalized system. The over-focus on 'high-risk' individuals has been critiqued by social scientists, practitioners, First Nations health care providers, expectant mothers, new mothers, and grandmothers. Their concern is that the intimate work of the women in the communities should be recognized for its contribution to health, not only in assisting physicians in their work, but in delivering a qualitatively different kind of care that is not available and may actually be undermined with overreliance on the medical system. Targeting 'high-risk' women in communities may actually work against the goals of the peer support workers since women will try to escape the social stigma that such programs generate.

A main strategy of these expanded prenatal care programs is the identification and training of individuals living in First Nations communities to carry out healthy pregnancy programming. Although peer support workers are hired at the community level, they are trained to deliver programmatic goals, objectives, and activities developed at international, national, and provincial levels. The peer support workers embody an interweaving of dominant discourses within the local contexts of individual and family life. Herein lies the struggle: with externally prescribed mandates and their greater perceived value to overall prenatal, maternal, and infant health, they unobtrusively prepare the main stage for the continuation of a medicalized approach to health care (see Benoit et al., this volume). Nevertheless, they remain true to self and cultural heritage, that is, they cannot help but execute their work from the basis of the experiential knowledge they possess. So they impart traditional family values, incorporate those values and the traditional functions of the family, and situate them within the space of locally administered government programs. Sometimes this can flow from a single consciousness; mostly, in the process of attempting a seamless delivery that consciousness intensifies and then begins to tear.

A purpose of the present study was to unravel system discourses to retrieve the significance of the intimate labour of the peer support workers as experienced and articulated by the women themselves and to assist in raising awareness of the intrinsic value of this kind of intimate work to enhancing the health of populations. Several questions inform the overall analysis, including: Who guides the women in their work? Who informs, supports, restricts them? How is this women's work connected to the 'bigger' picture of health for prenatal women, mothers, and infants in Canada? What factors infringe upon the original stories of pregnancy and childbirth in Aboriginal communities resulting in the overreliance on medicalization and risk discourses that exist today?

Findings

On Representing a Feminist Indigenist Standpoint

The following is a participant-observation scenario that allows for an investigation of the ways in which health care and social programs are delivered to clients and the impacts of this delivery. Within the story, we can perceive a world prescribed, a stage prepared with actors more or less uncritically assuming their roles, and get a glimpse of a situation that seems to contradict itself by withholding the very support that it was designed to bestow.

NANCY

Nancy is 47 years old. She is a First Nations woman and has spent her life with her family living off the land. Her father hunted, trapped, and fished and was able to teach these skills to his children. In her words, she was taught, 'all that a human being needed to know to be self- sufficient by the time [she] was 16 years old.' Nancy's life changed drastically when a major mining corporation entered the community and transformed the lifestyle of her people, rendering living off the land impossible. Nancy's father worked for the company until he was killed on the job in the mid-1970s. Several challenges started to weigh heavily upon her and by the time she reached adulthood, Nancy had turned to drink to 'numb the pain and help [her] escape the feeling that [she] had no control over [her] own life.' When Nancy's daughter announced to her that she was going to have a baby, Nancy made a life-changing decision,

> I decided I didn't want my grandchild to suffer like my children did. I wanted to make changes and to be able to share my story, hopefully so that it would give strength to the young people. Maybe they would see that if I could do it, so could they.

Nancy wanted to rediscover her traditional ways of childrearing. She wanted to reclaim her role as mother and grandmother, roles she felt she had long ago given away. By the time I met Nancy she had become a powerful community spokesperson in her own right and a support to her daughter and to other young moms in the community. None of this means that her struggle wasn't endless.

One summer, Nancy asked me to help her to relocate to the city so that she could register in an education program that would help her carry out her community work. I said that I would. Because Nancy was not entitled to the treaty right of government-funded education, she had to apply for social assistance to support her in her move. It was at the social assistance office that I witnessed a drastic change in a woman I thought I 'knew.' I was disgusted in the way that the social assistance worker spoke down to Nancy; in the way that he seemed to assume in her a lack of drive or personal direction. More so, I was astounded by the change I witnessed in Nancy: she had transformed from an autonomous woman with purpose and conviction to one docile and dependent. By the time we left the office, Nancy's vitality was washed away. Two weeks later, Nancy returned to the community with her task of enrolling in a continuing education that would provide her with the skills to accomplish her community work unrealized.

The scenario depicts a current framework that functioned to place Nancy, as a First Nations woman, in a power-imbued environment that could not only define her being, but also appropriated her self-confidence and her self-knowledge and replaced them with the negative one it held of her. The importance of this scenario is that it reveals 'possibility' within limited frameworks and points to exact locations and mechanisms that generate them. With such knowledge, change is possible.

The problem that Nancy faced in representing herself in her interaction with a government representative is one shared by other peer support workers, that is, to represent Aboriginal women as healthy, self-governing, and living according to specific ways of knowing and being in the world. For Nancy, by herself, the system was overbearing and encompassing. She lacked the support to be able to navigate through the system in order to meet her self-prescribed goals. This usurpation of power is precisely the strength upon which the role of the peer support worker turns.

The peer support worker's job is to assist women in self-representation, so that they can interact with the health care system as autonomous women. Their role is to liaise between everyday realities and system-implemented services so that women are able to access the best that the health care system has to offer and so that they can manipulate that system (i.e., to become agents within that system). This is no small achievement and requires of them an active analysis and interpretation of the multiple levels of governance within which their everyday intimate work is encased.

Problematization of the Everyday World as an Alternative to Pathologizing Individuals

Personal and community agency are central determinants of a population's health. And yet we are grounded in a neoliberal ideological framework that characterizes inefficiencies within persons as opposed to evaluating the conditions in which people live. This is another foundational element of the work of the peer support worker: to assist women in self-actualization through expanding their understanding of the multiple and interconnected circumstances of their lives. Rather than to label women as 'pathological' the focus of the work is on illuminating the contexts outside of the women to which they are connected but of which they may or may not be consciously aware (e.g., policies or lack of policies that lead to a decrease or perpetuation of the likelihood of domestic violence, poverty, and dilapidated housing). From this more contextualized perspective, pathologies are attributed away from the childbearing women and placed upon the situational contexts and environments within which they live.

In problematizing the everyday world, the women participants come to understand that the world we live and breathe manifests from our behaviours and experiences and, in turn, impacts them. Such an education builds within the women a sort of advocacy and interest in matters that were, to this point, unimportant to them and therefore excluded their active participation. With programming, women come to see that many of the factors that affect and are affected by our everyday lives exist beyond the scope of direct experience, meaning that we may not be able to see, hear, or feel all of the factors that affect our everyday lives and yet they affect us sensually.

Problematization of our social environments allows for a location of self inside a universe that links everyday experiences within the larger social and material structures of paternalism, colonization, and capitalism, including their most recent neoliberal form. By such a process, the peer support workers are able to engage in a process of knowledge building that fuses micro- with macro-levels of inquiry where the emphasis and impact lie at the most micro-level of analysis – the individually articulated and holistic experiences of pregnancy and motherhood.

The peer support workers expressed their discomfort with the current service delivery but could not explicate the reasons for their unease. For example, in a focus group, one of the peer support workers said,

> something's really wrong about the way they're treating us, but I can't really explain it.

She was referring to the interactions between prenatal women and their health care providers:

> You go into a prenatal [check-up] and you and your needs are no longer the focus of the consultation. Instead the focus is on the physician's busy schedule. Like, sometimes, the doctors don't really know what's going on with you. Or maybe they do but they don't say ... There was a few times where I had palpitations ... after I had my baby I figured out the reason

why that was happening 'cause my baby was pressed up against my heart.' Well, why didn't they tell me that? I thought I was going to go into heart attack! And I called the hospital a few times and here I am, a nurse, calling ... And they're telling me, 'Oh don't worry about it. It will go away. It's probably just due to stress. You probably had too much caffeine.'

This worker's inability to articulate her concerns can be attributed to her own personal acceptance that the physician's health interests must take precedence over her own. At some level, the medical system has been absorbed inside her consciousness to such an extent that even though she *knows* she requires a certain kind and degree of care, perhaps it is unfair to attribute fault to professionals who ultimately have a very central and important role in ensuring mother and infant health in pregnancy and childbirth. In the interaction, she was not given the opportunity to speak, to be heard. How could the medical staff have known that it could not have been the caffeine that was causing the palpitations, when it was not within their daily tasks to ask her? Rather than to press the subject with them, she left the appointment feeling not only misunderstood and unheard but that, indeed, her health might be failing her.

Valuations of Care: Differences between
What Women Feel They Need and What They Get

Reflections on health and wellness by the peer support workers revealed a lack of connection between personal conceptions of health and the type of health care services provided in the institutions. Although the women valued the knowledge, skills, and technologies of the medical practitioners, on the one hand, they felt alienated by them, on the other. Pregnancy and childbirth were transitions, life-changing occurrences, but these experiences seemed to escape the minds of experts more concerned with recording vital data. For most women, tensions between perceived need and feelings of alienation did not impact their utilization of physician-based prenatal care. Interestingly, according to the workers interviewed, the women most likely to refuse physician-based prenatal care were also most likely to reject community-based peer support programs as well. Bifurcated consciousness inherent in the tension described above was made apparent when the women described feelings that they had to consult the hospital or clinic-based physician, nurse, or obstetrician on matters regarding which they knew from experience the experts would not be able to offer assistance. In the focus groups, women described elaborate details of pregnancy and childbirth health care customs they would implement in the home, often under the care of grandmothers and other older women. Some of the stories included the specific roles of grandfathers, for example, in the selection of natural herbs and traditional medicines. Even with the conviction that these inherited practices were effective for health promotion (and at times, intervention), the women would explain that they would go to the clinic or hospital, 'just in case.' Reflecting further, the women would explain they felt they might be seen as neglectful if something was to go wrong with their pregnancy and they had not sought physician care. Following the medical discourse, the women, too, saw physician-oriented care as a safety measure for the reduction of risk to mother and infant – to them, this type of care was responsible care sought out by responsible women.

Women Expressing a Completely Different Kind of Care

Expression of the need for an intimate and involved kind of care ranges from complete resistance to adaptation and compromise. The woman in the following scenario reacted to a fear based on her own previous experience and one that she felt unable to express with her physician. Rather than take the risk of speaking out (and most likely, of doing so from a position of inferiority or disempowerment), she opted out of prenatal care all together:

> I had a young woman that refused to go see a doctor ... and then finally ... one of the family said something to me. I guess apparently what was happening was this woman ... had about four children already and each one they had to induce her and she was afraid to go see the doctor because she was sure they were going to induce her. That was her whole fear and that's why she kept the secrets ... She said, 'I'm not going to go.' And she didn't, and she did have her baby at home [in a nearby community].

Resistance as an approach to personal empowerment has several fundamental limitations, for example, the woman in the scenario above might have put herself in the precarious position of not being able to access essential health care services that could have benefited or saved her and her baby from severe consequences. Her resentment of physician-oriented treatment kept her from accessing any kind of care because, as the peer support worker explained, 'She figured that we would try and persuade her to go see the doctor.' To the resistant woman in the scenario, the whole system, from the level of community up was in cahoots to deliver a kind of care in which she had no voice. Expression, the sharing of stories, regarding pregnancy, childbirth, and mothering experiences is a critical determinant of health, 'because it provides alternatives to the oppressive model of motherhood provided and promoted by the dominant patriarchal culture, but also because it provides a position outside of the dominant culture from which to critique' (Lavell-Harvard & Lavell 2006: 3). Citing previous research, Lavell-Harvard and Lavell (2006: 4) further explain 'that the sharing of memories of violation and exploitation are pedagogically powerful because they have the potential to expose the oppressive ways in which our society is organized. Apparently the "personal" is not only "political," it is also powerful. Arguing that reality is itself subjective, empirical sociologist, Marcia Millman and Rosabeth Moss Kanter agree the "collective delusions" that support the inequity of society can be "undone by introducing fresh perspectives."'External expert and privileged control of the overall childbearing experience is evident in the existence of an essentially homogeneous official discourse for Canadian women. Within the policies and practices that stem from this discourse, there are noticeable silences that persist even in intimate settings involving women and their peers or within the family. For example, following one focus group that involved several sets of grandmothers, mothers, and daughters, one of the grandmothers approached me to say,

> I want to thank you so very, very much! I never shared these stories with my daughters before. Just having them to listen and for me to hear what they have to say and what they remember! This was such a wonderful experience for me to have.

This is not to suggest that dialoguing does not occur naturally, rather that it is not articulated widely nor present in its full capacity, thus resulting in limited impact within the official discourse and the policies and practices that stem from it. That women have more to say is evident through the stories shared by the peer support workers. For example:

> [Some women] plan [their] pregnancies right from before they got pregnant and take their folic acid and all that and going to the appointments. Sometimes ... seems like such a waste because all they do is they rush in,

check your blood pressure, ask you a few questions, and they're out the door in like ten minutes and the thing is after a few visits like that you kind of think, 'Well what's the point if they don't even tell me if my blood pressure is okay?' They just leave you in limbo like they didn't really talk to you. So, and even for myself, you just have to force yourself to keep going ... and ... if the doctors don't really have the time to really speak to you about some of the concerns that you have ...

The right to be visible and to be heard is a requirement for active engagement in health promotion. In the following excerpt, the woman is describing the impact of invisibility and marginalization within the health encounter:

... we have to consider the woman's time and be respectful of it. It's very stressful because you're thinking, 'Okay, I should be doing this, I should be doing that, and here I am sitting in your office ... You sit there ... and then ... [They say something like], 'Your blood pressure is high. You haven't lost any weight.' But, you already knew this. It's not enough.

Paradigms of Choice

The equitable inclusion of peer-delivered intimate labour within prenatal health care policy and practice is both a right and responsibility of those utilizing the services and their advocates. Inclusion of such assists governments in the ultimate goal of 'health for all' and is a vision that cannot be conceived without the active participation of communities, and specifically for the interests of the current study, of Aboriginal women and their families living in First Nations communities.

To assert that 'freedom of choice' is concealed inside current health promotion discourse is unoriginal. Lupton, for example, regards the new public health model as one that *appears* to be working in the best interests of individuals when, in fact, the converse is true: modern public health works to further neoliberal government interests focused on efficiency and accountability. Its concern with individuals is to encourage us to act in accordance with those interests, thus increasing governability. The characteristic outcome of power is not a relationship of domination of state over a subjected individual but the probability that the normalized subject will habitually obey (Lupton 1995). The symmetry of the modern state rests on the balance between the needs of the individual and the conglomerations of all individuals

within the state. Certainly, political structures that provide autonomy and choice for individuals are particularly valued in Western
cultures. However, having choices, making choices, and having the
ability to make the 'right' choice – always according to an index of
morality – are things that arise from understandings of freedom that,
in themselves, are central to the arrival of a particular conceptualization of the modern human being (Coveney 1998). To bring this point
down to the level of community programming, Lupton calls a major
strategy of the health promotion model, community participation,
'community manipulation.' It is thus that we can perceive health promotion, and in particular, prenatal support programs or childbirth
practices, as a form of governance that is productive in the sense that
it produces modern human beings, or modern and responsible pregnant women; in other words, it defines empirically what it means to be
healthy (in an ever expansive way) and it supervises proper routes to
health via a discipline that establishes for us a set of approved health
ethics (Coveney 1998).

One very central tenet of a bifurcated consciousness is the individual's ability to perceive and to understand multiple and more profound
levels of reality. Living from the angle of an alternative discourse forces
individuals to understand not only their own realities but also those
of the more powerful segments of society. Alternatively, those living
at the highest echelons of society rarely if at all need to pay attention
to the lives of those that society leaves marginalized. Living with such
understandings, however, may be a survival technique for marginalized individuals, but it is not necessarily emancipating.

An emancipating knowledge is rooted in an individual or community desire to confront the relations of oppression, gain independence,
and use knowledge to uplift circumstances for self and community.
According to the teachings of Paulo Freire, knowledge for liberation
must emanate from the people themselves and cannot be imposed
upon them from without. Through the medium of *conscientization,*
or consciousness raising, people can begin a process by which they
can become aware of the cultural context in which they exist and can
become challenged to work actively to bring about social change for
the better. Freire asserted that to incite individuals to fanaticism, conscientization 'enrolls them in a search for self-determination' (Dickson
1997). Emancipatory knowledge emerges from and embraces the social
histories of marginalized communities.

Locating opportunity for personal and community expression within the dominant government regime is an essential element of emancipation. Rose explains:

> It is in the space opened between the imposition of controls upon conduct by the public powers and the forms of life adopted by each individual that the vocabularies and techniques of the psycho-sciences operate. In the complex web they have traced out, the truths of science and the powers of experts act as relays that bring the values of authorities and the goals of business into contact with the dreams and actions of us all. These technologies for the government of the soul operate not through the crushing of subjectivity in the interests of control and profit, but by seeking to align political, social, and institutional pleasures and desires, and with the happiness and fulfillment of the self. Their power lies in their capacity to offer means by which the regulation of selves – by others and by ourselves – can be made consonant with contemporary political principles, moral ideals, and constitutional exigencies. They are, precisely, therapies of freedom. (Rose 1990: 257)

It is significant, therefore, that although the techniques of the self may be perceived to be subjectifying, they are so not because experts have co-conspired to dominate and subjugate the self through bureaucratic management of individual life, but because modern selves have come to identify with the project of freedom and actively search for it through the discourses supplied by those experts (Rose 1990). The concept of the care of the self implies a degree of agency that suggests that the techniques of governmentality are not simply imposed upon passive bodies but that resistance and change can be both generated and sustained (Lupton 1995).

The formulation of power-knowledge assists in informing an analysis of the role of First Nations women in experience articulating, a freedom that allows for the security of health in pregnancy and childbirth. It is the basis of an analysis that can situate First Nations women within the context of Canadian society and ask whether and to what extent 'official' discourses on pregnancy and childbirth health maintenance and personal responsibility are accepted in the construction of subjectivity and the practices of their everyday and every night real-life experiences. Understanding the macro-contextual factors that situate a female and indigenous standpoint is vital to this investigation.

Targeting Opportunities for Change

The sharing of experiences with the health care system during pregnancy and childbirth is a powerful indicator of health and well-being
and has potential for enhancing agency. Although available to all individuals within a democratic society, challenging the status quo requires
of the peer support workers a constant critical analysis of the elements
of their stories. Feelings of disconnect between what one feels and
what one ought to do for health promotion, as dictated by authorities
in the medical field (and often quoted by their community-based co-
providers), resounded in the interviews. Additionally, back-and-forth
thinking about what determines an effective health care service was
characteristic.

The next quotation is from a woman who had much more to say in a
prenatal health care interaction than she felt prepared to share:

> I don't know what was wrong with me. I never got a chance. He just said,
> 'I'm inducing you.' He was so rushing when I was there. I'd be trying to
> talk to him and he'd be walking out. And then I'd ask, 'Uh?' He just looked
> at my chart and ... He said, 'You are having a Caesarean.' I said, 'No, I
> uh, I don't know.' And he goes, 'I'll book you one.' And so that was it. I
> never really got to experience labour ... I never got to experience having an
> actual labour or birthing a baby the way it's naturally supposed to be.

The peer support workers could empathize with and share in the
experiences articulated by the women; however, they too experienced
difficulties that kept them from challenging the system. To illustrate,
one worker, a First Nations community-based nurse, told of her own
experience in a discussion with her obstetrician. After being told she
was to have her baby at a tertiary hospital in the city she cried, feeling
completely vulnerable and disempowered. Then,

> I said, 'wait a minute' I have some power here. I'm a nurse for heaven's sake!

The women desire to put more into the system, that is, to include a kind
of care that will enhance our understanding of individual health needs.
Interestingly, what they have to say is suppressed, a function of both
their own marginalized position within the system as well as larger
discursive and structural forces that devalue intimate labour and intimate care needs as unnecessary and/or indulgent. The frustration that

this induces in peer support workers was evident in the interviews, for example, one peer support worker said:

> You want to help the women, to get them to the point where they can sit down with the doctor and say, 'Look, I have a problem and I'm scared ... Can you tell me what's going on here?' Like to actually get the doctor to sit with you and help you work out what was going on is kind of like pulling teeth.
>
> When you are in that situation, you need to be able to ask ... But many women can't verbalize it. I think there's a lot of people like that.

Lack of perceived authority over personal health domains is perhaps evident in the peer support workers' own fear of asserting voice in the health care interaction. Even in situations where the peer support workers could clearly advocate for the program participants, they would often doubt their own abilities to make the changes necessary for an intimate and culturally informed provision of health care. For example, in the next excerpt, although the peer support worker clearly described what she saw as an important health care strategy, she finished by saying that she didn't know how to address the situation:

> I want the women to become more involved in their pregnancies and childbirths and to pick and choose their own needs. It's hard though to want them to come and participate in the prenatal program and then for all of the real important decisions, they have no say, no control of what happens to them ... and ... to be able to have a better understanding about the medical issues ... about having their babies that they don't have to run to the city. It's just the same as having their baby around home and it's not going to be any better [in the city] it might be worse ... than if they experience you know their whole birth experience at home. And [I'd like to] let them know that they have choices. I'd like them to have more choices in their birthing process ... if it's even offered where they don't have to take those drugs, like sometimes it's not even necessary. Women, long ago, didn't have to take any medication when they had their babies. They don't have to go and have their babies so far away; I'm not sure how to even go about changing or addressing that.

Another worker commented as follows:

> They take over ... it's your baby but when they take over how are you supposed to have it? It's like you lose control when you go away to have your

baby ... I hope that women become more aware of their choices, you know. They don't have to let, um doctors, I don't know how to say it, overpower them. But because ... they're the ones that are having the baby ... the point is, it's their baby and they have a say and they should have the birth, say, in the way that they want to be treated.

A fundamental element of the community-based peer support program is that it allows for expression and understanding of the holistic needs of women and their families within the contexts of home and community. From this knowledge base, medical/technological care can be better tailored to meet those actual needs of individuals. Although, the programs are still just finding their ground, and the women often repeated that they were unsure how to proceed, they were *doing it* and *talking about it* in their everyday work. Holistic and intimate knowledge of women could be of value independently and also in collaboration with the broader medical system. The two types of care should be regarded as qualitatively distinct but compatible.

How the Grandmothers Inform Health Care
Provision – Reinserting the Knowledge into Community-Based Care

Beyond a feminine bifurcation of consciousness, the current study focused on indigenous women, representatives of a culture system that diverges significantly, and often contradicts, mainstream Euro-Canadian ways of knowing and being in the world. For full expression of Manitoba Cree and Ojibway culture, many of the women interviewed took an about-face and re-examined a wisdom that was always available but perhaps not always accessible to them. Assimilation policies as well as the prohibition of traditional midwifery and medicinal remedies taught men and women to repress many of their indigenous customs. The peer support workers talked about these issues at length, remembering the lessons their Elders taught them, and reflecting on their importance in their current work. This final section of the chapter highlights some aspects of these stories and their potential for holistic health and overall wellness. The inclusion of traditional customs speaks to something far greater than an individual's physical health; according to Katsi Cook, midwife and traditional healer, the question to be pondered in our health work is not simply a matter of risk reduction, but of the woman's role in facilitating it and more: 'What threatens the sovereignty of the women; of the women's community? What threatens the self-sufficiency of women in matters of production and reproduction, not just of human beings, but of all our relations upon which we depend for a healthy life?' (Cook 1985: 14).

Infusing into the system this very different kind of health care provision, indigenous women address aspects of overall health until now overlooked by the medical system. The following citations reveal how some of the women began to incorporate these teachings and to use them to change the way they related to the medical health care system:

> They gave me a Caesarean but they induced me, and my mother told me, actually, my grandmother raised me, she told me, 'You weren't even ready to have your baby. You shouldn't have let those doctors do that to you.' She told me, 'That's why you couldn't have your baby and that's why you had a Caesarean.' She said, 'Your baby wasn't ready.' And so I tried to argue, well, I was just ... but she didn't understand, hey. Maybe I wasn't ready to have the baby. My grandmother was trying to teach me that I could challenge what the doctors were telling me ... that I could have an opinion.

The professionalization of intimate work was seen as a necessary aspect of bringing traditions back to the fore of community healthy living. With respect to culture, the workers incorporated traditional values and implemented them in their work as their grandmothers, mothers, and aunties would have done before them. One peer support worker explained:

> There has to be a vision for a future that is based in our past. I remember when we were kids and my mom was going off to have our sister. We knew she was in the hospital ... so we climbed up on that hill in front of the hospital thinking that if we could get high enough we might be able to see them, our mother and our sister. See, before that birth, we were all present at the births of our siblings. We need to have our children come into this world with our family around us, to remember and to live the sacredness of childbirth.

Beyond peer involvement, the women added the importance of involving the grandmothers in the programs:

> I wouldn't mind seeing more grandmothers involved in the program. To have them talk about how they grew up ... and how they were mothers to their kids. Just like to see different perspectives to see the different goals

of them being mothers. I would love to hear their birth stories and to see how they experienced having a kid.

Essentially, the peer support workers laboured to bond the bifurcation of consciousness, that is, to bring together the lessons of two dissimilar worlds but from the grounding of their own expression; their own being. One peer support worker explained this goal as follows:

> There are two sides to health ... In one way, we need the medical, the health promotion. Especially for those women who do not look after themselves, who end up getting gestational diabetes ... there are two sides to it. But the traditional side helps to get the women centred. It helps to get them to understand who they are, the responsibility for themselves and for others, for the baby and the family, for the unborn baby that they are nurturing already.
>
> I think that's where it's important, you should respect, like I strongly believe, what the client wants. If it can happen it should happen what the client wants. You should not take that away because you are de-powered. Like feeling I can't help myself; to take that dependency away. Like give the client choices. I think that would be better. Give them three or four choices. List them or point them out and say, okay, have you decided? Okay, what do you want? And I think that's where that independency will start to grow.

Summary and Conclusions

This chapter highlighted the significance of the intimate labour of peer support workers to maternal health policy and health outcomes for First Nations women and infants and discussed the role of bifurcated consciousness in mediating how peer support workers experience and perform their work. A bifurcated consciousness is understood to be an uncomfortable split of consciousness wherein a marginalized individual strives to work inside of a world that neither belongs to her nor makes intuitive sense to her. Absorbing the lessons of their everyday interactions with women, the peer support workers took back ownership of their terrain through active engagement in and re-creation of their work duties and responsibilities. They worked with Aboriginal women, as Aboriginal women. Instead of furthering susceptibility to a patriarchal framework, they began questioning its assumptions through dialogue and taking opportunities to build self-confidence, understand heredity, and take pride in difference. Some of the peer support workers knew they had something very valuable in the way of health enhancement that can be taught to medical practitioners.

The most powerful political message asserted through the study is that it speaks to the tendency of Canadian society to lean towards social homogenization. Neoliberal policies and programs have been delivered to Aboriginal women and yet disparities in virtually every area of health and wellness persist. This one-size-fits-all approach has further marginalized Aboriginal women and has undermined the relevance and importance of their work in fostering healthy communities.

The power of including the voices of Aboriginal women in health care and social discourses is that they have the potential to significantly change the system, to functionally redirect it so that it works for the benefit of their well-being. To this effect, Harding and others have emphasized the point that 'knowledge often arises through the adoption of different perspectives on nature and that this makes the cultural dimension of knowledge generation significant' (cited in Bala 2001:1). Paraphrasing Tuhiwai-Smith, the inclusion of voices outside male and Eurocentric knowledge frameworks leads to greater objectivity and is a goal of social justice that is expressed through a wide range of psychological, social, cultural, and economic domains. It is a process that necessarily involves the transformation, healing, and mobilization of peoples. The processes, approaches, and methodologies, while open to different influences and possibilities, are critical elements of a strategic health care agenda (1999: 116). The natural instinct of the women to share their stories and to express their interests creates the space for transformation to take effect. Through such practice, the women make a political and powerful statement regarding the need for change. The peer support workers in their ongoing work and their reclamation of the traditions of their Elders provide a fresh look at the fundamental role of intimate labour in enhancing health and reducing the health inequities that plague our nation.

REFERENCES

Anderson, K. (2000). *A Recognition of Being: Reconstructing Native Womanhood.* Toronto: Second Story Press.

Bala, A. (2001). *Harding and Standpoint Epistemology.* Retrieved June 2004 from http://courses.nus.edu.sg/course/phibalas/dialogue2001/Sciendtific Method/ Harding/Harding and Standpoint Theory.htm.

Brooks, A. (2003). *Dorothy E. Smith: Voice, Standpoint and Power.* Boston College Lecture Notes. Retrieved June 2004 from http://www.bc/edu/schools/cas/ sociology/vss/smith/.

Conway, K., & A. Kutinova. (2003). Maternal health: Does prenatal care make a difference? Unpublished paper, Department of Economics, University of New Hampshire, Durham.

Conway, K.S., & D. Partha. (2003). Is prenatal care really ineffective? Or, is the Devil in the distribution? Unpublished paper, Department of Economics, University of New Hampshire, Durham.

Cook, K. (1985). *The Women's Dance Reclaiming Our Powers.* Retrieved May 2004 from http://www.nativemidwifery.com/Articles.html.

Couchie, C., & H. Nabigon. (1997). A path towards reclaiming Nishawbe birth culture: Can the Midwifery Exemption Clause for Aboriginal Midwives make a difference? In F.M. Shroff, ed., *The New Midwifery,* 41–50. Toronto: Women's Press.

Coveney, J. (1998). The government and ethics of health promotion: The importance of Michel Foucault. *Health Education Research Theory and Practice* 13(3): 459–68.

Dennis, C., E. Hodnett, R. Gallop, & B. Chalmers. (2002). The effect of peer support on breast-feeding duration among primiparous women: A randomized controlled trial. *Canadian Medical Association Journal* 166(1): 21–8.

Dickson, G. (1997). *Participatory Action Research & Health Promotion: The Grandmothers' Stories.* Dissertation, University of Saskatchewan, Department of Community Health and Epidemiology.

Du Bois, W.E.B. (2007). *The Souls of Black Folk.* New York: Oxford University Press.

Eni, R. (2005). *An Articulation of the Standpoint of Peer Support Workers to Inform Childbearing Program Supports in Manitoba First Nations Communities: Institutional Ethnography as De-colonizing Methodology.* Dissertation, Community Health Sciences, University of Manitoba.

Frideres, J.S. (1986). Racism and health: The case of the Native people. In B.S. Bolaria & H.D. Dickinson, eds., *Sociology of Health Care in Canada,* 135–47. Toronto: Harcourt Brace Jovanovich.

Gjerdingen, D.K., & P. Fontaine. (1991). Preconception health care: A critical task for family physicians. *Journal of the American Board of Family Practitioners* 4(4): 237–50.

Heaman, M.I. (2001). *Risk Factors for Spontaneous Preterm Birth among Aboriginal and Non-Aboriginal Women in Manitoba.* Dissertation, University of Manitoba, Winnipeg, Manitoba.

Lake, M. (1996). The meanings of the 'self' in claims for self-government: Re-claiming citizenship for women and Indigenous people in Australia. Special Issue. *Law in Context* 14(1): 9–23.

Lavell-Harvard, D., & J. Lavell. (2006). *'Until Our Hearts Are on the Ground': Aboriginal Mothering, Oppression, Resistance and Rebirth.* Toronto: Demeter Press.

Lawrence, R.A. (2002). Peer support: Making a difference in breast-feeding duration. *Canadian Medical Association Journal* 166(1): 42–3.

Lupton, D. (1995). *The Imperative of Health: Public Health and the Regulated Body.* London: Sage.

Miles, A. (1991). *Women, Health and Medicine.* Philidelphia: Open University Press.

Mykhalovskiy, E., & L. McCoy. (2002). Troubling discourses of health: Using institutional ethnography in community-based research. *Critical Public Health* 12(1): 17–37.

Paul, G., S.M. Smith, D. Whitford, F. O'Kelly, & T. O'Dowd. (2007). Development of a complex intervention to test the effectiveness of peer support in Type 2 diabetes. *BMC Health Services Research* 7(136). Retrieved May 2007 from http://www.pubmedcentral.nih.gov/picrender.fcgi?artid=20 80630&blobtype=pdf.

Rose, N. (1990). *Governing the Soul: The Shaping of the Private Self.* New York: Routledge. 198.

Tuhiwai-Smith, L. (1999). *Decolonizing Methodologies: Research and Indigenous Peoples.* London: Zed Books.

PART FOUR

Unpaid Care Work in Intimate Settings

8 Mothers' Health, Responsibilization, and Choice in Unpaid Family Care Work after Separation/Divorce

RACHEL TRELOAR AND LAURA FUNK

Many Canadian social policies emphasize the obligation of individuals to care for their dependent family members, reflecting normative expectations that family members are responsible for providing support for one another. Such policies have particular implications for the economic, emotional, and physical well-being of those who do family care work, primarily mothers. In this chapter, we suggest that the concepts of familialism and responsibilization can help in understanding how care work after separation and/or divorce is highly gendered. We describe the implications of familialistic policies, practices and assumptions on mothers' health and dignity, with a focus on the Canadian context. In doing so, we draw on secondary data concerning mother's primary care work of parenting during separation and divorce as well as on other examples from Canadian family policy. Further, we suggest that the ways in which mothers exercise choice with regards to self-care and familial caring roles are both shaped by, and rooted in, the Canadian sociopolitical context of neoliberal reforms. We conclude by providing recommendations for future research, and health and social service policy and practice.

Familialism and the Gendering of Care Work

The boundaries between informal and formal care are becoming increasingly blurred. Formal (i.e., paid, non-family member or friend) care workers perform emotion work and increasingly provide in-home services; informal caregivers (i.e., family, friends, neighbours) can be paid and are encouraged to take on additional and more technical, skilled, and complex tasks, including work within formal care settings

(Henderson & Forbat 2002; Ungerson 1997; Ward – Griffin & Marshall 2003). However, one distinguishing characteristic of informal care is *who* performs this work in terms of their initial relationship to the care recipient, be it family member, friend, or stranger. This point of distinction is crucial, since being a family member has complex implications for the health and well-being of those receiving and providing care in this context.

A key influence on family care work is *familialism* (Segal 1983). This term is used to describe a set of ideological assumptions and expectations, operationalized in practices and policies that promote a particular view of what kind and how much of care work should be performed by the family (Esping-Andersen 1999; Lewis 2001). Familialism suggests that parenting and other forms of intimate labour performed in the home, such as elder care, are private relationships and moral imperatives. Households are viewed as having the primary responsibility for their members' welfare throughout the life course, as opposed to a broader understanding of collective responsibility (Esping-Andersen 1999), such as is found in the Nordic welfare states. Further, familialism, in both high-income and many low-income countries, is a highly gendered concept, including implicit and explicit assumptions about women's 'natural' ability for and knowledge about care. The caring role is seen to be an inborn trait for women, and is an important component of women's socialization (Olesen 1989). Indeed, dominant social ideas about care tend to promote a view that women should live through relationships, being 'selfless' in placing the needs of children and other family members before their own (Fineman 2005; Kline 1995; McMahon 1995). Leitner (2003) applies the concept of familialism to analyse the caring function of the family in child care (as well as elder care) in several European Union member states, including some of those that are the focus of the comparative studies that appear in this volume. Policies that explicitly support and promote the caring functions of family represent state responses to addressing needs in the context of the erosion of formal services, and are viewed as indicators of familialism. De-familial policy, in contrast, 'either socializes or "marketizes" the caring function of the family through public social services or market-driven care provision' (Leitner 2003: 357). In this regard, Leitner suggests that policies such as the public provision of child care are de-familializing; cash benefits for parental leave are familializing. By comparing countries based on a combination of these two indicators, Leitner generates a description of four types of familialism: strong familializing *and* strong de-familializing policies equate to 'optional familialism'; strong familializing *and* weak de-familializing policies equate to 'explicit familialization'; weak familializing *and* strong de-familializing policies equate to 'de-familialization'; and weak familializing *and* weak de-familializing policies equate to 'implicit famializiation.' Notably, Finland is described as 'a borderline case' between 'optional' (indicated indirectly by a combination of widespread formal child care, as measured by rates of use, combined with the presence of formal payments for family child care) and 'explicit' (poor rates of formal child care but formal payments for family child care are present) types of familialism. However, Leitner's ranking of countries as 'poor' or 'widespread,' with regard to the availability of formal child care, is a relative ranking of countries in comparison with one another, and Leitner did not consider non-European countries in her review. In Canada, some portion of parental leave is paid through employment insurance benefits, but only for those who have contributed through a salary position (e.g., not those working for contract or the under-or un-employed). Universal public child care is not available; however, there is some limited public funding for child care for low-income families, with provincial variations (the average Canadian province covers 38% of costs: Cool 2004). Based on Leitner's classifications, then, Canada might be described as having 'explicit familialism' in relation to child care.

Recent policy decisions in Canada, which are often referred to as *neoliberal*, emphasize private responsibilities and the need to reduce economic demands on the public purse: more and more tasks of care and support, provided in the period after the Second World War by the state in the form of health and social services, have been shifted back to families (Burchell 1996; McDaniel & Gee 1993). Tied to the restructuring of the welfare state and globalization of the economy, neoliberal policies have increased the emotional, economic, and physical burden of caregiving on the family (primarily women) and are often justified with reference to the principle of *family responsibility;* more specifically, individuals are encouraged to make independent yet 'responsible' choices (Baines et al. 1998). However, the concept of *choices* minimizes women's difficulties in navigating the tensions between their productive and reproductive lives, promoting a limited and neoliberal view of work (Calder 2007) that does not acknowledge the material costs associated with women's care work in contemporary society (Fineman 1995). This process of 'responsibilization' (Rose 1996) is addressed in this volume (Purkis, Ceci, & Bjornsdóttir) in relation to formal nursing care in the home setting. In relation to informal care, the concept of responsibilization directs our attention to changes in the operation of state power in the context of the erosion of the welfare state – this erosion of services allows for a less direct form of social control by state apparatuses; instead, individuals are socialized to 'take responsibility'– that is, to make the 'right' choices. This concept has been applied by others (Bjornsdóttir 2001) in relation to women's role in caring for the elderly, for instance, but remains to be fully explored in the context of women's role as mothers.

In a context of neoliberalism and responsibilization, familialistic policies pose a particular risk of further deepening the gendered nature of care work in Canadian society, since these processes represent structural and normative influences that constrain women to care for their immediate and extended families (Aronson 1992; Calasanti & Slevin 2001; Wuest 1997). Further, family work and intimate labour by women continues to be undervalued (Chappell et al. 2003), which has particular implications for mothers' dignity and mental health; in contrast, social and community recognition and acknowledgment for informal caregivers demonstrates they are worthy of esteem or respect. As Zelizer (2007) points out, intimate labour, though providing pleasure to both caregivers and care recipients, enhances the welfare of its recipients; therefore, it must be considered to be labour. However, both the invisibility of this work in the economic sphere, and its absence from dominant notions of social citizenship, highlight the lack of social value and recognition afforded to mothers performing this personalized work. Fineman (2005) argues that caregiving work is, in fact, a contribution to the public good; therefore, some of the costs of this work must be redistributed to the institutions of state and market. These institutions work as well as they do, in part, because they are subsidized by unpaid caretaking labour hidden within the private realm of families, and conducted primarily by women.

Despite the increased participation of men in child care, family care work is still conducted primarily by women, who tend to be differentially involved in this work (Armstrong & Armstrong 2004; Lewis 2005; Statistics Canada 2005). As Kershaw et al. (2008) note, an employment-oriented view of citizenship ignores this fact, failing as a result to account for the gendered implications of an employment-centred view. For instance, mothers face career – related costs as a result of extended employment absences (e.g., lower chance for promotions); and those giving up paid work lose the opportunity to pay into government-funded pension plans.

The effects of such costs are particularly salient when there is a separation or divorce. Further, mothers' ability to form autonomous households is increasingly eroded by welfare cuts, reduced eligibility for subsidized child care, and cuts to programs for women escaping domestic violence (Kershaw et al. 2008). Consequently, mothers' ability to participate in the labour market is compromised. Elsewhere, Kershaw (2004: 928) also points out that in British Columbia child care discourse 'the language of choice facilitates the articulation of neoliberal principles within a rhetorical framework that conveys a sense of political neutrality and individualizes responsibility for social inequalities.' As noted elsewhere in this chapter, in addition to having to bear the burden of these inequalities, mothers are often blamed for their consequences.

Although the focus of our chapter is on the Canadian context, there are parallels to be drawn with the Nordic countries. In contrast to Canada, the Nordic countries offer their citizens publicly funded child care, in addition to a wide range of social welfare provisions that reduce economic inequities and promote gender equality in employment and family life. Compared with Canada, Finland, for example, has enacted strong gender – sensitive labour force and social policies in recent decades, including a well-developed public child care system, which is especially helpful for single parents and other vulnerable groups. Neoliberal reforms that took place in Finland in the 1990s have, as in Canada, been similarly influenced by familialism, involving a shift to a gender-neutral, neoliberal emphasis on individual rights and personal choice, reductions to social provisions (such as public day care), and encouragement for mothers to stay home with young children (Pylkkänen 2007). Yet the impacts of these reforms have not been as pervasive as in countries such as Canada, where weaker welfare state structures exist and there is no national consensus on fundamental values such as economic equity and gender equality in employment and family life.

In this chapter, we explore the particular implications of neoliberalism and familialism for mothers who are separated or divorced. To date, most research on family caregiving has been concerned with the care of the frail and elderly. Some research demonstrates that women who provide elder care are likely to report negative job effects and longer term career opportunity costs as a result of care involvement (Martin-Matthews & Campbell 1995). Aronson (1988) also illustrates how familialism contributes to guilt and a reluctance to voice one's own needs and desires in relationships between daughters and their elderly mothers. Further, women tend to be judged (by family and others more generally) by higher standards in terms of the amount, extent, and quality of care and emotional investment in the caregiver role (Baines et al. 1998). Ironically, the expectedness of women's caring suggests that women may benefit less from the role: 'caring was what was expected of them and only failure to care brought attention' (Rose & Bruce 1995: 127). Women tend to have greater difficulty setting limits on care, feel more personal responsibility, and identify caring *for* with caring about (Hooyman 1990). These may be some of the reasons that women report more stress from care work (Martin-Matthews 2000).

Numerous studies, in Canada and elsewhere, provide evidence that informal caregivers may suffer economically, socially, and physically (Cranswick 2003; Dosman & Keating 2005; Keefe et al. 2005). Excess stress on informal care providers has also been shown to negatively affect care recipients, in the sense that their needs may not be as well met nor their dignity respected. Family care work is, in short, an important *public health* issue, not only because society depends upon family to provide informal health services, but also because caregiver strain negatively affects the health of caregivers as well as the quality of the care that they are able to provide. These findings remain to be confirmed in research on separated or divorced mothers caring for young children. Furthermore, the majority of studies conceptualize caregiving as an individual – level determinant of health, focusing on personal perceptions of burden and coping strategies. In contrast, care work, as a particular form of social support (Chappell et al. 2003), should at the same time be conceptualized as a *social and structural* determinant of health. In the next section, we explicate this societal-level perspective on care work, recognizing how policies and practices, infused with ideas about familialism, negatively impact the health of women after separation or divorce.

Familialism, Health, and Choice in Mothers' Care Work after Separation/Divorce

The data summarized in this section illustrate how care work can be conceptualized as a social determinant of health and well-being through examining how the ways in which mothers engage in post-separation parenting are influenced by broader contexts (such as familialistic, gendered policies and practices).

Considerable research explores the effect of divorce on parents' and children's psychological well-being (Amato 2000), yet less is known about the direct and indirect effects of divorce on individuals' physical health. Mothers are certainly not alone in coping with the impacts of divorce, which also affects fathers, children, and extended family members. Research documents the negative long-term effects of divorce on both parents' and children's physical and emotional health (Amato 2000; Lorenz et al. 2006). Indeed, it is well known that chronic and acute stressors can negatively impact on physical and emotional health (Cohen et al. 1998; Freemont, & Bird 2000), and it has been shown that divorce is one such stressor. Lorenz and colleagues (2006) found that divorced women reported significantly higher levels of psychological distress than married women immediately after divorce, but no differences in physical illness were observed between the two groups. However, a decade later, and controlling for prior health status and other key variables, the divorced women reported significantly higher levels of physical illness as well. These researchers conclude that physical illnesses accumulate gradually in response to the persistent stressors of divorce, which, particularly for mothers, include 'chronically disadvantaged social and economic circumstances' (Lorenz et al. 2006: 112). According to Avison (1997), it is not mothers' personal deficits that lead to high levels of psychological distress after divorce, but rather the constant exposure to stressors.

Research on the greater economic consequences of divorce for mothers is extensive (Finnie 1993; Statistics Canada 2006); family income is an important social determinant of both physical and mental health, and financial strain at separation has been associated with a long-term and cumulative effect on maternal morbidity (Avison 1997; Finnie 1993; Wickrama et al. 2006). A Statistics Canada report on women notes that lone-parent families headed by women have the lowest incomes of all family types, with 38% of these families below the low income cut-off (LICO). Their average income ($32,500) was 38% that of two-parent families and 60% that of male-headed lone-parent families (Statistics Canada 2006: 134). Increased household expenses, coupled with women's lower earnings and cutbacks to services and support agencies, and a tendency to blame women for their financial circumstances after separation and divorce, further contribute to their difficulties. Dunne and his co-authors suggest a need for improved social support services for separating couples and their children (2000), yet low (or no) cost services are rarely available even in larger Canadian communities. During the recent period of neoliberal reforms, some provinces have even eliminated legal aid for most family law issues, thereby constraining access to justice for low income single mothers and their children. If litigation is necessary, or if single mothers are required to respond to court applications, they must pay for legal services out of pocket, represent themselves, concede, or 'choose' to remain in an untenable situation for lack of real alternatives.

Divorces and separations that involve a high degree of conflict over children can be particularly stressful and damaging. Research in the United Kingdom (Smart 2003), the United States (Stacer & Stemen 2000), and Australia (Rhoades, Graycar, & Harrison 2000) indicates that legal conflict over parenting arrangements continues to increase. It is unknown if this increase is related to neoliberal reforms such as cutbacks to agencies that provide services to women, and further empirical exploration is warranted. Although no Canadian research specifically quantifies increases in legal disputes over children's arrangements, the jurisdictional context is similar here to that of the United Kingdom and Australia. Both familialism and responsibilization can contribute to this conflict. Parental autonomy in making arrangements for children only exists insofar as these decisions fit with prevailing views of child welfare (Diduck 2003), yet there are conflicting messages and interpretations about what is in a child's 'best interest.' One example is the conflict between the familialistic child welfare discourse that mothers must protect their children (or risk losing them) and family law, which insists that children spend time (sometimes unsupervised) with a parent who has placed that child at risk. These kinds of contradictions contribute to the challenges faced by abused women when separating (Irwin, Thorne, & Varcoe 2002).

Even in the Finnish context, where family policies have promoted shared parental responsibilities for earning and caring and have stressed the equal parental role of men for almost two decades, these policies have not always had the intended effect on men's equal participation in child care (Pylkkänen 2007). Most Finnish women combine full-time work with primary care work for children, as well as increasingly, of the elderly. However, regardless of 'choices' about the allocation of care work responsibilities while partnered, mothers' caregiving (seen as 'natural' beforehand) is problematized after separation. At this point fathers everywhere do, generally, expect to share responsibility for children (Pylkkänen 2007).

A further paradox is that of increased publicization (i.e., state control) alongside greater privatization of responsibility for care work that accompanies neoliberal reforms. An example of increasing publicization can be found in British Columbia's recent proposal to reform family justice services, and specifically, to make 'consensual dispute resolution' mandatory prior to an initial family court application (B.C. Ministry of the Attorney General 2005). Although currently in a testing phase in several communities, and likely to become law under proposed legislation, B.C. policy makers were explicit that underpinning this policy direction is the intention to shape post-divorce family practices as well as normative conceptions of the management of post-separation disputes. Another concern was the need to reduce 'subsidization' of court costs and shift the fiscal responsibility for these 'individual matters' back to the parties (ibid.). The Working Group notes that mediation is less costly to the public purse and proposes that government cover only the cost of a single session. A sliding scale would then be available for those with financial need who wish to continue. However, those with means would be 'free to use, and pay for, the services of a collaborative dispute professional who charges more, if they so choose' (ibid.: 50). If we consider the economic differences between women and men post-divorce (Statistics Canada 2006), this proposal affects mothers and fathers differentially. However, in the context of recent elimination or cuts to services for women (Teghtsoonian 2003) and community serving agencies in British Columbia, the elimination of family and poverty law legal aid (used primarily by women) (Brewin 2004), and the existence of ongoing economic and social gendered inequities (Armstrong 1997), these effects are compounded. The differential impact of cutbacks and service reductions on women, alongside a clear statement of government intent to shape the private sphere of post-separation parental behaviour and family life (i.e., 'publicization') has troubling implications for gender equality in family life, as well as the health and well-being, and 'choice' of mothers in these circumstances.

Among other things, familialistic policies, practices, and assumptions may have the consequence of idealizing father contact and devaluing or problematizing mothers' care work (Boyd & Young 2002; Rhoades 2002; Burck et al. 1996). Many clinicians believe that divorcing women create anxiety in children over father contact, and act out of anger and resentment (Chesler 1991). Negative bias about divorced mothers in information recall among family therapy trainees has also been documented (Schultz & Leslie 2004). Mothers tend to be held responsible for difficulties in the father-child relationship, for failing to ensure successful contact between father and children, even where the father has been abusive (Hardesty & Chung 2006; Silverman et al. 2004), and for failing to resolve or accede in a dispute (Burck et al. 1996; Boyd 2003; Gilligan 1982; Kaganas 1999). Gilligan and others critique this phenomenon as reflecting pressures for mothers to live 'guided by the perceptions of others' needs, where they can see no way of exercising control without risking an assertion that seems selfish and hence morally dangerous' (Gilligan 1982: 143).

One of the best predictors of children's psychological functioning after divorce is the psychological adjustment of custodial parents (Kelly & Emery 2003; Johnston 1994; King & Sobelewski 2006). Research suggests women who adjust best to divorce feel able to take control of their lives (Duffy et al. 2002). Mothers risk social and legal sanctions, punishment, and loss of custody if they depart from an idealized and normative version of motherhood, regardless of caregiving history (Kline 1995; Boyd 2003; Smart & Neale 1999). Yet legal decisions may deny either parent legitimate expression of their own needs, and hinder adults (and particularly women) from exercising self-care (Diduck 2003). Under these conditions, and in the broader context of familialism and responsibilization which place most of the responsibility on mothers but with little room for either control or choice, both 'caring for' and self-care may be problematic. As mothers' physical and emotional health is impeded, their ability to monitor and support their children is undermined (Lorenz et al. 2006). This is a further reason to ensure that Canadian social welfare provisions are adequate to support mothers through this difficult period. Specifically, this means ensuring not only that mothers have the financial means to raise their children, but also that services to provide legal and emotional support and information are available and, most importantly, affordable. Further, these need to be combined with a strong system of public child care and national economic and labour force policies that promote good jobs for both men and women, as well as the workplace flexibility required by single mothers.

Although self-care is a moral imperative for expectant and new mothers, once separation occurs, mothers are subjected to a different set of moral (and legal) imperatives, centred on a particular understanding of children's welfare. It is at this latter point that normative cultural discourses of 'good mothers' and 'good post-divorce parenting' are particularly evident: with this, mothers' parenting and decisions may be subject to public scrutiny in the form of legal decisions, professional assessment, and parent education programs. This publicization ensures the 'best interests' of children are met, according to contemporary psychological, social, legal, and political views. However, these views have little to say about mothers' own well-being, work-life balance, or capacity to make good decisions on their children's behalf, despite the connection between child and caregiver well-being. Why is it that at the point of separation, these factors cease to be relevant – even in the lives of children? What would appear to be individual-level health effects related to divorce are exacerbated by social and political contextual factors, such as increased responsibility and diminished economic and social support for mothers post-divorce (and, we would argue, more generally).

Christopher (2002), in comparing the treatment of single mothers in different welfare states, concluded that Canada ranks poorly in this regard. The Nordic countries scored much higher, related to their policies that allow single mothers both to form autonomous households if they wish, and to avoid poverty. Important factors included the Nordic tax and social transfer systems, as well as policies that support maternal employment. Both Sweden and Finland report very low rates of maternal poverty, with the proportion of single mothers living in poverty 4.4% and 5.1%, respectively. This is in stark contrast to Canada, with poverty among single mothers at 38.3%. Along with France, Finland and Sweden also have generous employment policies to support mothers of young children. These policies have a significant impact on poverty ratios of single mothers' and of mothers more generally. Although recent neoliberal reforms noted above are likely to have worsened the situation of single mothers in these Nordic countries to some extent (Pylkkänen 2007), we believe Canada can still learn important lessons from policy development relating to the increased care burden and its health effects on mothers undergoing separation and/or divorce.

Summary and Conclusions

This chapter has highlighted the health implications of mothers' care work after separation and/or divorce in Canada, within the context of eroding government responsibility and a moral emphasis on women's caregiving responsibility for their young children. Mothers face competing sets of expectations and must navigate the paradox of having autonomy while also feeling compelled to choose the 'proper' or 'responsible' route (Smart 2003). Yet this route, while ostensibly natural, has been shown to be highly problematic, and risks the health, well-being, and agency of this vulnerable group of women. Thus, both the privatization and publicization of responsibility have significant implications for mothers' health and autonomy, the welfare of those for whom they provide care, and for deepening gender (in)equality.

It is our argument that the physical and mental health and well-being of all family members are affected by the ways in which responsibilization and familialism in the sociopolitical Canadian context constrain the enactment of care work and the exercise of choice in this work. There is urgent need for further research that examines the links between broader ideological, political, and economic contexts and the experiences and health of mothers after separation and divorce, explicating the complex mechanisms involved.

As also shown above, the Nordic countries such as Finland have been more successful in developing economic and social policies that promote the health and well-being of single mothers and give dignity to their informal care work. Indeed, in many of the Nordic countries, intimate labour commands greater social recognition. Research is needed to identify in greater detail the contextual factors that give rise to this variation in policy environments and also assist in developing policies to better support mothers involved in family care work. Further, an exploration of differences between women is needed. For example, we know little about the experiences of separated and/or divorced mothers who are disabled, lesbian, and/or Aboriginal.

Many health and social service practitioners and policy makers may not have heard of terms like 'familialism' and 'responsibilization' or considered how they can support women in balancing their care work for others with self-care. Our aim has been to increase the awareness of these concepts and to offer a critical reflection on them in contemporary human service delivery systems, as well as to explore how the enactment of neoliberal reform policies negatively impacts mothers who separate and divorce. One possible avenue for the reconceptualization of care work is the feminist 'ethic of care' perspective (Gilligan 1982; Sevenhuijsen 1998; Hankivsky 2004), which promotes responsiveness to self *as well as* others and challenges the perceived disparity between selfishness and responsibility. Rather than further entrenching women's responsibility to care (Baines et al. 1998), this approach emphasizes interdependence and the collective (social) responsibility for care, in seeking to 'identify and make visible the social relations embedded in the decisions that involve obligation and responsibility' (17). Scholars such as Hankivsky (2004) are exploring the utility of such an 'ethic of care' approach in caregiving policy, making the case for greater, not the erosion of, state responsibility for care (i.e., providing services such as public child care). A full range of support services, child care, and labour market policies to assist mothers who provide informal care, particularly during difficult transitions such as separation or divorce from their partners, can buffer adverse health effects as well as promote real choice and reduce the unintended health effects of care work performed by women at various stages in the life course. In this way, we believe, mothers can retain both their health and dignity in this challenging period, and society can better support them in positively fulfilling the responsibility of raising healthy children.

ACKNOWLEDGMENT

Adapted, with permission from the Canadian Public Health Association, from the article by R. Treloar and L. Funk (2008), 'Mothers' Health, Responsibilization, and Choice in Family Care Work after Separation/Divorce,' *Canadian Journal of Public Health* 99 (Supplement 2): S33–S37.

REFERENCES

Amato, P. (2000). The consequences of divorce for adults and children. *Journal of Marriage and Family* 62: 873–907.

Armstrong, P. (1997). Restructuring public and private: Women's paid and unpaid work. In S.B. Boyd, ed., *Challenging the Public/Private Divide: Feminism, Law, and Public Policy*, 37–61. Toronto: University of Toronto Press.

Armstrong, P., & H. Armstrong. (2004). Thinking it through: Women, work and caring in the new millenium. In K. Grant, P. Armstrong, M. Boscoe, A. Pederson, & K. Willson, eds., *Caring for / Caring about: Women, Home Care and Unpaid Caregiving*, 5–44. Aurora: Garamond Press.

Aronson, J. (1988). Dutiful daughters and undemanding mothers: Constraining images of giving and receiving care in middle and later life. In C. Baines, P. Evans, & S. Neysmith, eds., *Women's Caring: Feminist Perspectives on Social Welfare*, 114–38. Toronto: Oxford University Press.

Aronson, J. (1992). Women's sense of responsibility for the care of old people: 'But who else is going to do it?' *Gender and Society* 6(1): 8–29.

Avison, W. (1997). Single motherhood and mental health: Implications for primary prevention. *Canadian Medical Association Journal* 156: 661–3.

Baines, C., P. Evans, & S. Neysmith, S. (1998). Women's caring: Work expanding, state contracting. In C. Baines, P. Evans, & S. Neysmith, eds., *Women's Caring: Feminist Perspectives on Social Welfare*, 3–22. Toronto: Oxford University Press.

B.C. Ministry of the Attorney General. (2005). *A New Justice System for Families and Children*. Retrieved 21 Aug. 2006 from http://www.bcjusticereview.org/working_groups/family_justice/final_05_05.pdf.

Bjornsdóttir, K. (2001). From the state to the family: Reconfiguring the responsibility for long-term nursing care at home. *Nursing Inquiry* 9(1): 3–11.

Boyd, S.B. (2003). *Child Custody, Law, and Women's Work*. Toronto: Oxford University Press.

Boyd, S., & C. Young. (2002). Who influences family law reform? Discourses on motherhood and fatherhood in legislative reform debates in Canada. *Studies in Law, Politics and Society* 26: 43–75.

Brewin, A. (2004). *Legal Aid Denied: Women and the Cuts to Legal Services in B.C.* Vancouver: Canadian Centre for Policy Alternatives.

Burchell, B. (1996). Liberal government and techniques of the self. In A. Barry, T. Osborne, & N. Rose, eds., *Foucault and Political Reason: Liberalism, Neoliberalism and Rationalities of Government*, 19–36. Chicago: University of Chicago Press.

Burck, C., J. Hildebrand, & J. Mann. (1996). Women's tales: Systemic groupwork with mothers post-separation. *Journal of Family Therapy* 18: 163–82.

Calasanti, T., & K. Slevin. (2001). *Gender, Social Inequalities and Aging*. Walnut Creek: Alta Mira Press.

Calder, G. (2007). The personal *is* economic: Unearthing the rhetoric of choice in the Canadian maternity and parental leave benefit debates. In S. Cowan & R. Hunter, eds., *Choice and Consent: Feminist Engagements with Law and Subjectivity*, 125–41. London: Cavendish.

Chappell, N., E. Gee, L. McDonald, & M. Stone. (2003). *Aging in Contemporary Canada*. Toronto: Prentice-Hall.

Chesler, P. (1991). Mothers on trial: The custodial vulnerability of women. *Feminism and Psychology* 1(3): 409–25.

Christopher, K. (2002). Welfare state regimes and mothers' poverty. *Social Politics* 9(1): 60–86.

Cohen, S., E. Frank, W. Doyle, D. Skoner, B. Rabin, & J. Gwaltney. (1998). Types of stressors that increase susceptibility to the common cold in healthy adults. *Health Psychology* 17: 214–23.

Cool, J. (2004). *Child Care in Canada: Regulated, Unregulated, Private or Public.* Ottawa: Parliamentary Information and Research Service, Library of

Parliament. Retrieved 21 Sept. 2008 from http://www.parl.gc.ca/information/library/PRBpubs/prb0418-e.pdf.

Cranswick, K. (2003). *General Social Survey Cycle 16: Caring for an Aging Society.* Cat. no. 89-582-XIE. Ottawa: Statistics Canada.

Diduck, A. (2003). *Law's Families.* London: Lexis-Nexis.

Dosman, D., & N. Keating. (2005). Cheaper for whom? Costs experienced by formal caregivers in adult family living programs. *Journal of Aging and Social Policy* 17: 67–84.

Duffy, M., C. Thomas, & C. Trayner. (2002). Women's reflections on divorce – 10 years later. *Health Care for Women International* 23: 550–60.

Dunne, J., E. Hudgins, & J. Babcock. (2000). Can changing the divorce law affect postdivorce adjustment? *Journal of Divorce and Remarriage* 33(3/4): 35–54.

Esping-Andersen, G. (1999). *Social Foundations of Post Industrial Economies.* New York: Oxford University Press.

Fineman, M. (1995). Masking dependency: The political role of family rhetoric. *Virginia Law Review* 81: 2181–2215.

Fineman, M. (2005). *The Autonomy Myth: A Theory of Dependency.* New York: New Press.

Finnie, R. (1993). Women, men and the economic consequences of divorce. *Canadian Review of Sociology and Anthropology* 30: 205–41.

Freemont, A., & C. Bird. (2000). Social and psychological factors, physiological processes, and physical health. In C. Bird, P. Conrad, & A. Freemont, eds., *Handbook of Medical Sociology,* 334–52. Upper Saddle River: Prentice-Hall.

Gilligan, C. (1982). *In a Different Voice: Psychological Theory and Women's Development.* Cambridge: Harvard University Press.

Hankivsky, O. (2004). *Social Policy and the Ethic of Care.* Vancouver: UBC Press.

Hardesty, J., & G. Chung. (2006). Intimate partner violence, parental divorce and child custody: Directions for intervention and future research. *Family Relations* 55(2): 200–10.

Henderson, J., & L. Forbat. (2002). Relationship-based social policy: Personal and policy constructions of 'care.' *Critical Social Policy* 22(4): 669–87.

Hooyman, N.R. (1990). Women as caregivers of the elderly: implications for social welfare policy and practice. In D.E. Biegel & A. Blum, eds., *Aging and Caregiving: Theory, Research and Policy,* 221–41. London: Sage.

Irwin, L., L. Thorne, & C. Varcoe. (2002). Strength in adversity: Motherhood for women that have been battered. *Canadian Journal of Nursing Research* 34(4): 47–57.

Johnston, J. (1994). High conflict divorce. *Future of Children* 4(1): 165–82.

Kaganas, F. (1999). Contact, conflict and risk. In C. Piper, & S. Day Sclater, eds., *Undercurrents of Divorce*. Aldershot: Ashgate.

Keefe, J., P. Fancey, & S. White. (2005). *Consultation on Financial Compensation Initiatives for Family Caregivers of Dependent Adults*. Final Report. Halifax: Mount Saint Vincent University.

Kelly, J., & R. Emery. (2003). Children's adjustment following divorce: Risk and resilience perspectives. *Family Relations* 52: 352–62.

Kershaw, P. (2004). 'Choice' discourse in B.C. child care: Distancing policy from research. *Canadian Journal of Political Science* 37(4): 927–50.

Kershaw, P., J. Pulkingham, & S. Fuller. (2008). Expanding the subject: Violence, care, and (in)active male citizenship. *Social Politics: International Studies in Gender, State and Society* 15(2): 182–206.

King, V., & J. Sobolewski. (2006). Nonresident fathers' contributions to adolescent wellbeing. *Journal of Marriage and the Family* 68(3): 537–57.

Kline, M. (1995). Complicating the ideology of motherhood: Child welfare law and First Nations women. In M. Albertson Fineman & I. Kappin, eds., *Mothers in Law: Feminist Theory and the Legal Regulation of Motherhood*, 118–41. New York: Columbia University Press.

Leitner, S. (2003). Varieties of familialism: The caring function of the family in comparative perspective. *European Societies* 5(4): 353–75.

Lewis, J. (2001). *The End of Marriage? Individualism and Intimate Relations*. Northampton: E. Elgaru.

Lewis, J. (2005). Perceptions of risk in intimate relationships: The implications for social provision. *Journal of Social Policy* 34(1): 39–57.

Lorenz, F., K. Wickrama, R. Conger, & G. Elder. (2006). The short-term and decade-long effects of divorce on women's midlife health. *Journal of Health and Social Behavior* 47: 111–25.

Martin-Matthews, A., & L. Campbell. (1995). Gender roles, employment and informal care. In S. Arbor & J. Ginn, eds., *Connecting Gender and Ageing*, 129–43. Milton Keynes: Open University Press.

McDaniel, S., & E. Gee. (1993). Social policies regarding caregiving to elders: Canadian contradictions. *Journal of Aging and Social Policy* 5: 57–72.

McMahon, M. (1995). *Engendering Motherhood: Identity and Self Transformation in Women's Lives*. New York: Guilford Press.

Olesen, V. (1989). Caregiving, ethical and informal: Emerging challenges in the sociology of health and illness. *Journal of Health and Social Behavior* 30: 1–10.

Pylkkänen, A. (2007). Transformation of the Nordic model: From welfare politics to gendered rights. *Canadian Journal of Women and the Law* 19(2): 335–54.

Rhoades, H. (2002). The 'no contact mother': Reconstructions of motherhood in the era of the 'new father.' *International Journal of Law, Policy and the Family* 16(1): 71–94.

Rhoades, H., R. Graycar, & M. Harrison. (2000). *The Family Law Reform Act 1995: The First Three Sears.* Sidney: University of Sydney and Family Court of Australia.

Rose, H., & E. Bruce. (1995). Mutual care but differential esteem: Caring between older couples. In S. Arber & J. Ginn, eds., *Connecting Gender and Ageing: A Sociological Approach*, 114–28. Buckinghamshire: Open University Press.

Rose, N. (1996). Governing 'advanced' liberal democracies. In A. Barry, T. Osborne, & N. Rose, eds., *Foucault and Political Reason: Liberalism, Neoliberalism and Rationalities of Government*, 37–64. Chicago: University of Chicago Press.

Schultz, C., & L. Leslie. (2004). Family therapy trainees' perceptions of divorced mothers: A test of bias in information recall. *Family Relations* 53(4): 405–11.

Segal, L. (1983). *What Is to Be Done about the Family?* Harmondsworth: Penguin.

Sevenhuijsen, S. (1998). *Citizenship and the Ethic of Care: Feminist Considerations on Justice, Morality and Politics.* New York: Routledge.

Silverman, J., C. Mesh, C. Cuthbert, K. Slote, & L. Bancroft. (2004). Child custody determinants in cases involving intimate partner violence: A human rights analysis. *American Journal of Public Health* 94(6): 951–7.

Smart, C. (2003). Towards an understanding of family change: Gender conflict and children's citizenship. *Australian Journal of Family Law* 17(1): 1–17.

Smart, C., & B. Neale. (1999). *Family Fragments?* Cambridge: Polity Press.

Stacer, D., & F. Stemen. (2000). Intervention for high-conflict custody cases. *American Journal of Family Law* 14: 242–51.

Statistics Canada. (2005). *Overview of the Time Use of Canadians.* Retrieved 23 Nov. 2007 from http://www.statcan.ca/english/freepub/12F0080XIE/2006001/tables/tab1_canada.htm.

Statistics Canada. (2006). Women in Canada: A Gender Based Statistical Report. *The Daily.* 7 March. Statistics Canada cat. no. 89-503-X. Retrieved 21 Nov. 2007 from http://www.statcan.ca/english/freepub/89-503-XIE/0010589-503-XIE.pdf.

Teghtsoonian, K. (2003). W(h)ither women's equality? Neoliberalism, institutional change and public policy in British Columbia. *Policy, Organisation and Society* 22(1): 25–47.

Ungerson, C. (1997). Social politics and the commodification of care. *Social Politics* 4(3): 262–81.

Ward-Griffin, C., & V. Marshall. (2003). Reconceptualizing the relationship between 'public' and 'private' eldercare. *Journal of Aging Studies* 17: 189–208.

Wickrama, K., F. Lorenz, R. Conger, G. Elder, W. Abraham, & S. Fang. (2006). Changes in family financial circumstances and the physical health of married and recently divorced mothers. *Social Science and Medicine* 63: 123–36.

Wuest, J. (1997). Illuminating environmental influences on women's caring. *Journal of Advanced Nursing* 26: 49–58.

Zelizer, V.A. (2007). Caring everywhere. Keynote Address, Conference on Intimate Labors, University of California, Santa Barbara, 4–6 Oct.

9 'Choice' in Unpaid Intimate Labour: Adult Children with Aging Parents

LAURA FUNK AND KAREN KOBAYASHI

In Canada, as throughout much of the Western world, the population is aging, with forecasts that seniors will almost double as a proportion of the population, from 13.2% in 2005 to 24.5% in 2036 (Turcotte & Schellenberg 2007). This demographic trend has generated concerns among policy makers and academics alike regarding the projected care needs of individuals in their later years. Although the proportion of men aged 45 years and older who reported providing some form of assistance to a senior remained roughly the same between 2002 and 2007 (19%), the proportion of women reporting providing such care increased from 18% to 22% (Cranswick & Dosman 2008).

A 2004 estimate suggested that just over 10% of Canadians aged 45 to 64 years were providing some form of care to their parents (Stobert & Cranswick 2004). In 2007, of caregivers aged 45 and older, 60% were providing care to an aging parent or parent-in-law (Cranswick & Dosman 2008). In fact, given increases in life expectancies, it has been suggested that Canadians will soon, on average, spend a greater period of their lives providing parent care than raising their own children (McDaniel 2005). The probability of providing such care continues to increase given the shift away from facility – based to home – based services that started in the 1980s (Marks, Lambert, & Jun 2001). Indeed, the majority of care for older adults has always come from family sources, particularly from daughters and/or daughters-in-law, and is often 'invisible.' Research has demonstrated negative impacts on the mental and emotional health of some family caregivers (Anderson, Linto, & Stewart-Wynne 1995; Cochrane, Goering, & Rogers 1997; Lee 1999). There is a particular need, then, to examine the broad contextual features that shape family care work, as well as the individual – level implications of providing such care.

Care work for aging parents represents a form of intimate labour within enduring family relations (Zelizer 2005). This term *intimate labour* was developed by Zelizer in order to counter the false binary between family care and paid care work – a binary that conceals, for example, the labour involved in what tends to be viewed as 'natural' unpaid family work (2007). In this chapter, we focus on another closely related false binary, that of choice (viewed as motivation for family care) and obligation. Most notably, quantitative approaches to predicting caregiving behaviour tend to construct and perpetuate a distinction between discretionary and non-discretionary motivations (Cicirelli 1993), while qualitative researchers have explored tensions between obligation and freedom experienced by women performing care work for parents (Aronson 1992; McGrew 1998). Others such as Armstrong and Kits (2001) argue that we need to ensure that family care work is voluntarily performed by both women and men. Throughout this literature, there tends to be both an implicit and explicit opposition set up between choice and obligation, individual freedom and external constraints, and indeed, between structure and agency. We will discuss some of the key tensions and conflicts that characterize the intimate labour performed by adult children with aging parents, linking these to meso – and macro – level contexts. Existing literature is supplemented with findings from our own research studies as we explore the implications of 'choice' in filial care work, as well as how such apparent choice frames the subjective experiences of care work and parent-child relationships. Ultimately, we argue that a binary between 'voluntary' and 'involuntary' motivations fails to reflect the complexities involved in family care work, even though the distinction highlights tensions experienced by individuals caught between competing discourses of obligation and independence, an argument that we illustrate and support with data from our own research programs in this area.

Enhanced Choice in Filial Care Work? The Individualization of Family Relationships

It has been suggested that cultural individualism, alongside social, economic, and demographic changes that have increased structural opportunities for individual choice, has contributed to the 'individualization' of family relationships in North America (Beck & Beck-Gernsheim 2001).

North American culture has, historically, been viewed in contrast to traditional Asian (i.e., Confucian) societies as more individualistic, that is, as focused on links between immediate family members rather than extended family, and with greater emphasis on the individual autonomy of family members, although there is uncertainty regarding the extent to which these differences are attributable to normative or structural forces.

Despite the fact that the individualization thesis addresses family commitments, which Beck and Beck-Gernsheim (2001) suggest are, in North America, increasingly 'voluntary,' it is rarely applied to the topic of informal care work. This is curious given that such commitments are perceived to be rooted in choice, preference, and interpersonal agreement and communication to a greater extent than was the case in the past, regarded as 'enhancements of the sense of individual well-being rather than as moral imperatives' (Bellah et al. 1985: 47). From this perspective, adult children reject ideas of obligation and seek independence from parents, with little sense of debt (Bellah et al. 1985). Individuals may conceptualize family responsibilities with abstract notions of individual rights, and as contractually based and voluntary (Silver 1998). Indeed, the social contract model of justifying moral responsibility to others, at the heart of which lies consent or agreement, is actually rooted in a cultural context of individualism (Smith 1993).

Relatedly, there has been some speculation that care work in this context is based to greater extent on 'discretionary' motives such as affection and closeness as opposed to economic necessity or obligation. However, such assumptions have not been conclusively confirmed empirically, particularly in the area of filial care work (Donorfio 1996; Lee & Sung 1997; Pyke 2000; Silver 1998). Folbre and Nelson (2000) draw on labour force and time-use data on child care work to suggest that care activities have been 'marketized' into the paid market; the resulting increase in parental time for other activities leads the researchers to suggest that parenting time in the home is given more freely now than in the past (Folbre & Nelson 2000). However, their research also implies that 'choice' in care work is still dependent on personal economic resources in market economies.

In sum, the individualization perspective reinforces a dichotomy between choice and obligation, implying that affection is a voluntary motivation. In the following section, we review other literature, most stemming from critical feminist perspectives, which tends to focus on obligation and/or constraints in filial care work.

Contextualizing 'Choice' in Filial Care Work

In fact, research on filial care work also suggests a number of macro-level influences that serve to contextualize choice in the enactment of intimate filial labour, findings that are often interpreted as suggesting that obligation, instead of choice and voluntary behaviour, motivate parent care. At the macro-level, the broader political economic and demographic contexts, structural factors such as gender and social class, and ideological and/or cultural influences are important considerations.

Demographic Contexts

Very broadly, demographic contexts and changing family structures in Canada influence the conditions under which care work for aging parents is initiated and conducted. With the age at first marriage increasing in Canada, the mean age at first birth for women has followed suit, topping out at just under 30 years of age in 2002 (Statistics Canada 2004). Further, with average life expectancy at almost 80 years (Statistics Canada 2005), Canadians are more likely to experience being 'sandwiched' between the needs of growing children and aging parents well into their forties and fifties. For some midlife adult children the stress of feeling 'caught' between competing demands can lead to negative financial and health outcomes (Gee & Mitchell 2003). This trend will likely continue as the pursuit of career as well as family interests becomes increasingly normative for Canadian women. Such demographic realities may limit the latitude for many adult children, particularly women, to exercise choice over the context and conditions in which they provide care. In addition, with the increasing trend towards one-child and childless families among contemporary generations of young adults (Mitchell 2009; Milan et al. 2007), the ability to 'choose' to care may be severely constrained for only-children, and may extend to nieces and/or nephews, some of whom may be only-children, for childless aunts and uncles in the future.

Parental support needs further influence the choices of adult children, regarding the timing of initial transitions to the caregiving role. At the point of the onset of chronic disease or disability in an older parent(s), support is transformed into care work requiring temporal, emotional, and financial sacrifices by middle-aged children, mainly daughters, who oftentimes make life-altering decisions regarding work and family in a very short period of time. According to the experiences of the twenty-eight adult children recently interviewed by Funk (2008), the onset of a sense of responsibility for parents (a motivator for care work) most often coincides with health declines in a parent. In sum, factors affecting the life transitions and health of older Canadians, through influencing parental support needs, indirectly impact children's sense of responsibility to provide care as well as parental expectations regarding levels and types of support. This reflects what life course theorists describe as the principle of interdependent or 'linked lives' (Bengtson & Harootyan 1994; Elder 1994), whereby events in one family member's life affect the lives of other family members.

Political, Economic, and Formal Service Contexts

The concept of 'responsibilization' (Burchell 1996; Rose 1996) also offers a more nuanced sense of individualization that incorporates a consideration of neoliberal political and economic trends and the particular forms of power operating in these contexts. Rose describes how neoliberal governance (in the sense of social control) occurs increasingly through the devolution of responsibility and monitoring 'through the regulated choices of individual citizens, now construed as subjects of choices and aspirations to self-actualization and fulfilment' (1996: 46); the goals of authorities are translated (e.g., through self-care) into what is perceived to be 'voluntary' individual responsibility. This perspective as well, then, directs our attention to structural and ideological constraints on choice in intimate labour.

A critical feminist perspective emphasizes constraints on choice that stem from a sociopolitical climate in North America of globalization and neoliberalism, which creates increased need for adult children to make choices to care given the erosion of formal supports and limited availability and affordability of other assistance (Baker 2007). In a contemporary context, cutbacks to health care and social services over the past decade in Canada have precipitated increased reliance on family at all levels for care provision for older adults.

As well as reductions in formal services, some evidence suggests that technical aspects of care work are increasingly transferred to family caregivers and practitioners seeking to 'activate' sources of family support (Ward-Griffin & Marshall 2003). In British Columbia, for example, funding of 'housekeeping only' services was cancelled in 1999. The implications of such decisions reverberate in the words of one woman interviewed by Funk (2008), who was concerned about her father's loneliness: 'Servicewise – it's very limited. It would really be great if even somebody could come once a week to clean. That would leave me the time then I could visit with him.' She later adds, 'When you walk in, you just wanna start *doing*, because the place needs some attention. But on the other hand, the bottom line is *he* needs some attention!'

When governments pull back from care work, more of the onus to care inevitably falls to midlife and older women, more of whom are also supporting co-resident adolescent and/or young adult children, and who increasingly face transitioning from full- to part-time employment or leaving the paid workforce altogether. Consequences of the transition to family care work are well documented (Fast et al. 1997; Keating et al. 1999), yet neither government nor employer-supported policies to date have adequately addressed the issue of paid elder care leave. Decisions about the provision of formal care and services to support care work restrict adult children's choices not only around how much to do, but the types and timing of these activities over the life course. Indeed, Aronson (1998a) claims that limited social policies create challenging relations involving both dependence and obligation between aging mothers and their daughters and, we would argue, their sons and/or daughters in law; this trend is likely to increase as Canada's fertility rate continues to decline to well below replacement level (Mitchell 2009).

These political and economic changes are reflected in constraints on choice that are particularly evident when considering the role of formal services (Arksey & Glendinning 2007:169): 'carers' opportunities to exercise choice over services appear to be closely circumscribed by factors outside their control. These factors include: the limited budgets of statutory services; tight eligibility criteria; a restricted range of service options; and the limited availability of agencies and paid care staff to provide the care required.'

In Canada, there is additional evidence suggesting the government's support for the 'legal' enforcement of family responsibility (Armstrong & Kits 2001). The World Health Organization, comparing Canada, the United States, and Sweden, noted that whereas Sweden repealed their filial responsibility laws, Ontario and some American states have chosen to maintain such laws, reflecting 'the belief that care is primarily a family responsibility' and underscoring efforts to protect the state financially (Lakra 2002). In practice, Canadian filial responsibility laws are rarely applied, although the report predicts their increasing application in the future. Indeed, in the face of increasing out-migration from rural to urban areas among younger people, countries such as South Korea and Japan are actively seeking to further legislate filial care for older parents (McDaniel 2008).

Gender and Social Class Inequalities: Implications for Choice

Whereas the individualization thesis aligns with ideas about traditional gendered assumptions becoming ungrounded in modern Western society, a feminist care work perspective suggests that ongoing reality involves a lack of real choice for women about whether to provide care in the absence of structural and ideological alternatives (Armstrong & Kits 2001; Aronson 1992; Calasanti & Slevin 2001). Further, the contexts in which women perform intimate labour tend to be more constrained, as women tend to 'provide care that is daily and inflexible while men provide care that can be more easily planned and organized around paid work' (Armstrong & Kits 2001: 12). The types of care work performed by daughters for parents (e.g., personal care and in-home tasks), for example, require greater amounts of time (Morris et al. 1999), reflecting the gendered nature of care in Canadian society more broadly (McDaniel 2005; Rosenthal, Martin-Matthews, & Matthews 1996). This, alongside research on women's personal sense of responsibility for parents, is used to suggest that women's greater involvement is externally pressured as opposed to 'freely' motivated (Calasanti & Slevin 2001; Hooyman & Gonyea 1995).

Constraints on family care work or intimate labour may be particularly salient for lower-income women, suggesting the intersectional nature of markers of inequality. Poorer women often have little choice in providing care (Morris et al. 1999), and working-class families, in British research (Arber & Ginn 1992), are more likely to provide co-resident care which involves greater constraints on the everyday lives of family caregivers. In contrast, higher income women can choose to enact more of a 'care manager' role (Rosenthal & Martin-Matthews 1999). For both daughters and those in lower socioeconomic strata, then, there may be even less 'choice' in family and filial care work. Further, in the political and economic contexts of neoliberalism, the financial costs of formal services that would assist filial care providers serve to narrow their range of alternatives.

Cultural and/or Ideological Contexts

Other factors potentially influencing choices in intimate labour are cultural and/or ideological, the most obvious of which is familialism, a set of ideals and norms about family and caring (see also Treloar & Funk, this volume). For example, ideas about reciprocity and 'paying back' those who cared for us promote parent care as a moral imperative (Selig, Tomlinson, & Hickey 1991). Indeed, research on ethnocultural families in North America underscores the salience of values of familialism and filial responsibility in, for example, Mexican American (John, Resdendiz, & de Vargas 1997), Korean American (Pyke 2000), Chinese Canadian (Ho et al. 2003), and Japanese Canadian (Kobayashi 2000) families. As a cultural norm, filial responsibility, as part of familialism, influences personal ideas about appropriate behaviour (Holroyd 2001). It is noteworthy, however, that research on Chinese and South Asian immigrant families in North America indicates that aging parents often have an equally strong sense of parental responsibility to continue to support young adult children, such as through co-residence (Gee & Mitchell 2003; Kamo 2000; Pacey 2002). In a study on parent-child relationships in Japanese Canadian families, it was found that both cultural (i.e., the expectation that the nuclear family will stay intact until children marry) and socioeconomic factors (i.e., economic necessity) shape young adults' preferences for co-residence (Kobayashi 1999). Such findings highlight not only the bi-directionality of familialism, but also the strength of cultural influences on co-residence, which serve to constrain 'choices' about the circumstances under which intimate labour within these families may be enacted.

Cultural ideas about familialism and filial responsibility can also be characterized as 'ideological' to the extent that they promote unquestioned assumptions about the appropriate sources of care for older adults and are used to justify shifting responsibility for care away from government onto families (and particularly women). Familialism is evident in day-to-day interactions, as this quote from a participant in Funk's (2008: 86) study illustrates: 'Every day you have people saying, you know how are your parents, it's so good that you're looking after them, yadda yadda yadda. It just comes nonstop. Yeah, and you sort of feel, well if I did decide I wasn't going to look after them, there's nowhere I could live like a human, and have any kind of respect whatsoever (laughs). I would be absolutely isolated.' The concept of familialism is also institutionalized within many of Canada's contemporary social and health care policies and practices. Those who view filial responsibility as ideology, from a critical feminist perspective, for example, focus on how it constrains women in particular (daughters and daughters-in-law) to provide parent care, thereby maintaining a division of labour that aligns with patriarchal and/or capitalist interests (Baines, Evans, & Neysmith 1998; Binney & Estes 1988). Familialistic beliefs in practice tend to posit care as women's natural ability and 'choice,' and judge negatively those women who do not provide care (Baines et al. 1998; Segall & Chappell 2000). Familialism, therefore, may deepen gender inequalities in care work, insofar as it defines 'good families' as those in which women in particular 'are able, available, and willing to assist other family members' (Killian & Ganong 2002: 1081). Indeed, Hooyman and Gonyea (1995) and Aronson (1992) argue that prescriptive assumptions about gender roles in family care work constrain women's actions and render such work obligatory, often through personal beliefs about what is 'right.'

Promoting family care work, the ideology of familialism, institutionalized in policy and practice, aligns with the 'goals of cost containment' (Hooyman & Gonyea 1995) to support cutbacks and/or a lack of expansion of formal care for the elderly. However, ideas inherent in familialism and filial responsibility are not in themselves 'wrong.' It is when they are applied as restrictive and concealing ideologies that they sustain existing structural inequities and limit alternative possibilities (Hooyman & Gonyea 1995). Further, these ideals are not always unquestionably applied, but serve as guidelines, and vary in the extent to which they are internalized as individual expectations (Finch & Mason 1993; Stein et al. 1998). Yet when they are accepted as internal standards, normative ideals serve as powerful self-regulators of behaviour. In one study, to avoid the guilt and shame that accompanied violations of their internal standards, female caregivers were reluctant to set limits or prioritize their own needs (Aronson 1998b). Connecting with a sense of identity, social norms as ideologies significantly influence choices from the inside.

Obligation in Filial Care Work: The Meso-Level Context of Family Relationships

We have described various macro-level influences that demonstrate how choice in intimate filial labour is contextual and may be restricted (and some would argue, severely so). In this section, we move to the meso-level, to consider the idea of choice in filial care work in the context of family relationships. For Smith (1993: 53), family membership implies involuntary obligations: 'it is acquiescence as opposed to agreement. Obligations are often like this. It is not that one agrees with the obligation, agrees willingly to assume it, or even agrees with the enterprise it is intended to promote, but instead that the obligation or enterprise comes attached to other things that are too important, too valuable to give up, so the person grudgingly acquiesces in assuming the obligation. That should not count as consent.'

Additional challenges to the individualization thesis stem from those who emphasize the importance of the family context for decisions about care work. Participants in Smart and Shipman's (2004) research on marital partnerships, for example, did not view care work and kinship as contingent; however, kinship ties and family culture can provide the contexts in which decisions are made. Indeed, one criticism of the concept of caregiving is that it ignores reciprocal exchanges and interdependencies that are part of the context of meaning of normal family relationships and interactions (Henderson & Forbat 2002). From this perspective, filial commitments, as all family commitments, stem from family interactions and largely implicit negotiations over the life course (Finch & Mason 1991, 1993; Piercy 1998).

The fact that filial care work is provided in the context of family relationships also has implications for the idea of choice in this work. This form of intimate care work is provided in the context of long-standing family relationships that can involve individual and structural ambivalence, relationship tensions, and even power struggles (Connidis & McMullin 2002; George 1986; Pillemer & Luscher 2004; Pyke 1999). Considerations about reciprocity, social exchange, and gender role patterns, as well as interests in protecting relationships and reputations are all important. Finch and Mason (1993) illustrate how some family members, often women, may initially choose to provide support but eventually become 'locked into' subsequent family care commitments over the life course. Further, Funk (2010) illustrates how adult children may seek to avoid 'pushing' their parents to accept formal services into the home, given concerns about causing conflict and potentially damaging the filial relationship.

As such, meso- or family-level influences can influence choices in family care work, including whether or not to provide care and how much. In fact, even adult children's choices around how they *feel* about care work can be constrained by normative and ideological 'feeling rules' (Gubrium 1989; Schott 1979) about the appropriateness of certain feelings within family relationships. For instance, when adult child caregivers feel anger or resentment towards parents, many struggle to manage such emotions, in order to avoid a sense of violating appropriate 'feeling rules' (and concomitant guilt, shame, and embarrassment).

Family members tend to define assistance as a normal, natural component of family relationships rather than care work (the latter tending to be associated with strain or negative emotion); for this reason, some family members do not even self-identify as caregivers (Harding & Higginson 2001; Henderson & Forbat 2002; Rose & Bruce 1995; Sheehan & Donorfio 1999). This phenomenon may, for many adult children, further negate the idea of 'choice' in intimate labour in filial relationships.

Love is often posited as a discretionary motivation by caregiving researchers. To the extent that such 'loving choice' is viewed as 'natural' to family care work, this fits with a 'separate spheres' perspective (Zelizer 2005) that conceals aspects of labour and obligation that are involved when filial care work is performed in unpaid family contexts. In other words, while the support of aging parents is often described as a 'loving choice' for many adult children, there is an element of compulsion, particularly where love for parents, coupled with a dearth of formal care services, contributes to situations in which there is no other choice but to provide support (MacLean, Cairn, & Sellick 1998). If children really had a choice, they may, for example, opt to spend more time visiting with parents instead of performing functional tasks. Indeed, the idea persists that if you do not take responsibility for (e.g., provide care for) your parents, you do not love them. As such, accounts of internal motivations (e.g., love and family ties) for parent care, particularly by women, are viewed by some as the internalization of familialistic ideals (thereby indicating obligation rather than choice) (Hooyman & Gonyea 1995).

In sum, a sociological perspective, and in particular a critical feminist approach, highlights the constraints on choice in intimate labour, often emphasizing the subjective experience of obligation and the objective experience of a lack of alternatives. Maureen Baker (2007: 162), for example, maintains that 'few of the new family patterns are entirely matters of choice. Our behaviour and even our personal ambitions tend instead to be influenced and modified by social and economic activities and events in the larger society ... constraints on relationships may relate to lack of money or power, new legal requirements, technological "advances," pressure from family and friends, feelings of obligation or entitlement.'

Moving beyond the Dichotomy

We have illustrated the polarization between the individualization perspective and another predominantly feminist perspective on the extent to which there is choice in intimate labour when performed in unpaid settings – in this case, filial relationships. Paralleling this broad-level polarization, there is a tendency in caregiving research to construct a dichotomy between 'filial responsibility' (conceptualized as a *non-discretionary* motivation, reflecting external pressures), and 'affection' or 'attachment' (conceptualized as a *discretionary* motivation, reflecting internal desires). However, *both* this empirical distinction, and the larger theoretical debate between voluntary and involuntary care work, does not adequately reflect the real complexities of intimate labour in filial relationships. Whether we can adequately disentangle the complex combination of obligatory and discretionary factors and motivations to provide care remains to be addressed. Although intimate labour in family relationships is often described as a 'loving choice,' it has been suggested that 'having to' and 'wanting to' are inextricably intertwined within a 'multiply determined predisposition to care' (McGrew 1998: 55).

The conceptual distinction between voluntary and involuntary care work and the broader debate about this predominates does, however, point to the tensions experienced by those caught between the competing ideals of obligation and independence. It also highlights the importance of understanding how normative and structural climates affect how we view family commitments, how we view 'choice,' and how we experience intimate labour in unpaid settings. For example, familialism and individualism are competing ideals, yet paradoxically, both are used as justification for shifting additional responsibility for care from governments and formal settings to families and informal settings. Individualism parallels 'responsibilization,' whereby individuals are 'offered' involvement in activities that were once government's role (such as care for older adults), but must assume responsibility for outcomes (Burchell 1996). The result is a society in which we should, as independent selves, voluntarily choose and want to provide care, yet are simultaneously pressured into both responsibility for family members as well as for self, and for independent yet 'responsible' choices

(Rose 1996). This contradiction may be reflected in the individual experience of the tension between having to and wanting to: 'in our individualistic society, we are ambivalent about kinship. We tend to value family highly as one of the few contexts within which one can count on others nearly unconditionally ... yet we are wary of the restraints on our individual decision-making that kinship involvements imply' (Bellah et al. 1985: 114).

Research by Funk (2008: 108) reveals that many of the twenty-eight middle-aged children interviewed constructed their sense of responsibility for their parent(s) as a 'choice.' The following quotations reflect respondents' beliefs that their decision to provide care was a choice, but also hint at underlying tensions and contradictions:

> There are times when I feel pressure I guess, but I think I choose to succumb to that pressure.
>
> It wasn't a negative like, 'oh now I'm painted in a corner and nobody else is gonna do it so now I've got to.' Not at all. It was an absolute choice. This would be best.
>
> I could choose not to care, and to not notice it.
>
> I can be a bad daughter if I want to, but that's my own evaluation of that.

Notably, these quotes emerged from female respondents, although males seemed similarly conflicted or uncertain when discussing choice. The construction of filial care work as a choice may stem from situational factors such as having siblings, a parent in good health, or financial resources allowing access to private care. However, the quotes also point to a different phenomenon – the tension between values of filial obligation and those of individual responsibility and independence in the parent-child dyad. First, the ideal of filial obligation can impinge on an adult child's sense of independence. Similarly, some respondents emphasized not being a martyr, and caring for oneself as well as others. The emphasis on choice may also help in coping with the realities of intimate labour within a culture that emphasizes the importance of family responsibility, as well as independence and control. One participant, who had conflicted feelings towards his mother, described how his counsellor told him not to do anything he didn't want to do. This participant expressed angst because he could not make himself want to provide care; he was caught between his sense of what is 'right' (filial care) and what another participant referred to as 'the counsellor's creed' which assigns primacy to self-focused motivations and desires.

The ideal of filial obligation can also impinge on the independence of parent(s). Some participants explicitly recognized that parents have responsibility for themselves, or emphasized 'not babying' the elderly (Funk 2010). This may help children cope with feelings of helplessness when parents resist or refuse help, but it may also represent a reinterpretation of the meaning and limits of filial responsibility in the context of increasing constraints (e.g., other work and family obligations) on the ability to provide significant amounts of parent care.

The emphasis on filial care as 'choice' by some of those interviewed by Funk may also represent attempts to de-emphasize the role of obligation in one's family relationships, and prioritize the role of love and enjoyment. This reflects the belief that caregiving should be based on affection rather than duty. For many respondents, this is a key reason why talking about responsibility does not fit with their personal understandings. Linda George (1986), who is a family sociologist, sees these kinds of normative conflicts (such as between family solidarity and duty/indebtedness) as generating personal stress. Responsibility was indeed seen by some respondents in Funk's study as incompatible with love – talk about supporting parents as a responsibility implies you 'have' to do it, which implies you do not love your parent. This may have been one reason why some respondents, while providing support and having a sense that they are responsible people, emphasized they do not 'feel' responsible (which led one respondent to express that he felt like a 'contradiction').

Because it is difficult to reconcile with the idea of obligation, love is often posited as a 'discretionary' motivation by researchers of caregiving. Yet the strangeness of equating love with choice is evident in one participant's query: 'I guess you could choose to love less?' (Funk 2008). Particularly in the context of the erosion of formal care services, love for parents can create a situation where there is no other 'choice' but to provide support.

Familialism and individualism might appear to be contrasting sets of ideals. Ironically, however, both can serve the interests of those seeking to shift additional responsibility for elder care from governments and formal settings to family members. As such, adult children are simultaneously pressured into providing care and 'taking responsibility' for aging parents as well as for making independent, voluntary choices to do so (Rose 1996). This contradiction is reflected in the tension that is experienced by individuals between having to and wanting to; as such, the above-mentioned examples reflect ambivalence (two opposing, irreconcilable forces) evident at the individual level but rooted in broader contradictions (Connidis & McMullin 2002) between individualism and familialism. Such contradictions serve to illustrate the complexities involved in the performance of intimate labour in unpaid family contexts.

Summary and Conclusions

In support of the work of individualization theorists, such a perspective does highlight changes that may have increased to some degree the amount of choice or flexibility in North American society for at least some adult children (e.g., those with private resources). And, at the very least, it points to the potential for increased choice. However, considering the greater weight of empirical research findings indicating constraints on choice, particularly in lower-income families, to maintain that family care work is now 'voluntary' is perhaps overstated. The decision by adult children to provide care for parents, and specific decisions around the levels and types of care they provide, is influenced by a number of factors: (1) the onset of the parent's need for assistance; (2) the lack of formal service alternatives; (3) cultural and ideological expectations; and (4) the nature of family relationships and related family-level processes. However, while the research findings presented in this chapter illustrate the ways in which choice is contextually based, we maintain that this does not necessarily support the idea that care work is experienced only as obligation. Further, just as there is a need to move beyond the dichotomy of 'separate spheres,' there is a need to move beyond the dichotomy between choice and obligation in research on intimate labour, and acknowledge that the two concepts are not mutually exclusive as motivations for parent care.

It is important that research on choice in intimate labour also clarify and refine its key conceptual definitions. First, it needs to distinguish between the idea of choice in motivations for adopting the filial caregiver role and the extent of choice available within that role. Second, the definition needs to distinguish between the concepts of objective and subjective choice. Third, it needs to move away from the idea of 'individual' choice, and focus instead on the extent, diversity, and accessibility of options available for individuals while acknowledging the relational and contextual nature of choice. Lastly, it is important to acknowledge the salience of 'choice' as a normative ideal enacted in participant accounts of intimate labour, particularly when this labour is performed in the context of family relationships. Indeed, the discussion and debate about choice highlights the importance of understanding how normative and structural contexts affect how we view family commitments, how we view 'choice,' and how we experience caregiving to aging parents.

Future research should focus on exploring how individuals themselves construct and experience 'choice' within a wide variety of intimate labour contexts. Research should also further explicate the circumstances which contribute to some adult children experiencing individual-level tension between choice and obligation, while others are able to reconcile the concepts. Although there is an emergent body of research considering the effects of control and empowerment on health that is relevant to caregiving, future studies should consider the effects of ambivalence and/or isolation experienced by adult children who feel caught between competing paradigms. In many instances, tensions experienced by these individuals, the result of broader-level forces, will have consequences for well-being that will be difficult if not impossible to quantify, because they operate at the complex level of emotional experience. Despite this, for some, these represent very real experiences, and we need to be sensitive to their potential impacts. For these individuals, mainly middle-aged women, it is important that governments address the underlying consequences of informal care provision through relevant health and social service policies and programs in the family and work domains. Such efforts will promote dignity in unpaid, intimate labour (Benoit & Hallgrímsdóttir, this volume).

Ultimately, caregiving discussions need to move beyond the debate over choice; while it is important to consider the ways individuals are constrained or supported in enacting care work, we should also consider how these broader dialogues are interpreted by adult children, and how they shape subjective experiences of intimate labour and the well-being of those providing it. Further, gender differences in this process are implicated and therefore need to be explored further. We also need to problematize the concept of 'choice' in intimate labour and explore the extent to which it is 'gendered.' Finally, we need a deeper understanding of intimate labour in unpaid settings than is currently characterized within quantitative research, one that moves us beyond the presentation of a simplistic 'internal' and 'external' dichotomy in more fully understanding the decision to provide care.

ACKNOWLEDGMENT

An earlier version of this chapter was published as '"Choice" in Filial Care Work: Moving beyond a Dichotomy,' by L.M. Funk and K. Kobayashi, in the *Canadian Review of Sociology* 46/3 (2009): 235–52.

REFERENCES

Anderson, C.S., J. Linto, & E.G. Stewart-Wynne. (1995). A population-based assessment of the impact and burden of caregiving for long-term stroke survivors. *Stroke* 26: 843–9.

Arber, S., & J. Ginn. (1992). Class and caring: A forgotten dimension. *Sociology* 26: 619–34.

Arksey, H., & C. Glendinning. (2007). Choice in the context of informal caregiving. *Health and Social Care in the Community* 15: 165–75.

Armstrong, P., & O. Kits. (2001). *One Hundred Years of Caregiving.* Retrieved 10 Sept. 2006 from http://www.cewhcesf.ca/healthreform/publications/summary/caregiving-100yrs.html.

Aronson, J. (1992). Women's sense of responsibility for the care of old people: 'But who else is going to do it?' *Gender and Society* 6: 8–29.

Aronson, J. (1998a). Dutiful daughters and undemanding mothers: Constraining images of giving and receiving care in middle and later life. In C. Baines, P. Evans, & S. Neysmith, eds., *Women's Caring: Feminist Perspectives on Social Welfare,* 114–38. Toronto: Oxford University Press.

Aronson, J. (1998b). Women's perspectives on informal care of the elderly: Public ideology and personal experience of giving and receiving care. In D. Coburn, C. D'Arcy, & G. Torrance, eds., *Health and Canadian Society: Sociological perspectives,* 399–416. Toronto: University of Toronto Press.

Baines, C., P. Evans, & S. Neysmith. (1998). Women's caring: Work expanding, state contracting.' In C. Baines, P. Evans, & S. Neysmith, eds., *Women's Caring: Feminist Perspectives on Social Welfare,* 3–22. Toronto: Oxford University Press.

Baker, M. (2007). *Choices and Constraints in Family Life.* Don Mills: Oxford University Press.

Beck, U., & E. Beck-Gernsheim. (2001). *Individualization: Institutionalized Individualism and Its Social and Political Consequences.* London, UK: Sage.

Bellah, R.N., R. Madsen, W.M. Sullivan, A. Swidler, & S.M. Tipton. (1985). *Habits of the Heart: Individualism and Commitment in American Life.* Berkeley: University of California Press.

Bengtson, V.L., & R.A. Harootyan. (1994). *Intergenerational Linkages: Hidden Connections in American Society.* New York: Springer.

Binney, E.A., & C.L. Estes. (1988). The retreat of the state and its transfer of responsibility: The intergenerational war. *International Journal of Health Services* 18: 83–96.

Burchell, G. (1996). Liberal government and techniques of the self. In A. Barry, T. Osborne, & N. Rose, eds., *Foucault and Political Reason: Liberalism, Neoliberalism and Rationalities of Government,* 19–36. Chicago: University of Chicago Press.

Calasanti, T.M., & K.F. Slevin. (2001). *Gender, Social Inequalities and Aging.* Walnut Creek: Alta Mira Press

Cicirelli, V. (1993). Attachment and obligation as daughters' motives for caregiving behavior and subsequent effect on subjective burden. *Psychology and Aging* 8: 144–55.

Cochrane, J.J., P.N. Goering, & J.M. Rogers. (1997). The mental health of informal caregivers in Ontario: An epidemiological survey. *American Journal of Public Health* 87: 2002–7.

Connidis, I.A., & J.A. McMullin. (2002). Sociological ambivalence and family ties: A critical perspective. *Journal of Marriage and the Family* 64: 558–67.

Cranswick, K., & D. Dosman. (2008). Eldercare: What we know today. Component of Statistics Canada catalogue no. 11-008-X. *Canadian Social Trends,* 48–56. Ottawa: Statistics Canada.

Donorfio, L.M. (1996). *Filial Responsibility: Widowed Mothers and Their Caregiving Daughters – A Qualitative Grounded Theory Approach.* Dissertation, University of Connecticut, Storrs.

Elder, G.H., Jr. (1994). Time, human aging, and social change: Perspectives on the life course. *Social Psychology Quarterly* 22: 233–45.

Fast, J.E., N.C. Keating, L. Oakes, & D.L. Williamson. (1997). *Conceptualizing and Operationalizing the Costs of Informal Elder Care.* Ottawa: National Health Research and Development Program, Health Canada.

Finch, J., & J. Mason. (1991). Obligations of kinship in contemporary Britain: Is there normative agreement? *British Journal of Sociology* 42: 345–67.

Finch, J., & J. Mason. (1993). *Negotiating Family Responsibilities.* London: Tavistock/Routledge.

Folbre, N., & J.A. Nelson. (2000). For love or money – or both? *Journal of Economic Perspectives* 14: 123–40.

Funk, L.M. (2008). *Responsibility for Aging Parents: Independence and Obligation within Filial Relationships.* PhD Dissertation, University of Victoria, Victoria, B.C.

Funk, L.M. (2010). Prioritizing parental autonomy: Adult children's accounts of feeling responsible and supporting aging parents. *Journal of Aging Studies* 24: 57–64.

Gee, E.M., & B.A. Mitchell. (2003). One roof: Exploring multi-generational households in Canada. In M.M. Lynn, ed., *Voices: Essays on Canadian Families*, 291–311. Scarborough: Nelson Thompson Learning.

George, L.K. (1986). Caregiver burden: Conflict between norms of reciprocity and solidarity. In K.A. Pillemer & R.S. Wolf, eds., *Elder Abuse: Conflict in the family*, 67–92. Dover: Auburn House.

Gubrium, J.F. (1989). Emotion work and emotive discourse in the Alzheimer's disease experience. In D. Unruh & G.S. Livings, eds., *Personal History through the Life Course*, 243–68. Greenwich: JAI Press.

Harding, R., & I.J. Higginson. (2001). Working with ambivalence: Informal caregivers of patients at the end of life. *Supportive Care in Cancer* 9: 642–35.

Henderson, J., & L. Forbat. (2002). Relationship-based social policy: Personal and policy constructions of 'care.' *Critical Social Policy* 22: 669–87.

Ho, B., J. Friedland, S. Rappolt, & S. Noh. (2003). Caregiving for relatives with Alzheimer's disease: Feelings of Chinese-Canadian women. *Journal of Aging Studies* 17: 301–21.

Holroyd, E. (2001). Hong Kong Chinese daughters' intergenerational caregiving obligations: A cultural model approach. *Social Science and Medicine* 53: 1125–34.

Hooyman, N.R. (1990). Women as caregivers of the elderly: Implications for social welfare policy and practice. In D.E. Biegel & A. Blum, eds., *Aging and Caregiving: Theory, Research and Policy*, 221–41. London: Sage.

Hooyman, N.R., & J. Gonyea. (1995). *Feminist Perspectives on Family Care: Policies for Gender Justice*. Thousand Oaks: Sage.

John, R., R. Resdendiz, & L.W. de Vargas. (1997). Beyond famialism? Famialism as explicit motive for eldercare among Mexican American caregivers. *Journal of Cross Cultural Gerontology* 12: 145–62.

Kamo, Y. (2000). Racial and ethnic differences in extended family households. *Sociological Perspectives* 43: 211–29.

Keating, N.C., J.E. Fast, K. Cranswick, & C. Perrier. (1999). Eldercare in Canada: Context, content and consequences. Ottawa: Statistics Canada, Housing, Family and Social Statistics Division.

Killian, T., & L.H. Ganong. (2002). Ideology, context, and obligations to assist older persons. *Journal of Marriage and the Family* 64: 1080–8.

Kobayashi, K.M. (1999). *Bunka no Tanjyo (Emergent Culture): Continuity and Change in Older Nisei (Second Generation) Parent-Adult Sansei (Third Generation) Child Relationships in Japanese-Canadian Families*. Dissertation, Simon Fraser University, Vancouver, B.C.

Kobayashi, K.M. (2000). The nature of support from adult sansei (third generation) children to older nisei (second generation) parents in Japanese Canadian families. *Journal of Cross-Cultural Gerontology* 15: 185–205.

Lakra, R. (2002). *Responsibilities for Care throughout the Life Span: A Brief Look at the Family and Long-Term Care Laws of Sweden, Canada and the U.S. with a Particular Focus on Aging.* Geneva: World Health Organization.

Lee, C. (1999). Health, stress and coping among women caregivers: A review. *Journal of Health Psychology* 4: 27–40.

Lee, Y.R., & K.T. Sung. (1997). Cultural differences in caregiving motivations for demented parents: Korean caregivers versus American caregivers. *International Journal of Aging and Human Development* 44: 115–27.

MacLean, M.J., R. Cairn, & S. Sellick. (1998). *Giving Support and Getting Help: Informal Caregivers' Experiences with Palliative Care Services.* Ottawa: Health Canada, Research and Knowledge Development Division.

Marks, N.F., J.D. Lambert, & H.J. Jun. (2001). The effects of transitions in filial caregiving on mental and physical health: A prospective U.S. national study. Madison: Center for Demography and Ecology, University of Wisconsin.

McDaniel, S. (2005). The family lives of the middle-aged and elderly in Canada. In M. Baker, ed., *Families: Changing trends in Canada,* 195–211. Toronto: McGraw-Hill Ryerson.

McDaniel, S. (2008). The conundrum of demographic aging and policy challenges: A comparative case study of Canada, Japan, and Korea. Paper presented at the Annual Meeting of the Canadian Population Society, Vancouver, 4 June.

McGrew, K. (1998). Daughters' caregiving decisions: From an impulse to a balancing point of care. *Journal of Women and Aging* 10: 49–65.

Milan, A., M. Vezina, & C. Wells. (2007). *Family Portrait: Continuity and Change in Canadian Families and Households in 2006.* Cat. no. 97-553-XIE. Ottawa: Statistics Canada.

Mitchell, B. (2009). *Family Matters: An Introduction to Family Sociology in Canada.* Toronto: Canadian Scholars' Press.

Morris, M., J. Robinson, J. Simpson, L. Martin, & M. Muzychka. (1999). *The Changing Nature of Home Care and Its Impact on Women's Vulnerability to Poverty.* Ottawa: Status of Women Canada.

Pacey, M. (2002). *Living alone and Living with Children: The Living Arrangements of Canadian and Chinese-Canadian Seniors.* Social and Economic Dimensions of an Aging Population (SEDAP) Research Paper #74, McMaster University, Hamilton.

Piercy, K. (1998). Theorizing about family caregiving: The role of responsibility. *Journal of Marriage and the Family* 60: 109–18.

Pillemer, K.A., & K. Luscher. (2004). *Intergenerational Ambivalences: New Perspectives on Parent-ChildRrelations in Later Life.* In F.M. Berardo, series ed., *Contemporary Perspectives in Family Research,* vol. 4. Oxford: Elsevier.

Pyke, K (1999). The micropolitics of care in relationships between aging parents and adult children: Individualism, collectivism, and power. *Journal of Marriage and the Family* 61: 661–72.

Pyke, K. (2000). 'Normal American family' as an interpretive structure of family life among grown children of Korean and Vietnamese immigrants. *Journal of Marriage and the Family* 62: 240–55.

Rose, H., & E. Bruce. (1995). Mutual care but differential esteem: Caring between older couples. In S. Arber & J. Ginn, eds., *Connecting Gender and Ageing: A Sociological Approach*, 114–28. Milton Keynes: Open University Press.

Rose, N. (1996). Governing 'advanced' liberal democracies. In A. Barry, T. Osborne, & N. Rose, eds., *Foucault and Political Reason: Liberalism, Neoliberalism and Rationalities of Government*, 37–64. Chicago: University of Chicago Press.

Rosenthal, C.J., & A. Martin-Matthews. (1999). *Families as Care Providers versus Care Managers: Gender and Type of Care in a Sample of Employed Canadians.* Social and Economic Dimensions of an Aging Population (SEDAP) Research Paper #4, McMaster University, Hamilton.

Rosenthal, C.J., A. Martin-Matthews, & S. Matthews. (1996). Caught in the middle? Occupancy in multiple roles and help to parents in a national probability sample of Canadian adults. *Journal of Gerontology* 51B: S274–S83.

Schott, S. (1979). Emotion and social life: A symbolic interactionist analysis. *American Journal of Sociology* 84: 1317–34.

Segall, A., & N. Chappell. (2000). *Health and Health Care in Canada.* Toronto: Prentice-Hall.

Selig, S., T. Tomlinson, & T. Hickey. (1991). Ethical dimensions of intergenerational reciprocity: Implications for practice. *Gerontologist* 31: 624–30.

Sheehan, N., & L. Donorfio. (1999). Efforts to create meaning in the relationship between aging mothers and their caregiving daughters: A qualitative study of caregiving. *Journal of Aging Studies* 13: 161–76.

Silver, C.B. (1998). Cross-cultural perspective on attitudes toward family responsibility and well-being in later years. In J. Lomranz, ed., *Handbook of Aging and Mental Health: An Integrative Approach*, 383–412. New York: Plenum Press.

Smith, P. (1993). Family responsibility and the nature of obligation. In D. Tietjens Meyers, K. Kipnis, & C.F.J. Murphy, eds., *Kindred Matters: Rethinking the philosophy of the family*, 41–58. Ithaca: Cornell University Press.

Statistics Canada. (2004). *Births, 2002.* Cat. no. 84F0210XIE. Ottawa: Statistics Canada, Health Statistics Division.

Statistics Canada. (2005). *Health Indicators, 2004.* Cat. no. 82221XIE. Ottawa: Author.

Stein, C.H., V.A. Wemmerus, M. Ward, M.E. Gaines, A.L. Freeberg, & T.C. Jewell. (1998). 'Because they're my parents': An intergenerational study of felt obligations and parental caregiving. *Journal of Marriage and the Family* 60: 611–22.

Stobert, S., & K. Cranswick. (2004). Looking after seniors: Who does what for whom? Component of Statistics Canada catalogue no. 11-008-X. *Canadian Social Trends* 74: 2–6.

Turcotte, M., & G. Schellenberg. (2007). *A Portrait of Seniors in Canada: 2006.* Cat. no. 89-519-XIE. Ottawa: Statistics Canada.

Ward-Griffin, C., & V.W. Marshall. (2003). Reconceptualizing the relationship between 'public' and 'private' eldercare. *Journal of Aging Studies* 17: 189–208.

Zelizer, V.A. (2005). *The Purchase of Intimacy.* Princeton: Princeton University Press.

Zelizer, V.A. (2007). Caring everywhere. Keynote Address, Conference on Intimate Labors, University of California, Santa Barbara, 4–6 Oct.

10 Spinning the Family Web: Grandparents Raising Grandchildren in Canada

PATRICIA MACKENZIE, LESLIE BROWN, MARILYN CALLAHAN, AND BARBARA WHITTINGTON

In the past decade, most provinces in Canada have experienced a dramatic increase in reports of child abuse and neglect. Government agencies report that they are consequently hard pressed to find additional out-of-home placements for children, particularly for children from poor families or from Aboriginal communities (Child Welfare League of Canada 2003; Ehrle, Geen, & Clark 2001). Seeking and making arrangements for the children to obtain 'kin care,' where members of extended families take on the care of children, is becoming an established practice. Kinship care, broadly defined as 'the full continuum of care of children by relatives within and outside of the child welfare system' (Gleeson 1999a), has provided a safety net for children in need across cultures and for centuries. Grandparents most often occupy this role and two out of three kinship caregivers are grandparents (Berrick, Barth, & Needell 1994). The 2001 Canadian Census reports that 56,790 grandchildren under the age of 18 were living with their grandparents without parents in the home; of these, 8,780 were from British Columbia. Several studies have identified maternal substance abuse as the leading reason grandparents must assume the responsibility of parenting their grandchildren. Less common reasons why grandparents are raising their grandchildren include parental death, homicide, incarceration, and mental illness (Burton 1992; Dowdell 1995; Jendrek 1994; Kelley 1993; Minkler & Roe 1993).

The rate of grandparent care varies among provinces and territories in Canada. More grandparent families are headed by single grandparents (50%), compared with the overall proportion of single-parent families (20%) in Canada. Fuller-Thomson, Minkler, and Driver (1997) determined that 77% of all caregiving grandparents in Canada were women.

Family Caregiving: Grandmothers Caring for Grandchilden

As was pointed out by Benoit and Hallgrímsdóttir in the introductory chapter of this text, family caregiving is a complex concept. The characteristics of family caring have been variously explored in feminist scholarship, welfare states research, and public and social policy. Caregiving has been variously understood as labour, as love, as duty, as obligation, and as a moral orientation (Daly 2002). Broadly, family care refers to the activity of looking after people who are not able to look after themselves. Orloff argues that scholars must also understand that the family is a central actor in the provision of welfare. She suggests that 'state provisioning that helps to shift the burden of welfare from the family to the state, or from women to men within the family furthers women's gender interests' (Orloff 1993: 312). The perspective put forward in this chapter is that family caregiving requires someone to do real work and involves labour whether it is recognized as such by individuals or institutions and whether it is paid or unpaid, physical or emotional in nature (Minkler 1999).

The parental surrogacy role now performed by many grandmothers (in some instances this role involved a set of grandparents) is in contrast to the traditional grandmothering/grandparenting role of supporting, monitoring family functioning, and intervening when needed. The precise nature of these roles may vary. For example, grandmothers may assume primary responsibility in a parental surrogacy role with or without legal custody. Grandmothers may live in the same home as grandchildren but do not have primary responsibility for raising these grandchildren. Alternately, grandmothers may be responsible for providing day care/babysitting for grandchildren. The data presented in this chapter are derived from an examination of the experiences of grandmothers who are raising their grandchildren on a full-time basis because of the inability of parents to assume care.

The ideologies and practices of familialism locate parenting as a private relationship undertaken by carers within the framework of the family (see also Treloar & Funk and Funk & Kobayashi, elsewhere in this volume). Included within familialism is the ideology of motherhood, the expectation that mothers will provide continuous, loving care to their children regardless of their circumstances, and place the needs of their children and families before their own (Kline 1995; Roberts 1995; Fineman 1995; McMahon 1995). Leitner (2003) suggests that familialistic policies attempt to strengthen the family in its caring role, while de-familializing policies work to relieve the family of providing direct care. We argue in this chapter that grandmothers are used to sustain the continuity of informal family care as an ideal and a practice, thereby reinforcing notions of familialism and familialistic policies. Among other things, this has implications for the recognition of how the caring work that occurs inside families is imbued with gender. Grandmothers experience the pervasiveness of familialism. There has been limited research that examines the caring labour associated with this type of family work and what assuming this role means for grandmothers in terms of challenges to their own health and well-being. These older women are expected to take on the long-term care of their grandchildren under conditions that are increasingly difficult and financially untenable, and they have few options to refuse to accept responsibility for this caregiving role. Grandmothers re-enter such caregiving arrangements under difficult circumstances and with varying degrees of support from family, friends, community, and social services. Significant effort and energy in providing caring labour is invested by caregiving grandmothers. These efforts are done with little understanding of the impact of the caregiving role on the physical, psychological, social, and financial well-being of older women.

Often, the lives to date of the grandchildren have been disrupted to such an extent that fears of loss and abandonment are ever present. Relieving their fears is partially dependent on the belief that their current caregivers are a constant and stable presence in their lives. However, a grandparent's declining physical condition has significant implications for the stability of the grandchild's family environment. According to several studies, the average age of grandparent caregivers is 55 to 57 years (Burton 1992; Dowdell 1995; Kelley 1993; Minkler, Roe, & Robertson-Beckley 1994). In a national study of kinship caretakers in the United States, of which 66% were grandmothers, 57% of the caregivers were age 50 or higher, including 29% over age 60, and 8% over age 70 (Feig 1997).

Data about the physical and emotional health of grandmother caregivers have been sparse until recent years. Less recent data suggest that grandparents raising grandchildren are profoundly affected by their caregiving responsibilities in several areas, including psychological stress, social and economic well-being, and physical health (Burton 1992; Dowdell 1995; Kelley 1993; Kelley & Damato 1995; Minkler & Roe 1993). These data reveal that these women may face a number of stresses and experience greater psychological distress and worse health than other women. Grandmothers' views of their overall health appear to be complex, with a need to carry on despite numerous health problems, perhaps neglecting their own health in the process. According to a recent study, grandmothers have reported increased anxiety and depression since assuming primary parenting roles; others report an increase in smoking and alcohol consumption and an exacerbation of pre-existing physical illnesses such as arthritis and angina (Hughes et al. 2007). Having fewer family resources, less social support, and poorer physical health produced greater levels of psychological distress among grandmothers raising their grandchildren. For example, Kelley et al. (2000) reported that psychological stress is exacerbated because of the social isolation and the restrictions inherent in the parenting/grandparenting role.

When Minkler and Roe (1993) queried grandparents regarding their psychological health, 37% reported it had worsened since assuming full-time caregiving of their grandchildren, and the vast majority (72%) reported feeling 'depressed' in the week immediately before data collection. Psychological stress stemming from grandparent/parenting roles often manifests itself in various physical symptoms such as headaches, fatigue, and increased blood pressure levels. Burton (1992) reported that more than one-third of grandparents have heightened medical problems since assuming full-time caregiving responsibilities for their grandchildren. Dowdell (1995) found a significant relationship between perceived caregiver burden and high levels of psychological distress, and over 45% of grandmothers identified themselves as having a physical problem or illness that seriously affected their general health. Minkler and colleagues (1992) noted that 85% of grandmothers reported their self-assessed health as good or fair but that 34% retrospectively evaluated that their health had worsened since caregiving began. Interestingly, those who indicated their health had worsened after assuming parenting responsibilities also reported financial problems and lack of family support. In their study of African American women raising grandchildren and great-grandchildren because of the crack cocaine epidemic, Minkler and Roe (1993) found that 28% of the caregivers reported that their health had deteriorated during the previous year. More important, 38% reported that their health had worsened since assuming full-time parenting responsibilities for grandchildren. The caregiving grandmothers in this study also admitted that they often put their caregiving duties ahead of their own health. Half of the caregivers reported that they had current concerns regarding their health yet had failed to keep a medical appointment during the past year because of child care responsibilities. One-third had not been to a doctor in three years or more.

Roe et al. (1996) suggested that many of the grandmothers caring for their grandchildren had a high sense of perseverance and determination to continue their responsibilities in spite of any physical limitations or symptoms. They not only had serious concerns about their current physical condition but also described more definitively the various physical symptoms endured while caring for their grandchildren, such as body pain, stiffness, high blood pressure, respiratory problems, and frequent headaches. In spite of these complaints, one-half of the grandparents reported that their physical state never interfered with their parental duties and responsibilities, but did interfere with their ability to maintain their own medical appointments.

Other research has suggested that there may be particular stressors and consequences of caregiving for custodial grandmothers with primary responsibility that differ from those who live with the grandchild but do not assume primary responsibility for their care (Kelley & Damato 1995; Minkler et al. 1992). For example, lack of reciprocal support by the middle generation, the need to care for multiple children (of multiple children), and conflictual relationships with the grandchild's parent(s) are likely to affect primary grandparent caregivers (Burton & Dilworth-Anderson 1991; Minkler et al. 1992). Further, grandparents with primary responsibility have reported high degrees of role restriction, social isolation, and financial difficulty (Kelley, 1993). Yet because the role of co-resident grandparents is less clear-cut, they may in fact experience greater, or perhaps different, stresses (Jendrek 1994).

As with caregivers of the elderly (Moen, Robison, & Dempster-McClain 1995), the effects of caregiver stress may be cumulative for grandmothers, which is particularly relevant since many grandmother caregivers can expect to provide care for up to 18 years. Many grandmother caregivers assume dual parenting and grandparenting responsibilities. Further, the grandmother's experience of caregiving is likely to be conflictual, with as many as 70% reporting feeling depressed, exhausted, or unable to get going, while concurrently feeling appreciated and worthwhile (Minkler et al. 1992). In addition, the ages and number of the grandchildren cared for and the length of time involved in caregiving may also affect stress, coping, and health outcomes.

In summary, the literature emphasizes the impact of caregiving on the health of grandmothers and raises questions about how this may (or may not) compromise their functional ability to carry out parenting responsibilities. Relative to the grandchildren, these health issues could also raise concerns about the quality of the family environment when grandparents with failing health raise young, active children.

Research Method

This chapter is based upon a study conducted in British Columbia, Canada. The project goal was to examine the experiences of grandmother-led families, explore the implications of their experiences for child welfare practice, and to apply a feminist policy analysis. The study gathered the experiences of a group of Aboriginal and non-Aboriginal grandmothers – the most dominant group of kincarers of children. Although conducted in British Columbia, we believe the findings have relevance to other parts of Canada, North America, and Europe, where similar trends can be seen. We used a grounded theory approach, beginning with in-depth interviews to create texts that were analysed to generate a descriptive, analytical, and interpretative account of the grandmothers' stories. According to Strauss and Corbin (1990: 23), 'a grounded theory is one that is inductively derived from the study of the phenomenon it represents.' Thus, a research project which is informed by grounded theory involves an analytical approach to text which results in a collection of categories or concepts and the relationships between and among these concepts (Glaser 1992).

Our reliance on the grounded theory approach required the researchers to closely examine textual material collected from a series of in-depth qualitative interviews. The purpose of the careful review was to discover the complex variables which lie beneath the experiences under examination. During the interview process, each of the twenty-two grandmothers who participated in the study described themselves, their grandchild's parents, and the grandchild in detail. A series of questions elicited the reasons the grandmother assumed care and whether the arrangements constituted private or public kinship care. Further prompts encouraged the grandmothers to reflect upon their experiences and provided insights into the rewards and challenges of engaging in this caring labour. We selected participants on the basis of diversity in terms of age (44 to 84); the circumstances under which they assumed care of their grandchildren (primarily mental health or addiction issues facing birth parent(s)); their income level and source (nine lived on limited incomes); marital status (13 lived with a spouse, three were widowed, and six divorced); age of children (4 years to over 19 years); duration of their care (8 months to over 9 years); legal status (nine of the grandmothers have full custody of their grandchildren, while in all other situations the arrangement was a voluntary one). Five of the grandmothers are First Nations women caring for First Nations children. A further five non-First Nations grandmothers are caring for grandchildren who are of First Nation ancestry. By examining each interview in depth we were able to see the daily processes involved in raising grandchildren, how the grandmothers maintained their own health and well-being, and how they juggled the multiple tasks of dealing with other family members, friends, the workplace, and the health care and social service systems.

Results

Drawing on the stories of the many grandmothers involved in our research, we direct attention to how grandmother caregivers deal with their amazingly complex situations. After analysing the interviews, we found consistent patterns emerging that illustrated the respective costs and benefits to grandmothers as they manage the challenge of revisiting the work involved in providing daily care for children. What we also found is that the grandmothers' caring work extended beyond child care to encompass a range of activities that make it possible for the extended family unit to stay connected, despite enormous odds and experiences of interpersonal pain and loss. A significant finding of this research study is that grandmother-headed families are dealing with the *unmaking* of one notion of family (the nuclear family of parents and children), and the *remaking* of new family within the grandmother's home. Tronto's (1993) conceptualization of caring includes caring about and taking caring of. These concepts were helpful in understanding the family-making processes that occurred in the grandmother-led families.

According to Tronto, 'caring about involves the recognition in the first place that care is necessary. Taking care of is the next step in the caring process. It involves assuming some responsibility for meeting the identified need and determining how to respond to it' (Tronto 1993: 106). Lewis (1997) suggests that Tronto's concepts allow for a deeper understanding of women's care giving work within families wherein 'the preservation of relationships and the avoidance of harm takes precedence over the rights and rules associated with an ethic of justice, and in which the focus of concern is to find an equilibrium between connectedness and empathy on the one hand, and the autonomous self on the other' (Lewis 1997: 171). From the narratives of the women interviewed, it became clear that preserving of relationships between and among the various members of an extended family unit and striving to minimize harm to children was their principal motivation for taking on this work. Hence, caring *about* their grandchildren was the very reason why it was essential for them to step up to the plate to care *for* these children. Grandmothers reported that they would have found it difficult to stand aside and merely watch the *unmaking* of the previous nuclear family unit. In the *remaking* of families, where grandmothers and grandchildren lived together, grandmothers became hands-on caregivers again, giving daily nurturing to their grandchildren. During the process of remaking families, grandmothers' narratives also illustrate the many dimensions of caring as they continue to care about and care for their adult children and other family members and seek opportunities to receive care from them as well. The new family form which results from this remaking must be flexible and allow for such contingencies as the potential return of children to their birth parents, the birth parents moving in with both children and grandmothers, or the addition of other extended family members to the grandmother-led family unit.

All grandmothers in our study reported that their primary reason for involvement is to provide a safety net for their grandchildren. The circumstances faced by grandmothers who become caregivers for their grandchildren are complicated and stressful. There are common threads in all grandmothers' stories that identify the reasons they are caring for their grandchildren. These reasons are related to factors that led to either the inability or unavailability of the birth parent to be a parent to her or his children. These factors include substance abuse (drugs and alcohol), child abuse and neglect, mental/emotional problems, physical illness, and death. During the interviews information was also collected regarding aspects of the birth parent's involvement including whether the birth parent(s) had lived in the grandmother's home during the past year, the amount of face-to-face contact between the grandchild and each parent, and the extent to which each parent had participated in decisions regarding the child and in actual child care. Generally speaking, the day-to-day involvement of the birth parents with their children was minimal, although the grandmothers' did their best to maintain a sense of connection and belonging between children and birth parents.

Maintaining this sense of connection between and among family members takes work. The grandmothers stories are filled with their descriptions of the physical, practical, emotional, and social labour involved in caring for the children (and other family members, including still 'mothering' the birth parent). The remainder of this chapter will focus on the themes in the data that capture how the grandmothers describe what we are considering to be grandmothers' caring labour in kinship networks.

We Are Family: Spinning the Family Web

The grandmothers often take on the responsibility of keeping all members of the family 'knitted together,' ensuring that a sense of family connection and belonging exists, even in very difficult situations. This requires engaging in the work of maintaining a family home; doing things to create a sense of belonging for grandchildren, self, and others; being responsible for the memory- and history-making activities of the extended family unit; and involving other family members to help and create good family times. Valuing family ways was a core theme in all of the interviews but was particularly strong in the interviews with First Nations grandmothers. In First Nations communities extended families play a huge role in defining who family is, and it is common to see children being raised by extended family units. The family definition using First Nations/Aboriginal knowledge and ways of being was beautifully stated by one of the First Nations grandmothers, who stated, 'family is family'; regardless of who gave birth to the child, we are all responsible for our children. Here the dynamics of family plays a huge part of parenting and how these relationships factor with grandchildren and extended families. Grandma's values, care, teachings, and expectations come into play. Within First Nations communities family dynamics plays an intricate part in everyday life. Many of the grandmothers reflect parenting by doing and role modelling to their grandchildren, passing strengths onto grandchildren and children. For many First Nations grandmothers, it seemed that the focus is not on themselves but rather on the children, grandchildren, families, and communities.

Grandma's Gaze: Attending, Watching, and Worrying

This important category in the analysis addresses the way grandmothers described how they 'watched over' their family situation, often for many years before stepping in to assume care of the children. Most grandmothers had spent a period of time as a part-time, temporary, or intermittent caregiver to their grandchildren before having the grandchild on a permanent or semi-permanent basis. Often these arrangements were unpredictable and distressing to everyone concerned. In the interviews grandmothers talked about their worries, apprehension, and need for vigilance while at the same time also including comments about the pride, love, and hope they feel for their grandchildren and other family members. Grandmothers related how much effort they put into watching over their grandchildren, keeping tabs on what was happening, and taking action when necessary (for example, when the children were exposed to dangerous situations involving substance misuse, driving under the influence, or inappropriate sexual activity). Many of the First Nations grandmothers stated that 'it just seemed natural' that grandmothers provided safety and protection of their grandchildren, foster children, and extended families' children. Some of the non-First Nations grandmothers expressed a sense of discomfort with this role but claimed that 'they had no choice' but to intervene when they thought the grandchild was at risk. The grandmothers reported many circumstances that arise when they need to be involved in keeping their grandchildren safe from people and situations that they (the grandmothers) felt were unhealthy or likely to cause harm. For instance, one grandmother watched how her grandson was being treated and disliked what she saw; she became proactive in his care and later shared joint custody with her daughter. Another grandmother set limits with her own daughter to make sure her grandchildren were safe and secure. In these situations, grandmothers reported that they had to spend time and effort re-teaching the birth parents how to make decisions that were in the best interests of the child. For example, making sure that children got to school, had access to good food, and had adult supervision for activities, while minimizing their exposure to alcohol, drugs, or other inappropriate behaviour.

Dancing Grandma

This is a category used to capture the comments made by grandmothers about the difficult task they face in juggling the needs and wants of many different members of the family system. Engaging in this task requires grandmothers to find a way to balance the often competing or contradictory needs of others. Grandmothers described how hard they work to ensure that everyone in the larger family unit feels valued, understood, and cared for. This category also refers to the other obligations grandmothers have, such as keeping their own outside-of-the-home jobs, maintaining their own marital relationship, and fulfilling their role as members of community and of other social groups. When talking about their lives, many grandmothers described how complicated the interpersonal relationships within the larger extended family network can be, For example, grandmothers reported that they felt like they often were 'walking on egg shells' when dealing with issues of loyalty between the generations. Grandmothers were concerned for the well-being of the child but were also aware of the need to make sure the birth parent (their child) was not completely cut out of all parenting roles. Balancing the expectations of their own child and the needs of the grandchild(ren) proved to be very difficult for many grandmothers. Many grandmothers found that they invested enormous energy in negotiating and mediating relationships among family members and between family members and those on the 'outside' (child protection workers, school and community helpers, health providers, legal personnel, etc.).

Dealing with the Burden and Coping with the Stress

Many grandmothers were reluctant to speak about what they considered to be the more negative aspects of their caregiving role but several did identify sources of stress, their efforts to cope, and aspects of their own physical, psychological, and social well-being. Since grandmothers with primary responsibility often considered themselves to be parent surrogates, many identified feeling stressed due to role-related confusion. Many grandmothers with primary responsibility indicated feeling somewhat trapped and restricted in their lives, and identified having to make real modifications in their lifestyle since they began caregiving. Some grandmothers expressed dissatisfaction with the 'way things turned out' and also admitted to having to make a decision to 'put others first' while running the risk of neglecting their own health.

Naming and Explaining 'Family': Shifting Family Forms

Grandmothers described how the composition and structure of their family shifted and sorted as people moved in and out of each other's lives and domestic space. For example, at times the birth parents and their grandchildren were sharing the grandparent's accommodation, while at other times they were keeping a household separate from the grandchild and grandparents. This moving in and out often leads to changes in roles: Who is the parent? Who else is involved in decision making? Who needs/receives care and from whom? New partners and other children may also be introduced into the family constellation and other extended family members are also involved at times. The grandmothers talked about how they interpreted these shifting family forms (and the resultant emotional and practical complications) to the grandchildren. As one grandmother said:

> It's a little more complicated and when we have to do a family tree at school you know, I said, well we're a very mixed up family.

Grandmother as Advocate: Taking Charge

Grandmothers work hard as advocates for their grandchildren, making sure they access all available supports. Other studies have found that many kinship carers suffer from 'service-neglect,' which shows up in the many unmet needs they have (McCallion & Janicki 2000). Many of the grandmothers described in detail the frustrations they encountered to make sure that their grandchildren had all the supports and resources needed and that they were kept safe from influences/situations that were not in their best interests. Knowing what to do and how to do it often proved to be a challenge that took time and effort. Grandmothers found that they had to interact with social agencies to obtain services for their grandchildren, but often encountered unanticipated obstacles. Overcoming the obstacles took work and usually required the grandmothers to assume the role of 'champion,' advocate, and leader in situations. Grandmothers described how they had to become quite ferocious and proactive, relying on their intuition, determination, and commitment to their grandchild to access services and resources from a not always helpful or accessible system of care. For instance, one grandmother did not have the firsthand knowledge of how to get her granddaughter away from her abusive mother until she used the telephone directory to access the help line. Another grandmother used every resource she could find in her community to help her with raising her grandchild including the school counsellor, volunteers from the Boys and Girls Club, a therapist from the local children's mental health program, respite care from child welfare, and structured programs in the recreation centre.

Setting Limits

Given the complexities of the family situation in which these caregiving arrangements take place, it is not surprising that the grandmothers are also faced with situations that require a clear head and a strong heart. We heard several examples of when grandmothers needed to establish clear boundaries defining everyone's respective roles, tolerable behaviour, and the conditions necessary for the child's well-being. Grandmothers were determined to put the best interests of the child first, even at the risk of compromising their relationship with their own child. One grandmother gave this example:

> I told her that I'm going to look after him [grandson] till she decides to get her life organized and until she decided to sober up. One of *my conditions* was I wasn't going to return the children back to her until she did make some changes in her life.

Keeping the Kids at Home

Grandmothers provide care tirelessly and keep many of their grandchildren out of the hands of the state child protection services through loving, nurturing, and caring. Many of the non-First Nations grandmothers knew that if they had not 'stepped up to the plate' to care for their grandchildren, the child would have wound up in the care of the formal child welfare system. From past experiences with the child welfare system, many families (especially First Nations people) feel they lost their children and that families and communities failed these children. In the 1960s and 1970s there was a dramatic increase in the number of children apprehended from First Nations communities and taken into the care of child protections services; these children were usually placed in non-First Nations homes as either foster children or as adoptees. For First Nations communities, the loss of children to what is referred to as the 'Sixties Scoop' and residential schools created loss of being and identity for many children, alienation across generations and communities, and resulted in tremendous personal and community tragedy. All of the grandmothers interviewed talked about the impact of loss and grief on family well-being and their own efforts to help family members heal through the pain associated with this. The First Nations grandmothers interviewed in this study believe that it is the responsibility of everyone to work together to keep family and community connected, thereby providing both community healing and a safety net for kids in the community. They also talked about how they provide leadership to their families in their work as teachers to the young. Grandmothers believe such teachings help children understand how respect is gained and values are maintained. It also provides history through story-telling, and provides children with a sense of belonging and a sense of identity. One of the First Nations grandmothers expressed the importance of getting an 'Indian' name and the ceremonies that go with it. Another talked about teaching her children and grandchildren how to fish, dry their catch, pick berries, and preserve food for later use.

Summary and Conclusions

Grandmothers interviewed for this study faced all the challenges that most parents experience and some distinctly different ones. Often, our participants tried to remain a parent and support to their children (the birth parent of the grandchild), in spite of disappointments. Although our participants may have been very unhappy because of their children's parenting, they had to nevertheless cope with the outcomes of difficult family situations while also trying to not blame their children or themselves. The findings from our interviews with both Aboriginal and non-Aboriginal custodial participants indicate a strong sense of commitment, duty, and responsibility for their grandchildren. Although the life circumstances between Aboriginal and non-Aboriginal grandmothers were different, both Aboriginal and non-Aboriginal grandmothers pointed out that the labour associated with caring for their grandchildren is poorly understood. Future research should question what the cost of this commitment may be and how this caregiving labour is perceived and valued in both Aboriginal and non-Aboriginal communities.

Recent scholarship, including many of the chapters in this volume, has focused attention on the unpaid, traditional, unvalued, and unrecognized labour of caring. Our study echoes questions raised by other authors about how relational models of kinship care need to be reconceptualized (Sands & Goldberg-Glen 2000). The themes that emerged from data reported by the women in our study show that 'second-generation motherhood,' whether in Aboriginal or non-Aboriginal communities, is complex and challenging in that it engages caregiving grandmothers in multiple layers of mothering as they strive to maintain a balance between competing generations while creating family environments in which all members feel valued and have a sense of belonging.

Running throughout all the narratives is a central dilemma that places two core values in conflict: family continuity (taking care of one's own) and generational independence. Our participants told us that, when they take responsibility for their grandchild, efforts must be made to ensure that the children remain connected to their birth parent(s). However, in doing so our participants said they worry that they usurp the role of the birth parents and risk fuelling intergenerational conflict. If the grandmothers choose not to take responsibility for their grandchild, the child may be adopted out of the family or be placed in foster care by the child welfare system, which in Canada is much more likely to be the case for Aboriginal children. This role conflict takes place in the context of a breakdown in intergenerational communication that inhibits its resolution and offers no perceived way for the grandmothers to exit the situation. Our participants maintained they work hard to avoid this conflict but often found that circumstances (usually a crisis point) precipitate the decision to act in the best interests of the child. However justified their actions, this may or may not be in participants' own best interests since it often required them to shoulder immense emotional stress. Their health was undoubtedly compromised, although few women in this study gave priority to this in their narratives. Some talked about their feelings of isolation, of having to 'do it all myself,' of experiencing 'retirement lost,' of longing to again have 'a room of one's own.' Participants also spoke of economic hardships, marital difficulties, lifestyle changes, and stress associated with multiple roles.

Overall, however, our participants reported that they enjoyed taking care of their grandchildren because it put meaning back into their lives. For many of them the situation also presented an opportunity to 'do it better or differently' the second time around. Several were very frank in their own admission of having failed as a parent in earlier days, and many felt a sense of guilt or remorse over decisions they had taken when their own children (the birth parents of the grandchildren) were young. Although the tasks of raising a child often left the participants tired and stretched, they also expressed a great deal of pride in their grandchildren and took pleasure in participating in grandchildren's activities. Several claimed to have a new focus in their life, and an appreciation for making sure that their child became accomplished and had 'a good start' in life.

Despite the absence of complaints from the participants in this study, there is no doubt that engaging in caring for their grandchildren has taken a toll on the physical, psychosocial, and economic well-being of the caregiving grandmothers. They reported elevated levels of stress that negatively impact their well-being (Hughes et al. 2007). Grandmother caregiver stress has been shown to be related to family resources, participants' physical health, and to a lesser extent, social support (Gleeson 1999a; Beeman, Kim, & Bullerdick 2000); however, the dearth of services available to private kinship families compounds the vulnerability of this group of caregivers. Our study supports these findings and suggests that greater attention be given to interventions aimed at decreasing psychological distress and improving the social and financial resources available to grandmothers raising grandchildren. If the state is going to continue to look to extended family networks to provide an alternative to putting children into the formal child welfare system, then a more comprehensive and integrated system of supports must be developed to support kincarers in this important work.

In conclusion, the social phenomenon of grandmothers raising grandchildren is receiving increased recognition. For these multigenerational families to thrive, health and social supports are critical. As society looks more to family caregivers to assume parental responsibilities as a preference over non-family relative foster care or institutional care, communities must deliver necessary health care and social services to support these families. Creativity, innovation, imagination, and consumer involvement in program design are key elements to facilitate and sustain positive change in the lives of grandmothers raising their grandchildren. This research points out the need for more information on the impact of engaging in caring labour on the physical, psychological, social, and financial well-being of grandmothers. The consequences of caregiving by grandmothers are not well understood but appear to be linked with psychosocial health. Additional studies, both qualitative and longitudinal, will provide deeper understanding of the complex situations faced by grandmother caregivers. Qualitative studies focused on the day-to-day experiences of grandmother caregivers will uncover the rewards and burdens of their role, while longitudinal studies will highlight the challenges they encounter at various phases of the process. Such inquiry will provide direction for designing additional ways to support grandmother caregivers in their work, with the aim of better outcomes for all family members. What must be understood is that even though they have the strong desire to complete their roles and responsibilities, there is the potential for serious health problems and that these may be avoided with proper care, attention, and efforts to strengthen the support network of women doing family work. Service interventions that may be effective in addressing the health needs of grandparents raising grandchildren should include an interdisciplinary team led by social workers and health care providers. Emphasizing familial and community strengths, support programs could be designed to facilitate better social and physical functioning. When assuming the responsibility of caring for their grandchildren, grandparents often must seek support for financial, social, recreational, and other needs. Such support could lessen the grandparenting/parenting burden, and improve intergenerational family relationships and overall life satisfaction. Finally, limitations of our sample meant that the differences between Aboriginal and non-Aboriginal grandmothers taking care of grandchildren were not studied in detail. This topic also presents an important issue for future study.

Policy and Practice Implications

Grandmothers who provide care privately (whether in non-Aboriginal or Aboriginal family units) appear to be serving a child welfare function outside of the public system. The child welfare system has utilized this tradition of private child protection in order to arrange care for children who would otherwise be wards of the state. Child welfare researchers point out the advantages for children of kinship care over non-family foster care as including stability, sibling togetherness, commitment to the child, and cultural and family continuity (Berrick et al. 1994; Le Prohn 1994; Gleeson 1999b). However, such arrangements also work to the fiscal benefit of the state since this very real labour cost is borne by those who have historically not been recognized as contributing an economic good – women who are the caregivers to vulnerable family members. Clearly the caring labour provided free of charge to the state by grandparents raising their grandchildren is an economic good that must be acknowledged and adequately supplemented with an integrated system of support. One could argue that this is especially urgent for Aboriginal grandparents who tend to be poorer than their non-Aaboriginal Canadian counterparts. An example of innovative approaches to this can be found in the United States. The Administration on Aging in the United States has earmarked 10% of funds from the National Caregiver Support Act of 1999 to develop programs for older (age 60 or over) relatives providing care to children This is the first time service designated for older adults will include 'respite' or child care funds (Generations United 2001).These programs focus on the entire family and are a beginning attempt to attend to the needs of different generations within a family context. As adults live longer and children continue to be at risk, attention should focus on the needs of multigenerational families and their members of all ages. A more holistic and interdisciplinary policy, program, and practice approach may allow for the prevention of more serious problems, treatment of abusive and neglecting parents, respite for grandparents, and mental health and educational resources for a family's youngest and most vulnerable members.

REFERENCES

Beeman, S.K., H. Kim, & S.K. Bullerdick. (2000). Factors affecting placement of children in kinship and non-kinship foster care. *Children and Youth Services Review* 22: 37–54.

Berrick, J.D., R.P. Barth, & B. Needell. (1994). A comparison of kinship foster homes and foster family homes: Implications for kinship foster care as family preservation. *Children and Youth Services Review* 16: 33–63.

Burton, L. (1992). Black grandparents rearing children of drug-addicted patents: Stressors, outcomes, and social service needs. *Gerontologist* 32: 744–51.

Burton, L., & P. Dilworth-Anderson. (1991). The intergenerational family roles of aged black Americans. *Marriage and Family Review* 16(3/4): 311–30.

Child Welfare League of Canada. (2003). *Children in Care in Canada: A Summary of Current Issues and Trends with Recommendations for Future Research.* Retrieved 27 April 2008 from www.nationalchildrensalliance.com/nca/pubs/2003/Children_in_Care_March_2003.pdf.

Daly, M. (2002). Care as a good for social policy. *Journal of Social Policy* 31: 251, 252.

Dilworth-Anderson, P. (1992). Extended kin networks in black families. *Families and Aging* (Summer): 29–32.

Dowdell, E.B. (1995). Caregiver burden: Grandmothers raising their high risk grandchildren. *Journal of Psychosocial Nursing* 33: 27–30.

Ehrle, J., R. Geen, & R.L. Clark. (2001). *Children Cared for by Relatives: Who Are They and How Are They Faring?* Assessing the New Federalism. Policy Brief B-28. Washington: Urban Institute. Retrieved 23 April 2008 from http://www.urban.org/publications/310270.html.

Feig, L. (1997). *Informal and Formal Kinship Care: Findings from National and State Data.* U.S. Department of Health and Human Services, Office of the Assistant Secretary for Planning and Evaluation. Washington: U.S. Government Printing Office.

Fineman, M. (1995). Images of Mothers in Poverty Discourse. In M. Albertson Fineman & I. Kappin, eds., *Mothers in Law: Feminist Theory and the Legal Regulation of Motherhood,* 205–23. New York: Columbia University Press.

Fuller-Thomson, E., M. Minkler, & D. Driver. (1997). A profile of grandparents raising grandchildren in the United States. *Gerontologist* 37(3): 406–11.

Generations United. (2003). *A Guide to the National Family Caregiver Support Program and Its Inclusion of Grandparents and Other Relatives Raising Children.* (September). Retrieved from http://ipath.gu.org/Kinsh6261201.asp.

Glaser, B.G. (1992). *Emergence vs Forcing: Basics of Grounded Theory.* Mill Valley: Sociology Press.

Gleeson, J.P. (1999a). Kinship care as a child welfare service. In R.L. Hegar & M. Scannapieco, eds., *Kinship Foster Care: Policy, Practice, and Research,* 28–52. New York: Oxford University Press.

Gleeson, J.P. (1999b). Kinship care as a child welfare system: What do we really know? In J.P. Gleeson & C.F. Hairston, eds., *Kinship Care: Improving Practice through Research,* 3–34. Washington: Child Welfare League of America.

Hughes, M., L. Waite, T. LaPierre, & Y. Luo. (2007). All in the family: The impact of caring for grandchildren on grandparents' health. *Journals of Gerontology,* Series B: *Psychological Sciences and Social Sciences* 62: S108–S119.

Jendrek, M. (1994). Grandparents who parent their grandchildren: Circumstances and decisions. *Gerontologist* 34(2): 206–16.

Kelley, S. (1993). Caregiver stress in grandparents raising grandchildren. *IMAGE: Journal of Nursing Scholarship* 25(4): 331–7.

Kelley, S., & E. Damato. (1995). Grandparents as primary caregivers. *MCN* 20: 326–32.

Kelley, S.J., D. Whitely, T.A. Sipe, & B.C. Yorker. (2000). Psychological distress in grandmother kinship care providers: The role of resources, social support, and physical health. *Child Abuse and Neglect* 24(3): 311–21.

Kline, M. (1995). Complicating the ideology of motherhood: Child welfare law and First Nations women. In M. Albertson Fineman & I. Kappin, eds., *Mothers in Law: Feminist Theory and the Legal Regulation of Motherhood,* 169–76. New York: Columbia University Press.

Leitner, S. (2003). Varieties of familialism: The caring function of the family in comparative perspective. *European Societies* 5: 353–75.

Le Prohn, N.S. (1994). The role of the kinship foster parent: A comparison of the role conceptions of relative and non-relative foster parents. *Children and Youth Services Review* 16: 65–84.

Lewis, J. (1997). Gender and welfare regimes: Further thoughts. *Social Politics* (Summer): 160–77.

McCallion, P., & M. Janicki. (2000). Grandparents as carers of children with disabilities: Facing the challenges. Preface. *Journal of Gerontological Social Work* 33(3): xix–xxi.

McMahon, M. (1995). *Engendering Motherhood: Identity and Self Transformation in Women's Lives.* New York: Guilford Press.

Minkler, M. (1994). Grandparents as parents: The American experience. *Aging International,* 21(1): 24–8.

Minkler, M., & K. Roe. (1993). *Grandmothers as Caregivers: Raising Children of the Crack Cocaine Epidemic.* Newbury Park: Sage.

Minkler, M., K.D. Berrick, & B. Needall. (1999). Impacts of welfare reform on California grandparents raising grandchildren: Reflections from the field. *Journal of Aging and Social Policy* 10(3): 45–63.

Minkler, M., K. Roe, & M. Price. (1992). The physical and emotional health of grandmothers raising grandchildren in the crack cocaine epidemic. *Gerontologist* 2(6): 752–61.

Minkler, M., K. Roe, & M. Robertson-Beckley. (1994). Raising grandchildren from crack-cocaine households: Effects on family and friendship ties of African-American women. *American Journal of Orthopsychiatry* 64: 20–9.

Moen, P., J. Robison, & D. Dempster-McClain. (1995). Caregiving and women's well-being: A life course approach. *Journal of Health and Social Behavior* 36: 259–73.

Orloff, A.S. (1993). Gender and the social rights of citizenship. *American Sociological Review* 58: 303–28.

Roberts, D. (1995). Racism and patriarchy in the meaning of motherhood. In M. Albertson Fineman & I. Kappin, eds., *Mothers in Law: Feminist Theory and the Legal Regulation of Motherhood,* 224–49. New York: Columbia University Press.

Roe, K., M. Minkler, E. Saunders, & G. Thomson. (1996). Health of grandmothers raising children of the crack cocaine epidemic. *Medical Care* 34: 1072–84.

Sands, R., & R. Goldberg-Glen. (2000). Factors associated with stress among grandparents raising their grandchildren. *Family Relations* 49(1): 97–105.

Strauss, A.L., & J. Corbin. (1998). *Basics of Qualitative Research Techniques and Procedures for Developing Grounded Theory.* Newbury Park: Sage.

Tronto, J. (1993). Care. In J. Tronto, *Moral Boundaries: A Political Ethic of Care,* 110–14. London: Routledge.

PART FIVE

Unpaid Care Work in Economic Organizations

11 Voluntary Caregiving? Constraints and Opportunities for Hospital Volunteers

MURIEL MELLOW

This chapter considers the role of volunteers as caregivers in hospitals. Many have argued that it is difficult for paid workers to combine the affective and instrumental components of care under the bureaucratic and time constraints imposed by economic organizations (Armstrong & Armstrong 2003; Brannon 1994; Browne 2003a, 2003b; Campbell 2000; Jones 1998). This leads me to ask how the unpaid work of hospital volunteers is also affected by such institutional regimes. To answer this question, I examine volunteer 'job descriptions' from four large teaching hospitals as well as data from interviews with volunteers. I show how hospitals define volunteer roles and also how volunteers work around and within certain constraints. Volunteers suggest that their unpaid status allows them to use time in flexible ways and relate to patients in a manner that differs from that of formal health care providers. This means they can provide forms of affective care that go beyond what is specified in the bureaucratic construction of their roles. Thus, they improve the quality of care for patients and increase their own sense of accomplishment or dignity in their work. Because most care work is done by women, regardless of whether it occurs in economic or intimate settings, I also ask how the work of volunteers may be gendered. I approach this question in two ways. First, I examine statistics on the gender of volunteers in four large teaching hospitals. Second, I consider how the content of volunteer work may be gendered, regardless of who does it. Even though hospitals specify that affective and instrumental care are a part of many volunteer roles, they do little to clarify the affective dimension or train volunteers for it. Does this presume volunteer caregivers who bring outside knowledge of caregiving with them – a kind of knowledge that is more frequently associated with the care work performed by women in other domains? This chapter addresses the central concerns of this volume by drawing attention to the formal rules that shape intimate labour, the ways in which the organization of this labour is gendered, and how workers – even unpaid ones – seek to maintain the quality of care for patients and maximize their own sense of dignity in their work (see Benoit & Hallgrímsdóttir, this volume).

Care Work in Hospitals and Beyond

Care work involves 'caring for' (instrumental tasks) and 'caring about' (affective labour) (Abel & Nelson 1990: 4; Graham 1983). This concept highlights the complexity of women's experience as caregivers across a wide range of settings; it also attempts to overcome the bifurcation of instrumental and affective tasks that arises from a masculine model of work. Care work involves dimensions such as social skills, trust, time, effort, and technique. It involves emotional labour (Hochschild 1983) since it relies on 'a sense of emotional attachment and connection to the person being cared for' (Badgett & Folbre 2001: 328). Personal knowledge of the person being cared for facilitates such work since it allows the caregiver to understand that person's unique needs and to adapt instrumental tasks accordingly. Caring labour is most effective when trust can develop between the caregiver and the individual who receives the care (Browne 2003a). Thus, time is also an important consideration; time allows trust to develop and provides the freedom to tailor care in individualized ways. The focus on personal knowledge and the development of trust means that care work may also be understood as a form of 'intimate labour' as defined by Zelizer (2005: 14–15; 2007). Most accounts of care work focus either on the labour which women perform for their own families (Abel & Nelson 1990; Blair-Loy & Jacobs 2003; Lan 2003) or on paid work. Paid care work has been discussed in relation to nurses (Reverby 1990), social workers (Baines 2004), teachers (Fisher 1990), day care workers (Einarson 1990; Nelson 1990), and domestic workers (Lan 2003).

The organization of care work and challenges associated with it may vary depending on whether it is paid or unpaid and whether it occurs in intimate settings or complex, economic organizations. Care work between family members is based on long-term relationships, intimate knowledge between individuals, and relative freedom to decide on how and when care is provided. However, when care work becomes paid employment and is situated within large institutions such as hospitals, tensions may arise between organizational constraints, managerial control, and the ethic of care which would otherwise guide such work. Many have argued that the particularity of caring fits uneasily within the standardized rules and impersonality of bureaucracy (Abel & Nelson 1990: 22; Baines 2004; Browne 2003a, 2003b). Standardized practices and close monitoring of work are used by organizations to ensure efficiency but may make care less effective and more stressful to provide. For example, Hochschild (1983) noted that the 'managed heart' – the codification and control of emotional labour – leaves workers feeling alienated and often means that emotional attentiveness and engagement is reduced to 'surface acting.' In contrast, Zelizer (2005) argues that instead of assuming that caregiving is at risk in large organizations or under the conditions of paid labour, we should inquire more closely to see how people negotiate caregiving relationships in these circumstances.

Those writing about paid work in hospitals have documented how rising costs and the introduction of neoliberal management paradigms from the for-profit sector have made it more difficult to provide effective care. The introduction of patient classification systems standardizes the number of staff, amount of time, and procedures required for particular types of patients – thus limiting nurses' ability to care effectively for individuals (White 2003). Care tasks have become more rigidly specified and limited in scope; a shift to quantitative accounting of these tasks is used to justify staffing levels (Armstrong & Armstrong 2003; Brannon 1994; Browne 2003a; Neysmith 2000). Treating work as discrete tasks overlooks the way that some aspects of care are best performed in relation to a broader scope of activities (Campbell 2000); for example, patient assessment is done while giving a bed bath. Average times assigned to tasks fail to account for the variations in individual needs and unexpected circumstances (Armstrong & Armstrong 2003; White 2003). In addition, White (2003: 131) points out that there is no way of identifying emotional support provided to patients or families in most classification systems. Thus, no time is allotted for emotional support and the demands of this work are not taken into account when staffing levels are determined (see Purkis et al., this volume).

Volunteers and Care Work

It is worth noting that in the past, volunteer work, like care work, was identified as a female domain, with women outnumbering men as volunteers (Abrahams 1996). However, more recently, the proportions of women and men who volunteer have converged. In 2004, in Canada, 44% of all men and 47% of all women over the age of 15, volunteer in some capacity (Statistics Canada 2006: 34). These data come from the 2004 Canada Survey of Giving, Volunteering, and Participating (CSGVP). The published report of the 2004 CSGVP tells us that the 26% of volunteers have roles that involve 'counseling or providing advice,' and 19% involve 'providing health care or support' though these proportions are not broken down by gender (Statistics Canada 2006: 39). Other authors suggest that there are distinct patterns of gender segregation across organizations (Baldock 1998; Millar McPherson & Smith-Lovin 1982; Popielarz 1999; Rotolo & Wharton 2003). For example, Baldock (1998) points out that women are more likely to volunteer in social welfare organizations, which entail a dimension of care, while men are more likely to volunteer in civic organizations such as sports clubs.

Discussions of care work performed by volunteers are less frequent in the literature than those that tie the same concept to paid work or to unpaid work in the family. Prentice and Ferguson (2000) consider mothers who volunteer in day care centres and how their caring labour structures their relation to paid workers and to the welfare state. Reitsma-Street and Neysmith (2000) look at volunteerism in community centres in impoverished urban neighbourhoods. Baines (2004) argues that because of the reorganization of welfare agencies, much caring labour formerly done as part of the job by social workers now happens outside of paid work hours, effectively becoming volunteer work. Abel and Nelson (1990: 22–3) briefly acknowledge the role of volunteers within 'circles of care,' although their discussion of this group is minimal compared with their discussions of care provided by family members or paid workers. Browne (2003b: 27) suggests that 'informal and formal care are complementary rather than alternative forms of support.' Browne explicitly uses informal care to refer to unpaid care provided by family and friends, although he also seems to place volunteers in this category.

The relatively minimal discussion of volunteers as care workers is an interesting gap in the literature because of the comparisons one might make to family caregivers and paid care workers. Like women in the home, volunteers are unpaid. However, this should not lead one to assume that volunteers have the same flexibility in how they provide care, given that volunteers may be in complex organizations. Inasmuch as their roles are defined by the organizations with which they are involved, and they are located in a division of labour that includes paid workers, it seems somewhat inappropriate to think of volunteers as 'informal' caregivers. Volunteers may differ from paid workers in regards to the level of skill, knowledge, discretion, and obligation that they bring to the task of caregiving, but they may be embedded in the same organizational regime. If tensions are created in regards to the performance of paid care work in more complex organizations, such as hospitals, it is possible that volunteers may be affected by similar dynamics. However, in keeping with Zelizer's caution against constructing false binaries in our analysis (2005, 2007), I do not want to assume an inherent opposition between caring and economic regimes. Instead I ask: when hospitals create job descriptions and rules that define the involvement of volunteers, does this enable or constrain the ability of volunteers to provide care? Examining the role of volunteers furthers our understanding of the ways in which intimate labour is carried out in economic organizations, such as hospitals.

Methodology and Data

The data for this chapter were gathered from four large hospitals in Alberta, Canada, between April and September 2003. I examine statistics on the numbers of male and female volunteers, the content of volunteer 'job descriptions,' and interviews with twenty-four volunteers. I also had shorter informal interviews with three volunteer coordinators. The hospitals in this study differ somewhat in size and scope of care. Each has its own volunteer resources department, and the range and number of volunteer positions varies between hospitals. Hospital A engages 473 volunteers; Hospital B, 469; Hospital C, 506; and Hospital D, 882. However, the four volunteer departments also work together and collaborate on a number of standardized policies. Thus, all hospitals classify volunteers into four main categories:

1 *Direct service volunteers* who have routine contact with inpatients, outpatients, or family members
2 *Indirect service volunteers* who provide office or program support in various ways including doing clerical tasks, attending to plants within the hospital, guiding school tours of the hospital, or providing layettes for newborns
3 *Revenue generating volunteers* who work in the gift shops or do fundraising

4 *Community-based volunteers* who are recruited by a variety of community organizations such as the Cancer Society or churches to provide services for patients.

Volunteers in the first three categories are recruited by the hospitals themselves. Hospitals also enumerate community-based volunteers because volunteer departments do security checks on these volunteers, provide them with identity badges, and monitor the hours they spend in the hospital. Each of these categories includes a variety of specific volunteer positions; for example, 'direct service' includes infant cuddlers, book cart attendants, and emergency room volunteers. The primary focus of this chapter is on direct service volunteers since this group is most logically engaged in care work and intimate labour. This is the largest group of volunteers in each hospital.

At my request, hospitals provided numbers of volunteers from their own databases; these databases are not completely standardized so hospitals varied in the degree of detailed information they were able to supply. Thus, while all hospitals could tell me the overall number of volunteers they engaged and the number in major categories, they could not all provide the number of women and men in specific positions. (I did not request statistics on the race or ethnicity of volunteers; it is unlikely that this information would have been available given the limited nature of hospital databases. There was only one person of colour among the volunteers interviewed.) More detailed statistics are available only for hospitals A and B. Since I was not allowed direct access to lists of volunteers and departments lacked the staff to compile these data for me, the gaps in the data are unavoidable. The incompleteness is interesting in itself; it raises the question of the extent to which the work of volunteers may fall under the radar of the hospitals even though volunteer tasks are formally specified in various documents. The written descriptions of volunteer positions take two forms. The first are one- or two-sentence 'program descriptions' that state the role of volunteers in different hospital units; these are often used for recruitment purposes. For example, the description for palliative care volunteers reads: 'Assist professional staff in providing the optimum quality of life for terminally ill patients and their families by offering companionship to patients and respite for family members' (Hospital D).

The second type includes one- to three-page 'volunteer assignment guides' (VAGs). These longer documents state the objectives of each volunteer program, the skills or qualities desired in the volunteer, the tasks that volunteers are expected to do, the work shifts involved, the person to whom the volunteer is responsible, and in some cases, the training provided by the hospital for that position. Volunteer positions and their descriptions are developed by the volunteer resources department in response to requests from staff and administrators on particular hospital units. I received short program descriptions from all four hospitals, and for all direct service, indirect service, and revenue-generating positions. Since my primary focus was to understand the role of volunteers in patient care, I only requested the more detailed VAGs for those programs categorized as 'direct service programs.' I was able to receive these from Hospitals A, C, and D. I have done a simple content analysis of both types of descriptions to understand how these hospitals formally define the volunteer roles. These descriptions have been reviewed for references to 'support,' for descriptions of instrumental and affective tasks, and for terms that describe volunteers' relationship to staff and to patients and family members.

Finally, I interviewed sixteen female and eight male volunteers. The selection criteria used for informants was being any volunteer in a direct service role – that is, anyone who had routine contact with patients or family members. Seven informants worked in the emergency room, six in specific adult hospital units such as geriatric units, five were infant cuddlers, three were general visitors covering a range of hospital units, and three more were assigned to positions that allowed them to move throughout the hospital but required only brief contact with patients or family members, such as volunteers who delivered items like water or books to bedsides. Participants were solicited by posters in the volunteer resources departments in each of the hospitals. Informants contacted me directly; the volunteer resources departments were not involved in their selection or informed of their participation. Interviews were taped and lasted from 60 to 90 minutes. Volunteers were asked to describe the tasks they did, their interactions with patients and their families especially around emotional support, and what they felt to be the most important part of their work. They were also asked to describe how they interacted with staff, and whether they felt their work complemented or differed from paid workers. Finally, I asked about their training and orientation, and if it prepared them for the tasks they undertook.

Volunteering as Gendered Work

In hospitals A and B, female volunteers appeared to predominate. In Hospital B, 79.1% of direct service volunteers were women. In comparison, women made up 75.4% of all volunteers in that hospital, and more specifically, 82.1% of the indirect service volunteers, and 63% of the revenue-generating volunteers. The high proportion of women in indirect service positions may be explained by the way many of these positions mirror paid jobs typically held by women; for example, many indirect service positions were related to clerical work, librarianship, and presentations to schoolchildren visiting the hospital. The lower proportion of women in revenue-generating positions may reflect cultural norms that link men, masculinity, and financial matters and, in contrast, link women with caregiving.

Hospital A only supplied detailed data for volunteers in direct service positions. Within direct service positions, women made up 68.6% of the volunteers. The overall proportion of male and female volunteers across this hospital is unknown, as is the proportion in indirect and revenue-generating categories. Informally, the volunteer coordinator estimated that women would be in the majority for all volunteers as well. So while women were in a majority in the direct service category in Hospital A, they were not as overrepresented here as in Hospital B. I could find no reason why the proportion of women in direct service positions should vary so greatly between the two hospitals. In examining the types of direct service positions filled by women and men, one common pattern emerges in both institutions. Men are disproportionately located in emergency departments, making up roughly 40% of the emergency room volunteers in both hospitals. In comparison, men constitute only 17% of the volunteers in all other direct service positions in Hospital B and 12% in Hospital A. (Although statistics on gender are not available for Hospital D, the volunteer coordinator suggested that a similar pattern was also true there.) Why might this be? I asked one coordinator if men were specifically recruited to fill these positions in the emergency department. I was told that they were not; rather the men themselves requested this placement. The coordinator suggested that many men liked the fast-paced nature of this position. She also pointed out that approximately half of these male volunteers were either medical students or training to be paramedics, and this volunteer placement was a way of gaining career-related experience. However, this latter explanation does not account for why women who enter medical school in increasing numbers would not also choose this volunteer option, and offset the proportion of men. Other possible explanations might be considered. The distribution of male volunteers parallels a similar pattern for male nurses. Edgeland and Brown (1989: 695) have documented the overrepresentation of male nurses in emergency units and suggest the 'heroic nature' of this type of nursing has a strongly masculine appeal. This heroic 'flavour' may also reframe the caregiving that men are called upon to do as emergency room volunteers. An additional explanation lies in an observation by Margolis (1979) about how volunteering in political parties is gendered; she found that men were more likely to be involved in highly visible public roles and women in behind-the-scenes work. Since volunteering in emergency is highly visible to the public it may have greater appeal to men than work in other units.

The high proportion of women among direct service volunteers in hospitals A (79.1%) and B (68.6%) suggests that here, as in the domestic sphere and in paid work, women are most likely to be the ones performing intimate labour. Note, as well, the overrepresentation of women in this type of volunteering compared with the proportion (51%) of all volunteers in Canada who are women (Statistics Canada 2006: 34). This reflects the patterns of gender segregation among volunteers identified by other authors, for example, Baldock (1998) or Rotolo and Wharton (2003).

How Hospitals Construct Volunteer Work

A review of the two types of volunteer job descriptions, described above, leads to several observations about how the hospitals define the direct service work performed by volunteers. First, the work of volunteers is formally positioned in the hospital's division of labour and constructed as contributing to the institution's goals. Second, the majority of descriptions include instrumental and emotional components of care. Third, many direct service positions also entail work associated with the bureaucratic processing of patients in addition to care work.

Program descriptions and volunteer assignment guides define the role of volunteers in the hospital's division of labour. Most of the shorter program descriptions state that volunteers 'assist' staff or 'complement and enhance quality care' and all VAGs identify the volunteer as a 'member of the hospital health care team' (Hospital A) or state that 'volunteers extend and enhance the work of the hospital's paid personnel in meeting the hospital's goals' for patients and their families (Hospital C). VAGs also list the staff person or department to which each volunteer is accountable. At some level, all volunteers are responsible to the volunteer resources coordinator, but some volunteers also are responsible to unit managers, nurses, recreational or occupational therapists, physiotherapists, or pharmacy technicians. Different hospitals vary as to whether they list the volunteer coordinators or unit-specific personnel first. Whatever the order of accountability, volunteers are explicitly embedded in a hospital's organization. Voluntary caregiving may be unpaid work, but, on paper at least, it does not mean that it is outside the lines of supervision.

Many descriptions of direct service positions for volunteers include instrumental and affective tasks, though there is variation in what these may include. In the sixty-three direct service programs across all four hospitals, forty-two of the short program descriptions state that volunteers should support patients or families, though the form of support is not always clearly specified. However, forty-three of the longer volunteer assignment guides are more explicit in describing instrumental and emotional dimensions of care. For example, a palliative care volunteer is to 'provide support and assistance to patients and their families by: offering companionship to patients ... [and] performing helpful tasks at the request of the patient, family or staff member (e.g., water flowers, refill water jugs, walk outdoors with able patient, run errands ... tidy rooms, take around coffee/juice' (VAG: Palliative Care Volunteer, Hospital D). A volunteer in a children's unit is to provide 'physical care such as feeding, bathing, and toileting under the direction of nursing staff ... [and] emotional support and comfort through such activities as cuddling, talking, spending quiet time (VAG: Unit Volunteer, Hospital C).

In outpatient clinics, volunteers 'welcome patients' ... [and] provide companionship for patients waiting for porters and drivers ... [as well as] provide cookies and juice for diabetic patients' (VAG: Ophthamology Clinic Friend, Hospital A). A rehabilitation unit volunteer is to 'lead patient in exercises once patient is taught by physiotherapist' while he or she provides 'encouragement' to exercising patients (VAG: Pulmonary Rehabilitation Exercise Program, Hospital A).

In contrast, nearly one-third of the direct service roles do not stress this combination of instrumental and emotional tasks. For example, a 'Patient Escort' volunteer travels with inpatients to offsite appointments; the tasks listed in this VAG do not identify any emotional component as part of this assignment (VAG: Patient Escort, Hospital A). The VAGs also highlight another set of tasks expected of many direct service volunteers which I will call the 'bureaucratic processing' of individuals. These activities ensure the smooth functioning of the organization as much as they are designed to provide care for patients. For example, volunteers in outpatient clinics lead patients to examination rooms, help them complete forms, tell them whether they need to disrobe, and ensure the patient's chart is available for the doctor or technician. In a children's clinic, volunteers receive the hospital's blue identification card, deliver it to the right location, and help to 'maintain "peace" in the waiting room' by providing 'orientation, cookies, surveying the area, general assistance' (VAG: Parent Services Volunteer, Hospital C). Emergency room volunteers serve as liaisons between those in the waiting room and triage nurses; they answer questions about where individuals are in the triage line-up and encourage people to be patient. These tasks serve to minimize interruptions and decrease pressure on nurses as much as they 'provide enhancement services' and support for the incoming public (VAG: Emergency Medicine, Hospital A).

Grant and Tancred have applied the label 'adjunct control positions' (1992) to many of women's paid jobs; in these front-line jobs, workers manage emotional and behavioural responses in clientele, in order to cushion professionals and bureaucrats from undesired behaviour. These workers extend the control of organizations over their clientele but are not directly given organizational power in their own right. Many volunteer positions can also be defined in these terms inasmuch as they prepare patients or family members for their encounter with medical staff and minimize undesired behaviour. Here, instrumental and affective tasks are combined but primarily for the benefit of the organization rather than the client. This observation speaks to an issue raised briefly by Abel and Nelson – that is, 'to what extent are services provided by volunteers tinged with elements of social control' (1990: 22). It seems that volunteers face the dual expectation of performing control work as well as care work: the *intimate labour they provide may achieve either control or care*. The question remains as to whether these two expectations potentially create contradictions for volunteers.

How Do Volunteers Accomplish the Work of Care?

Although hospitals lay out certain expectations for volunteer work, it is quite another thing to ask how volunteers actually accomplish the work of care. In the following sections, I consider how volunteers describe their work when interviewed, including the interplay between apparent constraints and alternate opportunities for providing care. Central to these descriptions are the differing degrees of discretion that volunteers have in regards to carrying out instrumental and affective care, and how volunteers work within institutional limits on the personal knowledge they may have of patients and the amount of time they can spend with patients.

Despite the stated lines of accountability in the volunteer assignment guides, only some informants said they 'reported in' to paid workers at the beginning of their shift. Respondents from neonatal units checked with the nurses upon their arrival, and those who worked with occupational therapists typically began by discussing the scheduled tasks for that day. Emergency room volunteers often responded to requests from nurses to run errands or settle patients into examination rooms throughout their shifts. Many volunteers, however, carried out their routines fairly independently; prior experience helped them decide what should be done. Such was the case with a unit visitor who looked for patients who seemed lonely. Much of the emotional caregiving seems left up to the volunteer's own discretion in terms of how it is accomplished, even though it is a stated expectation in the VAGs. For example, the VAG for emergency room volunteers states they should check on incoming patients and family members during long waits but both male and female respondents stated that they could decide how often to do this or how much attention to give to this task. In this sense, it seems that volunteers maximize the autonomy they may exercise in regards to providing emotional care thereby carving out greater dignity for themselves as workers than one might expect given their formally stated position in the division of labour. In contrast, most aspects of physical care offered by volunteers must be cleared with nurses, such as whether a patient can have water or can have their bed raised.

When volunteers described their training, they also seemed to suggest that hospitals took a greater interest in organizing instrumental rather than emotional care. General training by volunteer coordinators focused largely on protocols related to patient confidentiality, personal hygiene, and general rules about asking nurses or other staff what physical care could be provided for a patient. Unit-specific training usually consisted of a single shift where a volunteer shadowed the person they were replacing. Only minimal attention was given to preparation for emotional care. Volunteers – especially men – talked about how they gradually learned, on their own, 'to read' patients and family members' emotional cues and respond appropriately.

Personal Knowledge and the Care Work of Volunteers

Discussions of care work and of intimate labour emphasize how personal knowledge facilitates the act of caring (Browne 2003b; Zelizer

2005). For example, Campbell states that nurses 'recognize that their professional responsibility extends to knowing the patient holistically' (2000: 200). Many volunteer positions entail care work but hospitals also place strict limits on the amount of knowledge that volunteers are allowed to have about patients. This potentially creates a contradiction for volunteers: how can they manage to support patients if they are forbidden to know who they are supporting? This section considers how volunteers respond to this tension in the organization of their work. It also asks whether it is appropriate to consider the work of volunteers to be 'intimate labour' in the face of these formal constraints on their working knowledge.

Volunteers described the formal restrictions the hospital placed on what they might know about patients or their illnesses. The importance of patient confidentiality and how this constrained volunteers from asking about a patient's condition figured largely in informants' descriptions of orientation sessions for volunteers. Volunteers in emergency departments and outpatient clinics routinely transported medical charts but were not supposed to read them. Some respondents also stated that they were trained to avoid asking 'how are you' when entering a room in order to avoid upsetting patients. Decisions about physical care were always based on instructions received from nurses rather than on a volunteer's own knowledge and judgment. A few volunteers said that nurses or therapists occasionally revealed some details to help them better care for the patients, such as the fact that a particular patient was depressed or in a lot of pain. However, this depended on the working relationship of particular nurses and volunteers and was not a routine occurrence.

Despite these formal limits, volunteers described how they developed a different sort of knowledge about patients, which facilitated their ability to offer care. Within the context of carrying out other tasks, volunteers listened to patients reveal information about their physical condition, concerns about family members, or anxieties related to setting aside demands of the outside world during their hospital stay. One volunteer described visiting a patient who revealed he had just received word that his condition was terminal, and stated that she seemed to help the patient come to terms with that news 'just by listening.' A visitor to a neurological ward described playing cards with patients and trying to figure out 'what the patients' rules were' in order to judge their neurological health and guide future interactions. An emergency department volunteer told of an incoming patient with a minor injury who grew increasingly anxious during the long emergency room wait. In conversation, the volunteer discovered that this patient was considering leaving the emergency room without treatment because she had an important meeting scheduled and no one knew her whereabouts. The volunteer helped the patient phone her acquaintances, thereby decreasing her anxiety and convinced her to stay in the triage line-up. Volunteers working with long-term patients stated that an essential part of their work was to elicit and listen to accounts of people's lives beyond the hospital. By focusing on personal details, volunteers raised the spirits of a patient, making him or her feel like a whole person again rather than just the 'spinal cord injury in bed 28.' In this sense volunteers see themselves as providing a significant form of emotional care.

The kind of information to which volunteers gain access shares two significant features. First, it is the information that patients themselves decide to reveal rather than that which is requested by medical staff or contained in a standardized medical record. Since the patient self-defines this information, it helps to equalize the relationship between the cared for and the volunteer caregiver. Second, this information is more holistic and wide ranging than that which is prioritized in the medical chart. It allows volunteers to directly engage the patient as a person, rather than as a particular type of medical case. In doing so, volunteers do achieve a level of intimacy with and knowledge about a patient, even briefly, that allows us to consider their work to be intimate labour. Although volunteers tell many stories of how they respond to personal details revealed by patients, when asked if they convey this information back to the nurses, they offer very few instances of doing so. What is routinely conveyed to the nurses are requests for a bed pan, painkillers, or questions of a medical nature that volunteers are unable to answer. It is ironic that, while volunteers deal with a hospitalized individuals who self-define through the breadth of information they may reveal, the information that volunteers convey back to the nurses appears to be reduced to that which continues to focus on the individual as a patient requiring specific forms of care. Despite volunteers' recognition of the value of the alternative knowledge base that they develop about some patients, this knowledge and care work goes unrecognized within the hospital system.

Time to Care

Care work takes time and confounds rigid scheduling. James (1989) shows how this is so in family caregiving and in emotional labour in hospices. In a discussion of paid home care, Browne states that 'the essential gift a caregiver can provide is time, time to look after physical needs, to talk, especially to listen – time to build a relationship' (2003a: 188). In her discussion of intimate labour, Zelizer (2007) suggests that caring relationships are built on 'sustained and/or intense personal attention'; sustained attention implies that the length of the relationship matters although Zelizer's statement also suggests that there may a quality of interaction (its intensity) that is not simply about the amount of time available. Critiques of the health care system point to the way the pace of work has increased in recent years, undercutting the ability of paid staff to sustain or focus their attention on individual patients. Some authors have criticized the usefulness of volunteers within this system because of the limited shifts that they work and because they may be unreliable about their time commitments (Armstrong & Armstrong 1994: 47; Zweigenhaft, Armstrong, & Quintis 1996: 26).

The issue of time in relation to the performance of volunteer care work surfaces in various ways in the interviews. Volunteers typically work once a week for three to four hours, although this varies across units. Some volunteers make a habit of arriving early to be more helpful and stay late if the need arises. In addition to the length of the shift, the type of position affects the amount of time volunteers spend with patients. Only brief encounters with patients are likely for volunteers who work in outpatient clinics or as greeters at hospital entrances. Other positions, such as volunteer visitors in particular units, allow for more involved interactions. However, unless a volunteer is in a long-term care unit, a once-a-week shift usually means contact with a patient only once during a hospital stay because of rapid patient turnover. The rapid discharge of patients is one of the features of health care restructuring that spills over to affect volunteers as well as paid staff. It limits the ability of volunteers to develop rapport with a patient, which in turn limits their ability to support the patient effectively. Although most respondents seemed satisfied with the number of hours a week in their shift, three stated they would like more frequent shifts in order to be of more help to the patients.

Although the limited hours in a volunteer's shift may appear to constrain caregiving, most volunteers recognized that they provide a form of care that would otherwise be missing in the current system. Male and female volunteers felt the importance of their contribution lay in doing tasks that nurses did not have time to do, such as listening to patients tell stories of their lives, cuddling a child, or patiently helping stroke victims regain their ability to feed themselves. Informants pointed out that they were not as 'rushed' as the nurses. When asked what the most important thing was that he did, one male volunteer stated, 'I waste time on the patients.' A female emergency room volunteer explained, 'We're the only ones that patients see who don't have an agenda'; she said that this let patients relax in a different way with volunteers than with paid staff. Within any one shift, many volunteers have a certain amount of freedom in terms of how they allocate their time; they can spend as much time with a patient as the patient seems to need – a luxury that is not available to paid staff. This flexibility offsets the limited opportunity for repeat contacts with patients. Thus, even brief encounters with patients could present a significant opportunity to offer care to people at a vulnerable point in their lives. The intimate labour that these volunteers provide is not so much about sustained interaction as it is about focused attention, often in a short time frame.

Summary and Conclusions

The hospitals in this study include instrumental and affective care in their definition of many volunteer roles – and rely on a disproportionately female volunteer corps to do these tasks. Benoit and Hallgrímsdóttir (this volume) make the point that gender shapes the organization of health care in fundamental ways; including direct service volunteers in the division of labour within hospitals makes this all the more apparent. The gender composition of this group may be one reason why hospitals spend little time training volunteers in emotional caregiving despite the inclusion of this responsibility in many volunteer 'job descriptions.' Hospitals may assume that, because most volunteers are female, volunteers 'naturally' bring emotional expertise to bear on their work in the hospital. Thus, men who volunteer step into positions that are constructed in feminized terms; this means male (and female) volunteers are left to learn to read the emotional needs of patients as best they can. I also have pointed out how volunteering in emergency departments might be a better fit for men because of their more public and 'heroic' nature.

At the same time, there are limits in the extent to which hospitals organize volunteer work on a feminized model; women's work in families incorporates instrumental and affective tasks, but decisions about instrumental care are not left to the discretion of volunteers. This is understandable given the need to ensure safe and skilled physical care for patients. Nevertheless, differential attention to instrumental over affective tasks sheds light on how affective care gets lost in the hospital system despite its inclusion in the description of many volunteer positions. To some extent, volunteers collude in this erasure. Individually, volunteers may recognize the multidimensional aspects of care, but neither women nor men seem able to challenge the system by reinserting the affective dimension or their broader view of patients back into their communication with paid workers such as nurses. On paper, the stated content of many direct service positions seem to reflect a holistic approach to care work, but in practice, there seems to be little institutional support to help volunteers actualize this approach. One might consider how the assignment of such care to unpaid workers undercuts the struggles of paid workers to improve the remuneration they receive for caring. Many volunteers talked about declining conditions for paid workers, especially the time pressures that make it increasingly difficult for staff to provide care for patients. Some volunteers described how their positions might be seen as problematic from the perspective of unionized workers, but more often volunteers talked about themselves as a necessary stop-gap measure to off-set these worsening conditions. Moving beyond volunteers' own accounts, one could argue that the use of volunteers helps to justify the notion that care should be linked to altruism. If the care offered by volunteers can be untrained and unpaid – it makes it easier to see care as requiring little skill and little monetary value.

Instinct and altruism are qualities that often frame social conceptions of women's care work (see Benoit & Hallgrímsdóttir, this volume). These characteristics also seem to be intertwined in notions of how volunteers will perform. On the other hand, coordinators linked some men's motivation to volunteer to what these men would gain in terms of human capital: the experience of volunteering in an emergency unit could contribute to a future career. Coordinators did not talk about women's motivation in the same way. This raises the question of whether the care provided by male volunteers might be seen as somewhat less altruistic than that of their female peers.

I have suggested that the hospitals in this study may use various aspects of the work of direct service volunteers to enhance the institutional control and bureaucratic processing of patients. Though the control work performed by hospital volunteers is unpaid, it still serves an economic purpose if it eases the time or effort required for other paid workers to do their jobs. Adjunct control work (Grant & Tancred 1992), like care work, has typically been gendered work. In both instances, emotional and instrumental labour may be tied together. The mixing of control and care arises when care work is moved out of intimate settings and into large-scale organizations. It is interesting that volunteers in this study did not describe much conflict in doing both types of work. Their accounts suggest that the tensions and constraints they face are not as severely felt as may be the case for paid workers in hospitals, such as those described by Armstrong and Armstrong (2003) or White (2003). The experience of these volunteers underscores Zelizer's observation (2005, 2007) that researchers need to more closely examine how people manage the intersection of caregiving and intimacy with economic activity and contexts, including paying attention to variations in how intimate labour is performed.

The term 'intimate labour' (Zelizer 2007) highlights the way in which efficacious care work rests on the caregiver's access to in-depth knowledge about the person being cared for, and time to develop trust and adapt care to individualized needs. Both knowledge and time are more likely to be tightly controlled when intimate labour becomes paid and bureaucratically organized. Even as unpaid workers, volunteers in this study face bureaucratic restrictions on what they can do and know, and on the amount of available time to spend with patients in a weekly shift. Ironically, the interaction of these constraints with other features of their work open up alternate opportunities for providing care. Restrictions on the physical care offered by volunteers means that they have more time to spend listening, even though they work short shifts. Since volunteers are unpaid and not formally skilled workers, it may not be worthwhile for a hospital to closely account for their work. Fewer instrumental tasks, along with the under-specification of how emotional care is to be performed, frees volunteers to engage in informal conversations and develop a unique understanding of patients with whom they work. 'Not having an agenda' and being 'able to waste time on the patients' means their limited time is used in a more carefull way. In short, volunteers find ways of exercising autonomy and retaining dignity in their work (Hodson 2001), despite the constaints they face.

Hospitals define volunteer roles through written descriptions of expected tasks, lines of accountability, the length of volunteer shifts, and restrictions on access to knowledge and decision making about instrumental tasks. These organizational specifications mean that volunteers' care work is not entirely voluntary in regards to how or when it is performed. In some cases, these specifications create contradictions that volunteers must resolve, such as between the expectation to provide support to patients and limits on the length of shifts and the knowledge about patients to which they have access. But formal descriptions and protocols only partially help us understand how volunteers provide intimate labour and the relationship of their work to other forms of paid labour. Volunteers' own descriptions suggest ways in which they sometimes transcend these contradictions and constraints to find other opportunities for caregiving. In doing so, volunteers are able to create a more intimate connection with hospitalized individuals and their families than one might expect given the hospital's bureaucratic regime.

REFERENCES

Abel, E.K., & M. Nelson. (1990).Circles of care: An introductory essay. In E.K. Abel & M. Nelson, eds., *Circles of Care: Work and Identity in Women's Lives,* 4–34. Albany: State University of New York Press.

Abrahams, N. (1996). Negotiating power, identity, family, and community: Women's community participation. *Gender & Society* 10(6): 768–96.

Armstrong, P., & H. Armstrong. (1994). Health care as a business: The legacy of free trade. In P. Armstrong, J. Choiniere, G. Feldberg, & J. White, eds., *Take Care: Warning Signs for Canada's Health System,* 31–51. Toronto: Garamond Press.

Armstrong, P., & H. Armstrong. (2003). *Wasting Away: The Undermining of Canadian Health Care,* 2nd ed. Toronto: Oxford University Press.

Armstrong, P., H. Armstrong, & D. Coburn. (Eds.). (2001). *Unhealthy Times: Political Economy Perspectives on Health and Health Care in Canada.* Don Mills: Oxford University Press.

Badgett, M.V., & N. Folbre. (2001). Assigning care: Gender norms and economic outcomes. In M.F.Loutfi, ed., *Women, Gender and Work,* 327–45. Geneva: International Labour Organization.

Baines, D. (2004). Caring for nothing: Work organization and unwaged labour in social services. *Work, Employment and Society* 18(1): 29–49.

Baldock, C. (1998). Feminist discourses of unwaged work: The case of volunteerism. *Australian Feminist Studies* 13: 19–34.

Blair-Loy, M., & J. Jacobs. (2003). Globalization, work hours, and the care deficit among stockbrokers. *Gender & Society* 17(7): 230–49.

Brannon, R. (1994). Professionalization and work intensification: Nursing in the cost containment era. *Work and Occupations* 21(2): 157–78.

Browne, P.L. (2003a). Care power and commodification. In P.L. Browne, ed., *The Commodity of Care: Home Care Reform in Ontario*, 171–212. Ottawa: Canadian Centre for Policy Administration.

Browne, P.L. (2003b). The social division of care in a world of commodities. In P.L. Browne, ed., *The Commodity of Care: Home Care Reform in Ontario*, 1–22. Ottawa: Canadian Centre for Policy Administration.

Campbell, M. (2000). Knowledge, gendered subjectivity, and the restructuring of health care: The case of the disappearing nurse. In S. Neysmieth, ed., *Restructuring Caring Labour: Discourse, State Practice, and Everyday Life*, 186–208. Don Mills: Oxford University Pless.

Edgeland, J., & J. Brown. (1989). Men in nursing: Their fields of employment, preferred fields of practice, and role strain. *Health Services Research* 24(5): 693–707.

Einarson, E. 1990. Experts and caregivers: Perspectives on underground day care. In E.K. Abel & M. Nelson, eds., *Circles of Care: Work and Identity in Women's Lives*, 233–45. Albany: State University of New York Press.

Fisher, B. (1990). Alice in the human services: A Feminist analysis of women in the caring professions. In E.K. Abel & M. Nelson, eds., *Circles of Care: Work and Identity in Women's Lives*, 108–31. Albany: State University of New York Press.

Graham, H. (1983). Caring: A labour of love. In J. Finch & D. Groves, *A Labour of Love*, 13–30. London: Routledge and Kegan Paul.

Grant, J., & P. Tancred. (1992). A Feminist perspective on state bureaucracy. In A.J. Mills & P. Tancred, eds., *Gendering Organizational Analysis*, 112–28. Newbury Park: Sage.

Hochschild, A.R. (1983). *The Managed Heart.* Berkeley: University of California Press.

Hodson, R. (2001). *Dignity at Work.* New York: Cambridge University Press.

James, N. (1989). Skill and work in the emotional regulation of feeling. *Sociological Review* 37(1): 15–42.

Jones, L. (1998). Changing health care. In A. Brechin, J. Walmsley, J. Katz, & S. Peace, eds., *Care Matters: Concepts, Practice and Research in Health and Social Care*, 154–69. London: Sage.

Lan, P. (2003). Maid or madam? *Gender & Society* 17(7): 187–208.

Margolis, D. (1979). The invisible hands: Sex roles and the division of labor in two political parties. *Social Problems* 26(3): 314–24.

Millar McPherson, J., & L. Smith-Lovin. (1986). Sex segregation in voluntary organizations. *American Sociological Review* 51: 61–79.

Nelson, M. (1990). Mothering others' children: The experiences of daycare providers. In E.K. Abel & M. Nelson, eds., *Circles of Care: Work and Identity in Women's Lives*, 210–32. Albany: State University of New York Press.

Neysmith, S. (Ed.). (2000). *Restructuring Caring Labour: Discourse, State Practice, and Everyday Life*. Don Mills: Oxford University Press.

Popielarz, P. (1999). (In)voluntary association: A multilevel analysis of gender segregation in voluntary organizations. *Gender & Society* 12(2): 234–50.

Prentice, S., & E. Ferguson. (2000). Volunteerism, gender and the changing welfare state. In S. Neysmith, ed., *Restructuring Caring Labour: Discourse, State Practice, and Everyday Life*, 118–41. Don Mills: Oxford University Press.

Reitsma-Street, M., & S. Neysmith. (2000). Restructuring and community work: The case of community resource centres for families in poor urban neighbourhoods. In S. Neysmith, ed., *Restructuring Caring Labour: Discourse, State Practice, and Everyday Life*, 142–63. Don Mills: Oxford University Press.

Reverby, S. (1990). The duty or right to care? Nursing and womanhood in historical perspective. In E.K. Abel & M. Nelson, eds., *Circles of Care: Work and Identity in Women's Lives*, 132–49. Albany: State University of New York Press.

Rotolo, T., & A. Wharton. (2003). Living across institutions: Exploring sex-based homophily in occupations and voluntary groups. *Sociological Perspectives* 46(1): 59–82.

Salvage, J. (2001). Should we be recruiting volunteers to work in hospitals? No. *Nursing Times* 97(7): 25.

Statistics Canada. (2006). *Caring Canadians, Involved Canadians: Highlights from the 2004 Canada Survey of Giving, Volunteering, and Participating*. Ottawa: Minister of Industry.

White, J. (2003). Changing labour process and the nursing crisis in Canadian hospitals. In C. Andrew, P. Armstrong, H. Armstrong, W. Clement, & L.F. Vesca, eds., *Studies in Political Economy: Developments in Feminism*, 125–54. Toronto: Women's Press.

Zelizer, V.A. (2005). *The Purchase of Intimacy*. Princeton: Princeton University Press.

Zelizer, V.A. (2007). Caring everywhere. Keynote Address, Conference on Intimate Labours, University of California, Santa Barbara, 4–6 Oct.

Zweigenhaft, R., J. Armstrong, & F. Quintis. (1996). The motivations and effectiveness of hospital volunteers. *Journal of Social Psychology* 136(1): 25–35.

12 Volunteering on the Front Line: Caring for Sex Workers in Non-profit Organizations

RACHEL PHILLIPS, LAUREN CASEY, AND
CHRIS LEISCHNER

As the chapters in this volume demonstrate, intimate care is often received by populations who are vulnerable to a greater or lesser extent – children, the elderly, the infirm, and new mothers (Benoit & Hallgrímsdóttir, this volume). For some populations, intimate care needs arise from, and are intensified by, social stigmatization. Intimate care work in the context of persons with disabilities, addiction to illicit substances, mental health conditions, blood-borne and incurable infections, or for persons involved in income assistance and child welfare programs all takes place in the context of social stigma.

Goffman (1963: 3) defined *stigma* as an 'attribute that is deeply discrediting,' which reduces the bearer 'from a whole and usual person to a tainted, discounted one.' Stigma radically changes an individual's self-concept and tarnishes her or his identity, resulting in degrees of social exclusion that span from difficulty engaging in normal social interaction because of secrecy or shame, to being more completely socially ostracized and isolated (Link & Phelan 2001).

Goffman (1963: 30) further argued that stigma not only affects the individual bearing the stigma, but also, by courtesy, those who are in close relationship to the stigmatized individual or population: 'the problems faced by stigmatized persons spread out in waves of diminishing intensity among those they come in contact with.' The concept of *courtesy stigma* thus highlights how those closely associated with stigmatized groups also face systematic marginalization, and potentially, poorer health.

Courtesy stigma in the context of intimate care work is significant for a number of key theoretical and practical reasons. First, because of the interlocking nature of various axes of social and economic discrimination, persons representing stigmatized identities present intensified service needs, and experience more complex barriers to social participation, social support, and acquiring necessary resources such as housing and employment. Second, the structural and cultural marginalization of persons with stigmatized identities means not only that the demand placed on care providers is greater, and the solutions less obvious, but care providers themselves may experience less social and economic support for their care work, particularly when the population receiving care is a highly denigrated one. Care providers thus experience courtesy stigma, such that they – albeit to a lesser degree than those they serve – also experience downward social mobility, or find themselves blocked from social resources that may be available to workers serving other populations. This has many implications for both the occupational health and service practice of care providers in this context. The gendered underpinnings of the intersection of care work and stigmatization are significant as women are uniquely, and often disproportionately, burdened by the confluence of various sources of marginalization in stigmatized care contexts (Benoit & Hallgrímsdóttir, this volume). The non-profit service organization explored in this chapter provides a rich example of this as both the care providers and care recipients in this context are almost exclusively female. The stigma they face – the prostitute stigma – is one that has been historically focused on females (Hallgrímsdóttir et al. 2008).

Despite the challenges associated with social stigmas, care providers serving stigmatized populations also derive many rewards from their work; perhaps foremost, they see themselves as responding to a blatant and tangible need for support and social justice among those they serve. Further, despite stigma, such care providers also experience social support for their work from the broader mainstream community. In fact, they may even achieve an elevated status due to the perception that they are especially good-willed because they work with populations that others often fear, regard as dirty, or as hopeless. However, there are conditions attached to this valorization which emanate directly from the discursive boundaries of the stigmas associated with the client group. Specifically, social support for their care work pivots on their enactment of dominant narratives regarding how the stigmatized group ought to be managed or fixed.

This chapter takes a closer look at stigma and care work, drawing on the example of voluntary and paid care providers to persons involved in the sex industry. The organization examined – the Prostitutes

Empowerment Education and Resource Society (PEERS) – is particularly interesting as many of the paid and volunteer workers associated with this organization were formerly involved in the sex industry and therefore occupy multiple positions in relation to the stigmas that surround their work.[1] Care work to persons involved in the sex industry casts a unique light on the devaluation thesis of intimate labour – the idea that providing intimate care is a natural and moral female activity as opposed to a professional skill set motivated by financial rewards – as the moral overtones normally associated with intimate care are intensified by stigmas which may suggest that the population being served is deviant in some way or another (Benoit & Hallgrímsdóttir, this volume). Care providers working with persons in the sex industry are charged with the task of managing or correcting perceived abnormalities or deviance, so that members of the broader community do not have to be burdened by the varying offences and fears associated with the *prostitute* stigma. In this context, the rules and policies that govern the provision of intimate care are not only gendered, but are also marked by social control and resistance as it applies to deviant female sexuality and other deviant female identities (addict, single parent, etc.).

Stigma and Occupational Health among Care Providers

Stigma can be organized into three main forms: tribal stigmas, based on race or other identity categories; behavioural stigmas, based on deviant conduct; and bodily stigmas, conceptualized as observable disfigurement, disability, and other stigmatized health conditions (HIV/AIDS, mental illness) (Goffman 1963). Contemporary stigma theorists Link and Phelan (2001) conceptualize stigma as the co-occurrence of labelling, stereotyping, separating, status loss, and discrimination. Stigmas

---

1 The Prostitutes Empowerment Education and Resources Society was renamed PEERS Victoria Resources Society in 2009. This change reflected an ongoing tension between the original social change goal to reclaim and redefine the denigrated prostitute identity and the ongoing service goal to provide a safe environment to women who accessed the service. Over the years several clients expressed that they did not feel comfortable with the word prostitute on documents issued by the organization (such as support cheques and training certificates), and some had experienced discrimination or other harms because of their association with the organization. It was also felt that removing the word prostitute from the name of the organization might broaden funding opportunities for funds targeted for marginalized women more generally.

are standardized systems of belief that are constructed and disseminated through discourse, but when these scripts are enacted in everyday interaction, they take on a material presence in the lives of stigmatized persons; discriminatory beliefs are inevitably accompanied by discriminatory actions that result in limited access to social resources, including employment, education, earnings, housing, and health care (Link & Phelan 2001; Hallgrímsdóttir et al. 2006, 2008).

The historical origins and life course of various stigmas are complex and contextual, but generally – especially in the case of behavioural stigmas – involve a perceived threat to dominant ideas regarding the basis for social order. Studies examining the history of stigmas are infrequent in the stigma literature, which has tended to focus on the social psychology of stigma-based social interaction (i.e., examining avoidance, secrecy, and prejudicial behaviour between stigmatized and non-stigmatized individuals). Studying the historical and cultural origins of stigmas is of equal importance because it reveals how we must be critical of social welfare interventions for stigmatized populations, as they often reflect more about the fears, values, and politics of dominant subgroups than about the empirical reality of the stigmatized (Hallgrímsdóttir et al. 2006, 2008).

Scambler and Hopkins (1986) proposed that experiences of stigma could be subdivided into *felt stigma* (located in the perceptions of the stigmatized) and *enacted stigma* (observable instances of discrimination or discomfort by non-stigmatized individuals). Although acts of discrimination *(enacted stigma)* can be profoundly damaging to health, even in their absence, felt stigma plays a powerful role in reducing self-confidence, inhibiting social interaction, and reducing access to health resources as individuals engage in various forms of secrecy, covering, instrumental disclosure, and avoidance in order to limit their exposure to discrimination (Donkor et al. 2007; Gray 2002; Scambler & Hopkins 1986; McRae 2000).

Of equal importance to the stigma literature is the finding that stigmas are not necessarily experienced as profoundly or uniformly negative. A growing body of literature expands upon how stigmas have varying levels of influence, or a continuum of effects, on targeted individuals and groups. According to this perspective, stigma is experienced in varying, context-specific degrees, and negative labels are not necessarily internalized. Thus, more than simply *managing* or *reacting* to stigma, those bearing a stigma exercise both personal and collective agency in the context of negative labels, including, but by no means limited to, resisting negative stereotypes with counter-interpretations of their experience and derision of mainstream views (Camp et al. 2002; Kusow 2004; Reissman 2000; Shulze & Angermeyer 2003). Similarly, some scholars have drawn attention to the role of sociostructural variables – income, education, class – as mediators in the interpersonal and collective negotiation of stigma meanings (Link & Phelan 2001; McCormack 2004; Reissman 2000; Scambler 2004). This research asks basic questions such as why do some individuals experience more stigma-related harms than others, and why are some groups able to redefine and neutralize stigmas over time through collective action, whereas other negative stigmas seem more durable (Hallgrímsdóttir et al. 2008)? The available literature suggests that access to social resources buffers the impact of stigmas and facilitates resistance, whereas the coexistence of other forms of marginalization reinforces stigmas and limits the formation and impact of resistant ideas (Camp et al. 2002; Crocker & Quinn 2000; Kusow 2004; Link & Phelan 2001; McCormack 2004; Reissman 2000; Scambler 2004). Thus, stigmatized groups who collectively have greater access to education and economic resources (i.e., families with disabled children) are more likely to be able to intervene in negative stigmas than groups (i.e., women working in the sex industry) who collectively represent limited economic resources and education as well as powerful gender-based stigmas.

A smaller body of literature on the concept of courtesy stigma identifies many of the same core ideas as the literature on stigma. Courtesy stigma – also called *stigma by association* – refers to how persons in close association with stigmatized individuals are also subject to prejudice, stereotypes, and discrimination. In short, courtesy stigma in the context of care work refers to the devaluation of those who provide services to stigmatized groups, especially groups who offend social norms and values.

The courtesy stigma literature largely focuses on family members of stigmatized groups, noting, for example, how parents of children with disabilities feel blamed and ostracized because of their child's behaviour or support needs (Birenbaum 1970). Recent research indicates that parents of children with disabilities have been found to be at greater risk for depression and to attribute negative attitudes to other parents and service providers, even when there are no observable instances of discrimination (Norvilitis et al. 2002). Other research suggests that family members of stigmatized individuals curtail their own social interactions in order to avoid instances of enacted discrimination or the difficulty associated with having to confront others' misperceptions (Gray 2002; Green 2003; Khamis 2006; Turner et al. 2007). Thus, one of the main points found within the courtesy stigma literature is that it leads, not unlike stigma, to social isolation and loss of social support, both of which are in turn linked to poor physical and psychological health outcomes (Thomas 2006).

Another tenuous dimension of courtesy stigma that has been identified in the literature concerns the ascription of characteristics of the stigmatized to their associates – 'being known by the company we keep' (Kulik et al. 2008; Nueberg et al. 1994). Sigelman et al. (1991) found that students intolerant of homosexuality tended to assume that the voluntary associates of gay students were also likely homosexual, even when there was no direct evidence to suggest this. The same phenomenon likely applies to care workers serving stigmatized populations; the supposition that one possesses similar characteristics to those being served, or the idea that one has personal, extensive knowledge of a stigmatized issue may form the basis of more subtle forms of discrimination on the part of 'outsiders.' Although such assumptions of similarity may be unjustified at times, this issue is further complicated by the fact that it is also very likely that some persons working with stigmatized populations have first-hand connections to the stigmatized identity as personal experiences and social networks may influence opportunities in career selection.

A select few academic studies have taken up the topic of courtesy stigma and professional service provision to stigmatized populations. As might be expected, it has been documented that persons working with patients having HIV/AIDS – a highly stigmatized communicable disease – experienced reduced social support for their work from family and friends, resulting in high rates of worker burnout and employee/volunteer turnover (Brown et al. 2002; Synder et al. 1999). Another study found that nursing students had negative perceptions of both mental health professionals and their patients (Sadow et al. 2002). Interestingly, the authors also found that while education helped improve nursing students' attitudes towards mental health professionals, it deepened stigmas associated with mental health clients. This finding suggests that efforts to improve attitudes towards care providers may be related in some manner to vilification of the client group. This is not surprising as stigma narratives exhibit a preoccupation with defining culprits and a tendency towards fear-mongering (Hallgrímsdóttir et al. 2008).

Finally, several scholars have noted that one of the primary ways that stigma (and by extension, courtesy stigma) is structurally organized is in the provision of underfunded and inferior health and welfare services to stigmatized individuals (Birenbaum 1970; Crandall 2000; Link & Phelan 2001). Although all welfare states, including Canada, are struggling with escalating health care costs, there is a great deal of literature to suggest that services to vulnerable populations and the workforces who provide those services experience the most instability with regard to funding, and are the hardest hit by budget reductions (Hall & Banting 2000; Saunders 2004). In Canada, services to vulnerable populations have been increasingly downloaded to the non-profit and private care sector, and government funding tends to focus on costly crisis-oriented services, with little opportunity to develop innovations that focus on upstream health determinants (Raphael 2004). The relevance of the latter point to the concept of courtesy stigma is that it suggests that one of the significant ways service providers experience courtesy stigma is in the very organization of their work environments, including having to carry out their work with stigmatized populations with inadequate resources and limited intervention modalities to draw on. This environment contributes to the widespread feeling among care workers that they have been set up to fail those they serve.

Although the above paints a bleak picture for care providers to stigmatized populations, it is just as likely that, not unlike primary or direct stigma, the negative ramifications of courtesy stigma cannot be considered an inevitable fact, and it is likely that they vary greatly according to a number of contextual variables such as education, the existence of organized support, and the ability of the individuals involved to advance authoritative counter-interpretations of their care work and the characteristics of the client group.

It would be remiss at this point to not at least briefly review the literature on determinants of occupational health among helping professionals as it contains both parallels with, and complements to, the literature on courtesy stigma.

For most occupations, autonomy, decision-making authority, social support, and skill utilization have been found to contribute to occupational health (Wilkins & Beaudet 1998; Karasek & Theorell 1990). Therefore, regardless of other workplace rewards and stressors, those individuals who are able to exercise personal control over their work and draw upon their unique assets in the performance of their jobs are more likely to have good occupational health. A balance between workplace demands and rewards is also an important determinant of occupational health, with rewards such as wages, benefits, social support, occupational prestige, and personal fulfilment helping to buffer against stressful, dangerous, or demanding work conditions (Siegrist 1996). Thus, people who provide care work in highly demanding contexts, including contexts where exposure to danger or abuse is prevalent, for lower wages, poor benefits, or in the absence of other workplace rewards, such as feelings of efficacy and social recognition, are at the greatest risk for job strain and poor occupational health (Jackson 2004; Quick et al. 1992; Reskin & Padavic 1994; Hodson & Sullivan 2002; Oktay 1992; Bennet et al. 1996; Lloyd & Chenoweth 2002; Siefert et al. 1991).

In addition, for those engaged in intimate care work, a significant body of research suggests that the emotionally laden nature of the work is a source of strain for them, leading to low job satisfaction and workplace exhaustion (Acker 1999; Maslach & Jackson 1981; Lloyd & Chenoweth 2002; Shulze et al. 1995; Baird 1999). However, other research suggests that the emotional content of care work is a source of workplace reward for those who enjoy the social interaction and associated emotions they experience at work (Messing 1998). This apparent contradiction in the literature underscores the necessity of examining the specific conditions under which workplace demands such as emotional care become risks to health, while at the same time looking at the role restorative resources and support can play in minimizing the harms caused by emotionally demanding work.

Although it is accepted that care work is often demanding, there is some division in the literature regarding whether or not this demand results from the severity of needs presented by the client population, or other contextual workplace variables such as management practices and organizational structures (Maslach & Jackson 1981; Shoptaw et al. 2000). Although it is certainly the case that some client groups – particularly the most marginalized – present high needs for support, combined with difficult histories of abuse and trauma, which undoubtedly emotionally impact the care workers who become privy to these experiences, a focus on client 'burden' is unproductive because it both 'blames the victim' and provides few avenues for thinking about improving occupational health. Again, given that some workers derive satisfaction from responding to those who require help, it is more likely that contextual and structural workplace variables, specifically limited rewards and resources for care workers, is the more likely cause of poor occupational health, and therefore a more important target for policy change.

Bearing in mind the array of risks and rewards associated with both courtesy stigma and providing care work to vulnerable populations, we now turn to a brief discussion of the specific context of the sex industry, including the durable and widespread stigma that surrounds this form of activity, especially for women who are the primary targets of the prostitute stigma (Pheterson 1989, 1996).

Stigma and the Sex Industry

In Canada it is legal to sell sexual services; however, many of the practical activities associated with selling sex – communicating, operating a bawdy house, living off of the avails – are illegal (Lowman 1987, 2005). The legislative framework surrounding the sex industry in Canada can be viewed as an ongoing compromise between conflicting historical discourses regarding who the real culprits in the sex industry are – sex workers, clients/johns, or pimps – and calls for community order and control (Lowman 1987, 2005; Shaver 1994).

Academic scholarship on the sex industry has similarly been influenced by the stereotypes and generalizations associated with the prostitute identity and has thus been polarized between those who regard commercial sex exchange as inherently oppressive or risky to health and those who regard it as a valid economic activity that is problematic mainly because those involved are marginalized and lack access to social protection (O'Connell Davidson 1999; Pateman 1988; Pheterson 1989; Scambler 1997; Shaver 1994). The policy frameworks associated with these positions range from *abolition* advocated by those who regard the sex industry as inherently oppressive, *regulation and surveillance* advocated by those who are concerned primarily with the health risks and crime associated with the sex industry, and *legalization* or decriminalization advocated by those who regard the harms of the sex industry as primarily the result of social marginalization.

What is especially important in the context of this chapter is that the 'expert' and public stakeholder positions that have informed the law, research, and other forms of societal intervention into the sex industry are rooted in stigmatized constructions that have been in circulation since before the 1900s (Hallgrímsdóttir et al. 2006, 2008; Vanwesenbeeck 2001). For over a century, the sex industry has, to a greater or lesser extent, signified urban decay, crime, community disorganization, and moral failure (Hallgrímsdóttir et al. 2006, 2008). Further, sex workers have been alternately and contradictorily cast as infantilized victims of pimps, abuse, and poor upbringing, morally reckless, and financially shrewd sexual entrepreneurs (ibid.). One of the ways that sex work has been titillating and fear inducing for the public is by the co-linking of sex work narratives with other forms of deviancy and social stigmas based on race, substance use, disease transmission, or the corruption of middle-class morality regarding marriage, family, and appropriate sexual behaviour (ibid.). Narratives about the sex industry, especially those found in the popular media, inevitably construct female sex workers as 'other,' characters who exist in a distant, criminal world where the same provisions and social rights expected in the 'normal' world do not apply (Vanwesenbeeck 2001; Hallgrímsdóttir et al. 2008). Thus, the violence, social isolation, and myriad other harms enacted against women (and men) working in the sex industry are both neutralized and regarded as inevitable.

Although there may be some truth to the stigmatized characters and narratives associated with the sex industry (e.g., a minority of sex workers are also affected by chronic substance abuse), what is problematic about them, as noted earlier, is that they limit what can be known, and by extension, what can be enacted in policy, program interventions, and day-to-day interaction. Marginalization is both produced and reinforced as negative, simplistic ideas about the sex industry are materialized in social welfare services, the law, the media, research, and other important social institutions of knowledge. Further, the clandestine nature of the sex industry ensures that the vast majority of citizens both receive and propagate prostitution stigmas in the absence of any real empirical knowledge of, or contact with, the sex industry (Hallgrímsdóttir et al. 2008). Thus, care workers to persons in the sex industry find themselves at the centre of tensions regarding the seemingly incontrovertible stigmas associated with the sex industry, and the tacit, experiential knowledge they possess as a result of their direct contact with the sex industry, either as care workers, or for many of the workers quoted below, as former sex workers.

In sum, as we turn to our case study, it becomes important to keep a number of key considerations in focus as they make up some of the unique challenges faced by intimate care workers to vulnerable, stigmatized populations. Stigmatized populations, because of the intersectional processes of marginalization, experience complex barriers to health and wellness. Intimate care workers to stigmatized populations are charged with the task of addressing these care needs, but they often receive less social support, both at the individual and organizational levels, for their work as negative stigmas suggest that certain populations, such as sex workers, are wilfully deviant, burdensome to the community, and therefore undeserving of social resources. The stigmas associated with the sex industry are particularly durable because they are formed and disseminated in popular culture in the absence of meaningful contact with or knowledge of the diverse empirical reality of the sex industry. Care workers are uniquely located in this struggle as potential advocates because of their direct contact with sex workers, but they also experience considerable pressure to enact stigmas associated with how to help those in the sex industry, especially because only by doing so are they able to garner social support for their work.

There are also notable gaps in the limited literature on courtesy stigma in addition to an overall lack of information regarding its presence among health and social care professionals. One notable gap stems from the tendency to regard those who experience courtesy stigma as a distinct group who would not otherwise experience stigma except for their association with a stigmatized group. It is more likely the persons working with stigmatized populations have varying levels of similarity to those they work with along a number of key demographic and sociocontextual variables – including income, education, gender, and ethnicity. The presence of a range of stigmas among those providing care – female, single parent, Aboriginal, limited formal education, disabled, etc. – is especially likely because, as the chapters in this volume demonstrate, undersupported work environments are more likely to be populated by vulnerable workers (Hallgrímsdóttir et al., this volume). There is similarly little discussion regarding the impact of co-occurring stigmas, both with reference to those who experience courtesy stigma at work, as well as among the stigmatized groups they serve. In addition to potentially providing insights into why some workers are harder hit by workplace health risks than others, locating care workers and those they serve according to broader socioeconomic categories (and related stigmas) reveals important information about how marginalization, even within the care sector, is systemically organized along gender, ethnic, and class lines, both for workers as well as for clients.

We now turn to a description of the Prostitutes Empowerment, Education and Resource Society (PEERS) – Victoria.

The Prostitutes Empowerment Education and Resource Society

PEERS began in 1995 based on the work of a small group of volunteers, most of whom had formerly been involved in the sex industry (Rabinovitch & Strega 2004; Rabinvotich & Lewis 2001). Importantly, the group was supported by a community activist with extensive experience in grassroots organizing and innovative community-based social services. (See Rabinovitch and Lewis (2001) for biographical information.)

After receiving $200,000 in 1997 from the provincial government, PEERS formally opened its doors as a service agency providing programs for those currently and formerly involved in the sex industry. The mission statement of PEERS encompassed the following key foci: empower, educate, and support sex workers; educate the public; improve working conditions for sexworkers; provide alternative employment for those seeking to leave the sex industry; and create a safe, supportive place for persons currently or formerly involved in the sex industry (Rabinovitch & Lewis 2001).

With core funding in place, the agency applied for, and received several federal grants to expand their program portfolio to men involved in the sex industry, sexually exploited youth, various types of employment and pre-employment programming, and special issue projects concerning topics such as fetal alcohol spectrum disorder, the indoor sex industry, the criminal code, and Aboriginal and public education (Rabinovitch & Strega 2004). Private donors also helped to support PEERS programs and have remained a crucial supplement to government grants (Benoit & Millar 2001).

Despite its vigorous start and many grant successes, like other non-profit organizations, PEERS constantly struggles to maintain program funding. In the early years, while most of the federal grants PEERS received were one-off, time-limited funding opportunities, PEERS could always rely on the core funding provided by the provincial government to get them through times of scarcity. But in 2001, PEERS lost its primary source of provincial funding during a time of widespread cutbacks to provincially funded social services (Creese & Strong-Boag 2005). Since then PEERS has been competing with other non-profit agencies for limited government and private donor dollars, which are increasingly being linked to outcome frameworks that impose specific parameters for success, many of which are not well aligned with the diverse needs of their target clientele. For example, today PEERS operates two core programs – outreach and an employment rehabilitation program – but it has no specific funding to support clients who walk through the doors seeking general services (lunches, bus passes, general support counselling, etc.), who are in crisis, or who present other needs that fall outside the scope of employment training and street-based outreach. Since it would be unreasonable to not provide these essential services, PEERS staff stretch already-scarce program resources to cover these service expenses, while at the same time fulfilling core program requirements

(Hallgrímsdóttir et al., this volume; Baines 2004). An additional problem associated with outcomes-based funding, particularly when funding is connected to enrolment in successive stages of rehabilitation, is organizations such as PEERS are put in the position of turning away potential clients who may not be able to meet the rehabilitative outcomes imposed by funding bodies.

However, one of the advantages of the stigma and sensation that surrounds the sex industry is that public and government interest in program interventions has remained fairly consistent in recent years (Hallgrímsdóttir et al. 2008). Thus, even within a neoliberal political climate of welfare state retrenchment, PEERS has been able to locate a fairly steady stream of program funding (Rabinovitch & Strega 2004). The downside is that funding for innovative programs that challenge dominant ideas about the sex industry is more difficult to secure. Interestingly, at the same time, PEERS staff indicate that in the current climate of short-term funding, locating long-term funding for programs that are effective, but not considered 'innovative' can be equally difficult to secure. PEERS staff are forced to strike a delicate, and perhaps unachievable, balance between securing necessary program dollars to meet the service objectives of the organization, while at the same time resisting the hegemonic and stigmatizing narratives that accompany these initiatives, most notably that supporting persons in the sex industry can only mean helping them to leave the sex industry, or otherwise focusing on the deviance and harms associated with the prostitute stigma.

PEERS is an innovative organization for at least a couple of key reasons. First, rather than insist on hiring social service experts as is the case across helping professions to vulnerable populations, PEERS was, and continues to be, largely staffed and managed by 'experiential' persons who were formerly involved in the sex industry (some of who are also formally educated, social service experts). The rationale for this was three-fold: to provide opportunities to former sex workers seeking to expand their career opportunities, to increase the chances of engaging the stigmatized target population by decreasing the social distance between service provider and client, and to subvert stereotypes that would suggest that persons working in the sex industry are not contributing community members. In doing so, PEERS adopted the stance that first-hand, life experience was key to effective service delivery and social change (Canadian HIV/AIDS Legal Network 2005; Rabinovitch & Strega 2004). This ethos, combined with a commitment to refuse a position within the academic and political debates described earlier regarding the origins and appropriate legal response to the sex industry, has been key to the longevity of PEERS as a service organization. Although individual members of PEERS no doubt hold an array of opinions regarding the sex industry that resemble variations on the abolitionist, legalization, and decriminalization positions noted above, it is agreed that PEERS as an organization does not take a public position on these issues, and instead strives to maintain an exclusive focus on delivering services that respect, and build on, the choices of their clients, while at the same time reducing harm and building capacity (Rabinovitch & Strega 2004). PEERS' reluctance to take a position on certain aspects of the sex industry is both imperfectly practised and limiting in terms of a social activist response to stigma, but it has nevertheless proven essential to surviving internal conflicts and maintaining a focus on the primary goal of providing peer-based, front-line support services (Rabinovitch & Strega 2004).

There are currently fourteen staff employed by PEERS, all of whom are female except, at the time of the interviews, one male to female transgendered individual. This finding mirrors other estimates that suggest that over three-quarters of paid and unpaid workers in the non-profit and care sectors are women (Benoit & Hallgrímsdóttir, this volume; Mellow, this volume; Saunders 2004). In addition to these staff, there are six contractors who supplement the core staff in the employment program by delivering a variety of therapeutic and pre-employment workshops as part of the curriculum of the main employment program offered by PEERS. It is important to note that the number of staff and contractors at PEERS fluctuates in accordance with the availability of program funding.

At any given time, there are also approximately five or more active program volunteers and social work practicum students who help with the daily lunch program, housekeeping, outreach, and fundraising activities, as well as additional volunteers who are recruited for specific fundraising events. Practicum students, all of whom have been female in recent years, have become increasingly necessary to carrying out the essential duties of the organization, reflecting the sector-wide pattern of downloading care work to unpaid, female workers in times of funding scarcity (Baines 2004; Mellow, this volume). Although PEERS has on occasion had male volunteers help primarily with cooking and maintenance of the building, and has employed males as part of short-term program aimed at men in the sex industry, it has been unable to sustain a consistent male presence in the organization over the long term. The almost exclusively female makeup of the PEERS staff, volunteers, and clientele is undoubtedly reinforced by the notion that the 'prostitution problem' is essentially female. Although the lack of social welfare interventions aimed at male sex work may, on the one hand, be justified by the notion that, as a result of gender inequality, female sex workers are more vulnerable, both within and outside the sex industry, it is also an important example of how gendered social welfare interventions have the power to re-inscribe social stigmas by targeting certain populations as problematic over others.

Observation of paid and unpaid workers at PEERS suggests that they exercise a high degree of autonomy and skill discretion in the performance of their jobs with relatively basic paperwork and service policies guiding them as they interact with clients compared with larger, more bureaucratized organizations. The seemingly high levels of autonomy and skill discretion among PEERS workers likely contribute to workplace health.

PEERS has been very successful in designing and adapting their services to the emerging needs of their clientele and is frequently called upon to educate other professionals about the sex industry and how to address the needs of those who have been in the sex industry. However as noted earlier, this autonomy is often constrained by the ongoing need to attract short-term funding dollars and generate other forms of social support for their work. Thus, while PEERS has a strong sense of the client-centred services it would like to deliver and experiences relatively few intraorganizational barriers to change, generating public interest and securing ongoing funding for their ideas is problematic. Further, while workers attempt to bridge this gap with their service practices, there is an inevitable disjuncture between the mission of the organization to support the diversity of needs among women and men in the sex industry, and the actual services delivered.

In addition to ongoing organizational change, high staff turnover has also historically been a characteristic of PEERS and is a well-known feature of the non-profit human service sector, presumably because of th fluctuations in program funding, the demands of the work, and the limited resources made available to care providers to offset workplace stressors (Saunders 2004; Hallgrímsdóttir et al., this volume). Apart from the general demands and strains associated with the underresourced non-profit sector, there are a number of additional factors that likely contribute to staff turnover at PEERS. First, as a training ground for persons who may have recently left sex industry work, it is likely that many PEERS staff move on to other types of employment, or in many cases, similar employment in other organizations.

Second, as will be explored in more detail below, it is also likely that courtesy stigma plays a part in staff turnover as workers leave to seek less controversial forms of work, for which there is greater social support. Thinking about the strains associated with courtesy stigma it is interesting to note that while workers at PEERS associate many benefits with their women-centred work environment, they also cite it as a factor contributing to organizational conflict, not only because gender scripts likely have a hand in shaping interpersonal communication, but also because the organization is populated largely by women who have experienced many forms of structural disadvantage in their lives. Drawing on the notion of lateral oppression – the idea that one manifestation of internalized oppression is the enactment of harms against other oppressed persons – it is likely that workplace conflict is heightened in care work organizations serving stigmatized populations as workers and clients seek to manage the various forms of devaluation and resource deprivation they face (Bishop 2002). Indeed, workers at PEERS often note that while their own gendered experiences of violence, addiction, poverty, single parenthood, sex work, etc. are, on a good day, resources in their service practice, on a bad day, these same experiences are also implicated in poor workplace health and interpersonal conflict.

Adding this to the concerns raised by Hallgrímsdóttir et al., in the final chapter of this volume, regarding how poor support to workers is inextricably linked to provision of care, there is reason to pay special attention to the availability of restorative supports within organizations such as PEERS, where histories of various forms of marginalization are common to those employed, as well as those served. Recognizing the unique constellation of risks and assets among their staff, PEERS has recently experienced an increase in staff retention, which they link to the introduction of a more formalized staff support, training, and supervision program. In the final section of this chapter, we explore staff perceptions about providing care work to persons involved in the sex industry, specifically for themes regarding courtesy stigma on the job.

Care Workers' Perspectives

The findings presented below are based on preliminary analysis of qualitative data compiled by the first author as part of an ongoing ethnography of PEERS, feedback from current and past volunteers, and participant-observation. In total, ten staff and three volunteers answered a number of questions aimed at understanding the challenges and rewards of their work environments. Although the data presented below represent an early and incomplete investigation of the role of courtesy stigma in the context of care to marginalized populations, a number of important themes have emerged that provide insight into the toll created by the devaluation of intimate care, poor material resources in the care sector, and the additional complications posed by stigma.

Before investigating some of the challenges reported by care workers at PEERS, it is important to note that volunteer and paid workers alike articulated that the opportunity to help others, participate in social change, and be part of the PEERS community were the main attractions of the job, verifying the body of work that suggests that some care work has normative rewards for those who engage in it. Workers described being drawn to the work in order to 'be able to give back to people that were still kind of stuck where I had been stuck' and see 'shortcomings, like having an addiction problem, and having been involved in sex trade work all of a sudden became my asset.' PEERS workers additionally described times when they felt they had provided tangible assistance as one of the foremost rewards they experienced in their line of work, for example:

> We like hearing about the success of the clients, you know. It's good to hear when a client moves on, you know, goes to treatment, when a client leaves an abusive relationship, when the client gets a job or any success in that person's life, we love to hear. And they [successes] do happen, right, so that's always really rewarding.
>
> It just makes me so proud to see that, be apart of that and be someone the girls know will always be there that they can feel loved and not judged.

Such comments underscore the notion that for some individuals, intimate labour has significant normative implications that impart meaning and dignity to their work. Others similarly described how relationships with staff and clients were rewarding aspects of their work at the organization:

> The opportunity to come and work here and be part of the team and meet the people. I've met some amazing women coming through the doors and really bright, really wise, very kind people ... I take away a whole lot more than I come in with, so, I mean that's a no-brainer.
>
> It was not feeling rewarded by what I contributed so much as being very humbled by what I learned from both clients and staff, and feeling the privilege of being welcomed and accepted into this piece of their lives.

However, equally apparent was that the intrinsic rewards experienced by responding to others' needs, developing relationships, and witnessing moments of client success were not enough to sustain workers over the long haul. Workers unanimously noted that the helping sector as a whole is underresourced and fundamentally incapable of meeting the needs presented by clients. Thus, PEERS workers are not unlike other workers in the care sector who find that the extrinsic rewards and support associated with care work were lacking (Saunders 2004). As one worker described:

> But then you start breaking down what supports they need, well, you can't get them ... so the supports instead of being given to these people are taken away. It's the opposite of the way it should be ... The burnout comes from the system ... [which is] so big that we feel totally powerless and helpless.

Another similarly noted that:

> ... it's hard to work for PEERS. Really hard. You've got the women that are begging for help, and you got the government that says 'Prove that you can make these people walk out of here well and [with] a job.' You just can't. It takes years.

Another noted that providing care was demanding, especially because the environment and context of the clients' lives was so far from her own:

> [The work] has an emotional cost, both from a caring aspect, and from the perspective of it feeling like I was in a foreign country while there!

Workers also experienced challenges associated directly and indirectly with the stigma that surrounds the sex industry. Although some workers were comfortable providing services to street-based sex workers, many of whom are also affected by addiction and homelessness, other workers lamented that the organization was unable to reach a more diverse population of people working in the sex industry. As one worker noted:

> There's not enough support there for women who you know, [aren't] necessarily the street-addicted, highly entrenched population, I mean that's only 10%, what about the 90% that we're supposed to be helping?

At the same time, workers felt pessimistic about the availability of funding for alternative sex worker identities or supports for persons seeking to stay involved in the sex industry. One worker noted:

> When talking about strengths and decriminalization, lots of people are kind of angry, but when I talk about it in terms of women being victims, when I start telling these sad stories, then everyone is like 'oh,' like there's no animosity. Very little. So it's like okay for me to present having been in sex work, [but] I have to come from a place of being a victim in order to get funding, and that's huge. You don't come from a place of victim, you don't get funding.

Another noted:

> ... all you get back is a letter says, 'No we didn't pick you,' you know, they don't say, 'Cause we hate your issues,' (*laugh*) or anything like that, but I do think there is an impact.

From a service perspective, the downside of representatives of PEERS feeling pressured to frame the sex industry in particular ways to gain social support – often invoking images of persons in the sex industry as victims – is that the organization has developed a reputation of being an organization that supports highly marginalized women to leave the sex industry. Thus, while it is not their intention, PEERS staff, in their funding and public education endeavours, find themselves not only invoking stereotypes about the sex industry, but also limiting the relevance of their services to many of the people they hoped to support.

In addition to feeling pressure to frame the sex industry for potential supporters, workers also report that they and their clients are judged by others as they take their work into the community, leading to a heightened sense of vigilance. As one worker described:

> Lots of non-profits do advocacy work, but I mean usually you don't have to advocate at the hospital level, right, and it's like that ... we have to advocate at every level for people.

Another worker similarly described:

> We have to work really hard here, a lot harder in this environment to get help for the clients or to move issues forward. We have to work way harder

than other agencies or other causes do and ... some days I will go home from work thinking did I get anything accomplished today?

At the same time as they noted that they had to work hard to help their clients access community resources, workers also noted venturing into the community as a representative of PEERS might mean that they too would be subjected to discrimination, especially if their personal involvement in the sex industry was raised. Thus, courtesy stigma poses an additional barrier to dignity at work as workers' reputations and identities are – to varying degrees depending on their ability to simultaneously distance themselves from the prostitute stigma – sullied by their proximity to the sex industry and the organization's practice of hiring 'experiential' staff (Hallgrímsdóttir et al., this volume; Stacey 2005). One worker described her encounter with another social service worker this way:

I saw the look on her [social worker's] face and I knew that if I gave her the 'yes' answer she would see me as less than professional, so I gave her a, 'not everybody at PEERS has to [have a history] in the sex trade,' which is actually true.

Another felt that anyone associated with PEERS could be subjected to assumptions about background and identity:

Even identifying that I work at PEERS, right, has you know [implications]. Depending upon how much the population knows about PEERS already they will have formed an idea in their head of who I am and what my background is.

Assumptions about background were less a concern for workers who had other credentials to draw on when challenged about their source of expertise on the sex industry. For example, one worker described how her professional education offset the stigma she might otherwise experience as someone with a history in the sex industry:

But again unfortunately because I have letters after my name, there is a little more respect and that's sad because sometimes I feel that I have to use that, my academia, to stand up and say, 'I [was] a sex worker.'

Another worker, who did not have a background in the sex industry, similarly felt that she used her credentials to distance herself from the assumption that she had been a sex worker. However, doing so felt like a betrayal to those she served as it revealed her own reluctance to bear the prostitution stigma.

Some workers also described receiving less support for their work from family, alongside concerns that their work might impact their families. For example, one worker described how her work was a potential source of shame for her children:

> I have [children] and they know where I work and they know who I work with and they know what I do, but they don't want their friends to know where I work and who I work with.

Another worker described how friends did not want to talk about her work because she believed it challenged their lack of action towards helping vulnerable members of the community:

> Although my friends were very supportive of my involvement at PEERS, it seemed difficult for them to express interest in what I was doing there without needing to justify their own interests and busy schedules. Since guilt was never my intention, I seldom said anything to anyone unless they asked, so at times it felt like a lonely venture.

Workers additionally described how public responses to their work could include varying, unpredictable views, which could be valourizing, belittling, openly disdainful, or voyeuristic, leading to reluctance to talk about work with others and strategic articulation of their work to persons who inquired. For example, one worker who also described great pride and satisfaction in her work, relayed a surprising experience where she felt hesitation to speak about her work in a public setting:

> I was in a store with my husband, [I] think it was an electronics store, and we were buying something, and the guy said to me, 'Where do you work?' and I said, 'PEERS,' and he said 'What is that?' and there was a lot of people at the counter, and it was the first time that I stopped myself before right out saying prostitute, you know, and I could feel my face flushing bright red and I don't know why that was ... And it was quite embarrassing, it was really embarrassing.

For workers with a history of involvement in the sex industry experiences of courtesy stigma overlapped with direct stigma. One respondent noted how she internalized belittling views about the sex industry because of her previous experience as an escort:

> The perception [that] 'Oh, so you're saving those victims' ... it stigmatizes me because then I feel like I'm being put into the same category.

It is not surprising, then, that when leaving PEERS, workers articulated a desire for less controversial and more anonymous forms of work with fewer political and identity implications. As one worker described after moving on from the organization:

> It's nice to have work that I can talk about. Part of what I wanted was to sort of square up, right. I have the skills now, I could work anywhere. Let's go see who I am when I'm not connected to this issue.

Similarly, another noted:

> For somebody like me who comes from the world and who had a chronic drug addiction, to have that in my face over and over and over. For me it was like reliving my past over and over and over, and I'm trying to move in a new direction now.

In sum, preliminary analysis of feedback from paid and unpaid workers at PEERS suggests that courtesy stigma is a significant determinant of their occupational experience alongside other occupation-based health determinants. The findings of this research suggest that courtesy stigma plays a role in high turnover, with one of the most devastating aspects of courtesy stigma being PEERS' inability to secure sufficient community support for their work in the form of diverse program funding and collateral resources for their clients such as housing, substance use rehabilitation, education, and supported employment. Another important finding is that courtesy stigma overlaps with other sources of stigma, leaving some workers more vulnerable to the strains associated with their work environment than others. In particular, while PEERS workers strongly believe in the benefits of a peer-based model of service, it is also apparent that workers with a background in the sex industry and limited formal employment experience are especially vulnerable to the stresses associated with their work, especially if they do not have access to social capital such as professional credentials or strong support networks. Yet, it should not be assumed that the negative aspects of courtesy stigma are debilitating to workers in stigmatized environments. Despite being worn down by the array of challenges associated with working in the context of stigma and inadequate resources, workers also described an offsetting commitment to their work, which was fuelled by positive service encounters with their clientele, opportunities to educate the public about the sex industry, and their steadfast belief in the need for grassroots, peer-oriented services for the largely hidden population of women and men working in the sex industry.

Summary and Conclusions

The preliminary data analysed for this chapter demonstrate that paid and unpaid workers at PEERS face similar challenges to care workers in other non-profit organizations in achieving dignity at work, but they also experience additional indignities arising from the stigma that surrounds both their work and their work-private life interface (Benoit & Hallgrímsdóttir, this volume). The search for funding – and the increasingly targeted, short-term and outcome-oriented nature of program funding – is a constant source of pressure and insecurity for program staff, that must be balanced with their primary mission of providing responsive front-line services.

  The current neoliberal funding climate detracts from care work by not allowing for the full maturation of programs, leaving organizations without core operating support, imposing stringent reporting requirements, and by discouraging the grassroots development of program innovations that challenge the scope of existing funding initiatives (Armstrong & Armstrong 2003). For PEERS, funding for ideas that do not resonate with dominant stigmas about the sex industry, or focus on identities of lesser interest – for example, male indoor workers – is harder to come by, as the public at large remains most interested in interventions that promise to respond to the most visible and startling harms associated with the sex industry. In addition, while private donations and public fundraising events can be a good source of income for smaller programs that cannot secure government funding, this arena is especially sensitive to controversy and thus is only appropriate for widely sanctioned program interventions. In fact, PEERS is disciplined by the knowledge that donors will withdraw support if the organization becomes involved in contentious initiatives such as providing safer working environments for those who wish to continue working in the sex industry, and must strategically market itself in public fundraising to maintain public interest and sympathy.

In addition, workers in non-profit organizations across Canada suffer from an imbalance between extrinsic and intrinsic rewards, high turnover, and limited resources for training and recruitment (Saunders 2004). This is also the case for PEERS workers who are highly discouraged and disillusioned by the structurally underresourced nature of the sector, including limited income, benefits, and supports for workers. PEERS workers report frustration with the limited resources they must work with, and are especially concerned about a lack of allied supports and services in the broader community to complement their work. Aware of the discrimination their clients face accessing other services, PEERS staff feel additional pressure to advocate for their clients in the health care and child and family service systems, places that should be sources of support.

In addition, PEERS workers are disadvantaged by the distinct possibility that they too may be subject to derision and discrimination when accompanying their clients into other service environments. For example, while public education presentations can be a positive experience for staff who derive pride from using their experience in the sex industry to educate others, it can be very distressing for staff who are unprepared for the implications of speaking publicly about a stigmatized topic; this is especially the case because the discriminatory ideas they are often asked to respond to in public forums have immediate implications for their own identity and dignity, both as workers and as persons who may have formerly been involved in the sex industry. Perhaps more intensely than workers in other non-profit organizations, PEERS workers experience limited social support for their work and some feel devalued by others' misunderstanding of the sex industry and their role as care providers. Workers at PEERS are especially vulnerable to inadequate resources to support their work as not unlike their clients, they often represent an intersection of marginalized and stigmatized identities – female, Aboriginal, former youth in care, history of domestic violence, recovering from substance abuse, limited formal education, learning disability, low income, single parent, former involvement in the sex industry, chronic health condition, etc.

Workers at PEERS also experience difficulties related to essentialism in identity politics as they attempt to strike a balance between, on the one hand, elevating and promoting the 'experiential voice' as unique and privileged and, on the other, working against the 'othering' and distancing processes that form the basis of discrimination. This poses an additional strain for workers who feel defined by the identity politics surrounding how they make a living or where they volunteer.

In sum, PEERS represents a rich example of how the devaluation of intimate care intersects with the stigmas surrounding one vulnerable client group – persons working in the sex industry – resulting in a situation where those providing services are subjected to similar processes of marginaliztion as those they serve. Given the gendered subtext of PEERS and its client population, combined with the emphasis within this organization on experiential staff, the situation is in many respects one of marginalized women serving other marginalized women (Benoit & Hallgrímsdóttir and Hallgrímsdóttir et al., this volume).

In the face of these challenges, it is important that PEERS and similar organizations look for ways to support and train staff regarding how to identify and respond to the presence of stigma in their work environments. Sufficient time for staff development, including opportunities for debriefing and strategizing around common challenges are essential, as are other restorative benefits. In addition to program funding, it is essential that the organization also have sufficient resources set aside for supervision, mentoring, and counselling/coaching for service staff as well as management. Further, as is the case with other organizations, some employees are more vulnerable to the stresses and strains of the job than others because of their specific responsibilities, their rank within the organization, and their personal background. Identification of positions associated with poor occupational health and specific health risks is an important step towards designing support programming for staff who fill these positions. PEERS continues to work with an alliance model where 'experiential' and 'non-experiential' staff and volunteers work alongside each other. In addition to providing opportunities for co-education and skill transfer, ensuring that diverse groupings of staff and volunteers have opportunities to work together is also an important intervention into the pitfalls of essentialism, namely, the tendency for political organizing to reify a discriminated identity.

On a more structural level, however, policy change impacting the broader non-profit care sector is imperative as PEERS and other organizations are severely limited by the current funding climate, and an apparent belief that front-line services to marginalized populations are a matter of charity, rather than an essential aspect of an organized, proactive, and economically efficient social welfare regime that responds to the needs of the most marginalized citizens because it is socially responsible to do so.

Finally, while this study has identified some important themes with regards to courtesy stigma and the implications for occupational health among those working with vulnerable populations in the non-profit sector, it is not without important limitations mainly due to the incomplete and preliminary nature of the data. In particular, the research noted above fails to examine whether or not courtesy stigma leads to depersonalization with regards to clients, a risk noted in the literature on burnout among helping professionals (Maslach & Jackson 1981). Although all service workers are likely to experience depersonalization from time-to-time on the job, preliminary observations suggests that the female-dominated, grassroots ethos found at PEERS contributes to emotionally laden care, frequent displays of empathy, a protective view towards their clients, and increased resistance to bureaucratization and other forms of social control that typically permeate social welfare services (Mellow, this volume). Although the stigma surrounding PEERS' client group and gendered expectations of care may at times contribute to greater empathy and intimacy flowing from workers to clients, this is subject to variation, and it is likely that workers' intimate identification with those they serve has additional positive and negative implications for their service practice and occupational health that have not been explored in this chapter (Baines 2004). Moreover, it is unclear how workers at PEERS individually reconcile the potentially contradictory economic and social justice imperatives that permeate their intimate care context (Hallgrímsdóttir & Benoit, this volume). Future research will look more closely at how courtesy stigma impacts the micro-environment of co-worker and worker-client interaction, with a specific interest in a gendered analysis of how various forms of stigma, including courtesy stigma, shape the quality of care provided.

REFERENCES

Acker, G.M. (1999). The impact of clients' mental illness on social workers' job satisfaction and burnout. *Health and Social Work* 24(2): 112–19.

Armstrong, P., & H. Armstrong. (2003). *Wasting Away: The Undermining of Canadian Health Care*. Toronto: Oxford University Press.

Baines, D. (2004). Caring for nothing: Work organization and unwaged labour in social services. *Work, Employment and Society* 18: 267–95.

Baird, S. (1999). 'Vicarious Traumatization, Secondary Traumatic Stress, and Burnout in Sexual Assault and Domestic Violence Agency Staff and Volunteers.' University of Northern Texas. Retrieved December 2004 from http://www.library.unt.edu/theses/open/19992/baird_stephanie/thesis.pdf.

Bennett, L., M.W. Ross, & R. Sunderland. (1996). The relationship between recognition, rewards and burnout in AIDS caring. *Aids Care* 8: 145–54.

Benoit, C., & H. Hallgrímsdóttir. (2008). Engendering research on care and care work across different social contexts. Special Supplement: Finding Dignity in Health Care and Health Care Work. *Canadian Journal of Public Health* 99 (Suppl. 2): S7–S10.

Benoit, C., & A. Millar. (2001). *Dispelling Myths and Understanding Realities: Working Conditions, Health Status, and Exiting Experiences of Sex Workers.* Funded by BC Health Research Foundation, Capital Health District, and BC Centre of Excellence on Women's Health.

Birenbaum, A. (1970). On managing a courtesy stigma. *Journal of Health and Social Behavior* 11: 196–206.

Bishop, A. (2002). *Becoming an Ally: Breaking the Cycle of Oppression in People.* Halifax: Fernwood.

Brown, L., J. Shultz, G. Forsberg, S. Kocit, & R. Butler. (2002). Predictors of retention among HIV/hemophilia health care professionals. *General Hospital Psychiatry* 24: 48–54.

Camp, D., W. Finlay, & E. Lyons. (2002). Is low self-esteem an inevitable consequence of stigma? An example from women with chronic mental health problems. *Social Science and Medicine* 55: 823–34.

Canadian HIV/AIDS Legal Network. (2005). *Nothing about Us without Us: A Manifesto by People Who Use Drugs.* Toronto: Author.

Crandall, C. (2000). Ideology and lay theories of stigma: The justification of stigmatization. In T. Heatherton, R. Kleck, M. Hebl, & G. Hull, eds., *The Social Psychology of Stigma,* 126–50. New York: Guilford Press.

Creese, G., & V. Strong-Boag. (2005). *Losing Ground: The Effects of Government Cutbacks on Women in British Columbia, 2001–2005.* Prepared for the B.C. Coalition of Women's Centres, University of British Columbia Centre for Research in Women's Studies and Gender Relations and the B.C. Federation of Labour, Vancouver, B.C.

Crocker, J., & D. Quinn. (2000). Social stigma and the self: Meanings, situations, and self-esteem. In T. Heatherton, R. Kleck, M. Hebl, & G. Hull, eds., *The Social Psychology of Stigma,* 153–83. New York: Guilford Press.

Donkor, E., & J. Sandall. 2007. The impact of pStigma and mediating social factors on infertility-related stress among women seeking infertility treatment in Southern Ghana. *Social Science and Medicine* 65(8): 1683–94.

Goffman, E. (1963). *Stigma: Notes on the Management of Spoiled Identity.* Englewood Cliffs: Prentice-Hall.

Gray, D. (2002). 'Everybody just freezes. Everybody is just embarrassed': Felt and enacted stigma among parents of children with high functioning autism. *Sociology of Health and Illness* 24: 734–9.

Green, S. (2003). What do you mean 'what's wrong with her': Stigma and the lives of families of children with disabilities. *Social Science and Medicine* 57: 1361–74.

Hall, M., & K. Banting. 2000. The non-profit sector in Canada: An introduction. In K. Banting, ed., *The Non-profit Sector in Canada: Roles and Relationships.* Kingston School of Policy Studies, Queen's University.

Hallgrímsdóttir, H, R. Phillips, & C. Benoit. (2006). Fallen women and rescued girls: Social stigmas and media narratives of the sex industry in Victoria, B.C., 1980–2005. *Canadian Review of Sociology and Anthropology* (Special Issue) 43: 265–80.

Hallgrímsdóttir, H, R. Phillips, C. Benoit, & K. Walby. (2008). Sporting girls, streetwalkers, and inmates of houses of ill-repute: Media narratives and the historical mutability of prostitution stigmas. *Sociological Perspectives* 51: 119–38.

Hodson, R., & T. Sullivan. (2002). *The Social Organization of Work.* Belmont: Wadsworth.

Jackson, A. (2004). The unhealthy Canadian workplace. In D. Raphael, ed., *Social Determinants of Health: Canadian Perspectives,.* 79–94. Toronto: Canadian Scholars' Press.

Karasek, R., & T. Theorell. (1990). *Healthy Work: Stress, Productivity and the Reconstruction of Working Life.* New York: Basic Books.

Khamis, V. 2006. Psychological distress among parents of children with mental retardation in United Arab Emirates. *Social Science and Medicine* 64: 850–7.

Kulik, C., H. Bainbridge, & C. Cregan. (2008). Known by the company we keep: Stigma by association effects in the workplace. *Academy of Management Review* 33: 231–51.

Kusow, A. (2004). Contesting stigma: On Goffman's assumptions of normative order. *Symbolic Interaction* 27: 179–97.

Link, B.G., & J.C. Phelan. (2001). Conceptualizing stigma. *Annual Review of Sociology* 27: 363–85.

Lloyd C., R. King, & L. Chenoweth. (2002). Social work, stress and burnout: A review. *Journal of Mental Health* 11: 255–65.

Lowman, J. (1987). Taking young prostitutes seriously. *Canadian Review of Sociology and Anthropology* 24: 99–116.

Lowman, J. (2005). *Submission to the Subcommittee on Solicitation Laws of the Standing Committee on Justice, Human Rights, Emergency Preparedness and Safety.* Retrieved 22 Sept. 2008 from http://mypage.uniserve.ca/~lowman/.

Maslach, C., & S.T. Jackson. (1981). The measurement and experience of burnout. *Journal of Occupational Behaviour* 2: 99–113.

McCormack, K. (2004). Revisiting the welfare mother: The power of welfare discourse and tactics of resistance. *Critical Sociology* 30: 355–83.

McRae, H. (2000). Managing courtesy stigma: The case of Alzheimer's. *Sociology of Health and Illness* 21: 54–70.

Neuberg, S., D. Smith, J. Hoffman, & F.J. Russell. (1994). When we observe stigmatized and 'normal' individuals interacting: Stigma by association. *Personality and Social Psychology* Bulletin 20: 196–209.

Norvilitis, J., M. Scime, & J. Lee. (2002). Courtesy stigma in mothers of children with attention-deficit/hyperactivity disorder: A preliminary investigation. *Journal of Attention Deficit Disorder* 6: 61–8.

O'Connell Davidson, J. (1999) *Prostitution, Power and Freedom.* Ann Arbor: University of Michigan Press.

Oktay, J.S. (1992). Burnout in hospital social workers who work with AIDS Patients. *Social Work* 37: 432–39.

Pateman, C. 1988. *The Sexual Contract.* Cambridge: Polity Press.

Pheterson, G. 1989. *A Vindication of the Rights of Whores.* Seattle: Seal Press.

Pheterson, G. 1996. *The Prostitution Prism.* Amsterdam: Amsterdam University Press.

Phillips, R., & C. Benoit. (2005). Social determinants of health care access among sex industry workers in Canada. *Sociology of Health Care* 23: 79–104.

Quick, J., L. Murphy, J. Hurrell. (1992). *Stress and Well-being at Work.* Washington, DC: American Psychological Association.

Rabinovitch, J., & M. Lewis. (2001). *Impossible, eh? The Story of Peers.* Vancouver: Save the Children Canada.

Rabinovitch, J., & S. Strega. (2004). The PEERS story: Effective services sidestep the controversies. *Journal of Violence Against Women* 10: 140–59.

Raphael, D (2004). *Social Determinants of Health: Canadian Perspectives.* Toronto: Canadian Scholars' Press.Reissman, C. (2000). Stigma and everyday resistance practices: Childless women in South Africa. *Gender and Society* 14: 111–35.

Reskin, B., & I. Padavic. (1994). *Women and Men at Work.* Thousand Oaks: Pine Forge.

Sadow, D., M. Ryder, & D. Webster. (2002). Is education of health professionals encouraging stigma towards the mentally ill? *Journal of Mental Health* 11: 651–65.

Saunders, R. (2004). *Passion and Commitment under Stress: Human Resource Issues in Canada's Non-profit Sector: A Synthesis Report*. Ottawa: Canadian Policy Research Networks.

Scambler, G. (1997). Conspicuous and inconspicuous sex work: Neglect of the ordinary and mundane. In G. Scambler & A. Scambler, eds., *Rethinking Prostitution: Purchasing Sex in the 1990s*, 105–20. London and New York: Routledge.

Scambler, G. (2004). Re-framing stigma: Felt and enacted stigma and challenges to the sociology of chronic and disabling conditions. *Social Theory and Health* 2: 29–34.

Scambler, G., & A. Hopkins. (1986). Being epileptic: Coming to terms with stigma. *Sociology of Health and Illness* 8: 26–43.

Schulze, B., & M. Angermeyer. (2003). Subjective experiences of stigma: A focus group study of schizophrenic patients, their relatives and mental health professionals. *Social Science and Medicine* 56: 299–312.

Shaver, F.M. (1994). The regulation of prostitution: Avoiding the morality traps. *Canadian Journal of Law and Society* 9: 123–46.

Shoptaw, S., J.A. Stein, & R.A. Ronson. (2000). Burnout in substance abuse counselors: Impact of environment, attitudes and clients with HIV/AIDS. *Journal of Substance Abuse Treatment* 19: 117–26.

Siefert, K., S. Jayaratne, & W.A. Chess. (1991). Job satisfaction, burnout and turnover in health care social workers. *Health and Social Work* 16: 193–202.

Siegrist, J. (1996). Adverse health effects of high effort / low reward conditions. *Journal of Occupational Health Psychology* 6: 27–41.

Sigelman, C., J. Howell, D. Cornell, J. Cutwright, & J. Dewey. (1991). Courtesy stigma: The social implications of associating with a gay person. *Journal of Social Psychology* 131: 45–56.

Synder, M., A. Omoto, & A. Crain. (1999). Punished for their good deeds: Stigmatization of AIDS volunteers. *American Behavioral Scientist* 42: 1193–1211.

Thomas, F. (2006). Stigma, fatigue and social breakdown: Exploring the impacts of HIV/AIDS on patient and carer well-being in the Caprivi Region, Namibia. *Social Science and Medicine* 63: 3174–87.

Turner, J., B. Biesecker, J. Leib, L. Biesecker, & K. Peters, K. (2007). Parenting children with Proteus Syndrome: Experiences with, and adaptation to, courtesy stigma. *American Journal of Medical Genetics* 143A(18): 2089–97.

Vanwesenbeeck, I. (2001). Another decade of social scientific work on sex work: A review of research 1990–2000. *Annual Review of Sex Research*. 2001 Online journal. Retrieved 22 Sept. 2008 from http://findarticles.com/p/articles/mi_qa3778/is_200101/ai_n8932379/pg_1?tag=artBody;col1.

Wilkins, K., & M. Beaudet. (1998). *Work Stress and Health*. Health Reports 10, 47- 62. Cat. no: 82-003. Ottawa: Statistics Canada.

PART SIX

Public Policy Implications and
New Directions for Research

13 Neoliberalism, Gender, and Care Work: Trends and Challenges

HELGA HALLGRÍMSDÓTTIR, KATHY TEGHTSOONIAN,
DEBRA BROWN, AND CECILIA BENOIT

In this concluding chapter we draw on the theoretical and empirical materials presented by the contributors in earlier chapters of this volume to develop a gendered understanding of how neoliberal policy contexts shape the working environments and practices of those who provide health and social care in public and private domains. Our central interest is in highlighting the complex and context-sensitive political and social conditions that provide for – or undermine – dignity in performing care work/intimate labour work or receiving care or intimate services. We consider dignity for workers to flow from equitable and healthy working conditions, and remuneration that adequately recognizes the skill and expertise involved in the work. Dignity for the recipients of care rests on equitable and timely access to appropriate care in environments that contribute positively to well-being, recovery, and quality of life. As evidenced by the chapters in this volume, dignity understood in these ways has not been at the forefront of neoliberal policies regarding the provision of health and social care that have been pursued by governments in Canada and elsewhere in the industrialized West in recent years.

There are three important premises that have informed the analyses developed by the contributing authors in this volume and that underpin our discussion in this final chapter. First, gendered assumptions about the nature of caring practices and relationships in the workplace shape the organization of care work and the delivery of health and social care services. Second, the well-being of those receiving care is inextricably linked to the economic, social, and personal well-being of those who provide care. In a context where both paid and unpaid caregivers are predominantly female, gender is clearly significant in shaping the extent to which care providers enjoy equitable working conditions that support their quality of life. Third, the larger historically changing policy context in which intimate labour is organized also has gendered dimensions, which take on a range of configurations within and across countries at different points in time. The chapters in this collection offer an opportunity to explore the common threads and differences in the gendered dimensions of public policy and its effects on the provision of intimate labour, across countries with differently configured welfare states, geographical regions within countries, arenas of practice, and organizational sites where care is provided.

This is a timely moment to have this discussion in Canada. The media report almost daily on the apparent crises facing Canada's publicly funded health care system, including long wait times for necessary surgeries, overcrowded emergency rooms and hospitals, and declining hygienic standards, as evidenced by the spread of the new 'superbugs.' Reactions to these crises have ranged from the implementation of new policies aimed at standardizing wait times for surgery and cancer treatment, to hand-washing training sessions for health care staff (CDC 2002; Noseworthy et al. 2003; Balka et al. 2004; Duffy 2005). These developments contribute to understandings of the Canadian health care system as distended, inefficient, and in ongoing crisis. In the current political context in Canada, these representations have contributed to a particular framing of the health care system in media and policy discussions, one which suggests that the system can only be made more efficient and cost-effective through reforms that involve further privatization and the downloading of work to contracted employees and/or to the family members of people who are ill and/or in need of care (McMahon & Zelder 2002; Esmail & Walker 2006). Similar trends have characterized the provision of care and support to the elderly, persons with disabilities, and dependent children. Thus, underresourced home care services are substituted for care provided in institutional settings where workers are more generously compensated (Duncan & Reutter 2006; Lilly 2008), and unpaid care and support provided by volunteers or family members must fill the breach left by inadequate public funding and services (Neysmith 2000; McDaniel 2002a; Baines 2004a; Chouinard & Crooks 2008). Lost in these discussions is what these crises, and the solutions proposed for them, might mean both for those providing health and social care and for the quality of the services that they provide in settings that are highly gendered. This is a significant oversight, particularly in light of the well-established and growing body of work analysing the gendered and racialized dimensions of health and social care policies and services, and of proposals for reforming them (Armstrong et al. 2002, 2003; Baines 2004a; Hankivsky 2004; Stinson et al. 2005; Ad Hoc Working Group on Women 2006; Armstrong et al. 2008). This literature has clearly established that we need to attend to gender, along with other dimensions of marginalization, in order to understand and redress inequities in the working conditions and in the accessibility and quality of care work/intimate labour.

Scholars have conceptualized the relationship between gender and care work in several ways. A key theme in this literature is that a central pathway through which gender shapes the provision of health and social care is via the devaluation of skills, expertise, and physical strain associated with caring work. This devaluation is first and foremost a function of how the activities associated with caring work are generally conflated with what are assumed to be universal and natural female characteristics (England et al. 2002). Women engaged in intimate labour are thus understood to be expressing their natural aptitudes and inclinations rather than drawing on acquired skill and expertise. As a result, much of the work performed in these jobs is invisible to both employers and policy makers (Campbell 2000; McKie 2001).

A second conceptualization of this relationship focuses on gendered assumptions regarding the motivations that lead women to engage in intimate labour and the kinds of rewards they seek – and derive from – this type of work. Here, scholars have argued that the care sector relies, both implicitly and explicitly, on an assumption that women who seek out caring work are motivated primarily by an altruistic orientation to others and by the emotional rewards of this work (Baines 2004a). In this framing, aspects of work that are understood to motivate people employed in other sectors of the economy – wages, benefits, reasonable hours of work – appear to be secondary considerations for women engaged in care work. As a result, such women face moral pressure to continue to provide care in the face of reduced compensation and deteriorating working conditions and to meet a range of care needs over and above formal job responsibilities (White 2001; Noseworthy et al. 2003; Baines 2004a).

This gendering of intimate labour carries with it serious consequences for the status, remuneration, and quality of health and social care work in Canada and elsewhere. For example, it is undoubtedly linked to undercompensation – what effectively amounts to the 'wage-penalty of caring' (McKie 2001; England 2005). Moreover, as Bourgeault and Wrede have illustrated in this volume, poor remuneration of care work is linked to both out-migration of skilled care labour, as well as an impending shortage of trainees (Burke 2003; Shamian et al. 2003).The gendered devaluation of care work also leads to a systematic underestimation of the amount of physical labour, stress, and skill involved in caring. As a result, care workplaces are under-resourced and caregivers overworked and more likely to experience high job stress, rates of injury, and job dissatisfaction (Denton et al. 2002; Balka et al. 2004). Thus, for example, it should come as no surprise that Canadian nursing suffers the highest absenteeism rates of any employment sector. Furthermore, overworked health care practitioners who experience significant levels of stress in their workplace are at higher risk of injury and have lower health expectancies overall, and are thus less able to provide appropriate and effective care to their patients and clients (Baines 2004a).

Clearly, the policy goal of creating systems for effective health and social care delivery cannot be divorced from the need to provide those that perform the intimate labour that it involves – in all its guises, whether paid or unpaid, public or private – with safe, rewarding, and dignified working conditions. By extension, then, effective health and social care systems are ones that take seriously the need to address these gender inequities in the way that work in these sectors is organized and delivered. This means, among other things, ensuring that it is appropriately remunerated, that care workers enjoy both autonomy and intellectual challenge in applying their skills, and that they do so in working environments that are safe and supportive of their health and well-being. Public and organizational policies have a pivotal role to play in ensuring that the necessary resources are made available to achieve these goals.

The chapters in this volume contribute to our understanding of these issues in three important ways. First, the range of topics they consider conveys a strong sense of the pervasiveness of gender as a feature of the organization and delivery of health and social care across a number of different contexts, from the paid work of primary care physicians and nurses in formal settings to the unpaid work of relatives in family homes. Second, the diversity of the contexts examined illustrates not only how significant intimate labour is to the health and social care sectors but also how the gendered assumptions that structure intimate labour are embedded into the institutional frameworks through which health and social care are provided. Third, the international case studies provide a crucial comparative dimension to the discussion, allowing us to explore the ways in which different welfare state regimes and policies at different points in time mediate how gender shapes the structure of health and social care services and the conditions under which intimate labour is carried out. This comparative perspective is of particular importance because it opens up opportunities for considering a variety of policy interventions that may be effective in addressing gender inequities in caring work that appear as natural and immutable.

Below, we draw out four themes from the chapters in this volume that are visible across the diverse contexts discussed by our contributors. These themes are: (1) the downloading of care work from relatively more generously compensated practitioners to those whose skills are less valued and who receive less, if any, financial compensation for their work; (2) deteriorating conditions of health and social care work and their problematic effects; (3) the increased prominence of practices of responsibilization and familialization in health and social care policy; and (4) the different ways that these processes, and the policies shaping them, play out when implemented in the context of populations already stratified in terms of their racialized identity, age, class, and spatial location. We then discuss the potential for alternative policies and practices in the health and social care sectors, drawing on the comparative perspective across countries and across fields of practice offered by the chapters in this book. To provide a backdrop against which these themes and alternatives can be understood, we begin by identifying key features of the political and economic context within which health and social care policies are being developed in high-income countries, in particular, those that flow from the orientation to policy, broadly labelled as neoliberalism, that currently dominates these policy discussions.

Neoliberalization, Public Policy, and the Provision of Care

As noted in the opening chapter, neoliberalism, or more accurately, neoliberalization, 'denotes a politically guided intensification of market rule and commodification' (Brenner, Peck, & Theodore 2010: 3). Neoliberalization involves regulatory experimentation, interjurisdictional policy transfer, and the formation of transnational rule regimes. All of these processes have played out to a significant extent in the organization of care work in each of the countries examined here.

As a political orientation informing the policy directions that governments pursue, neoliberalization is neither homogeneous in form or in its effects. Cross-national differences in political institutions, class structure, gender relations, and welfare state programs and histories means that neoliberalization is differentially taken up and resisted across national contexts (Blomquist 2004; McDaniel 2002b; Coburn 2004). Rather than suggest that this temporally and contextually sensitive process involves an invariant set of specific policies, then, it is perhaps more useful to identify a cluster of normative commitments and discourses that are generally associated with it. These may include an enhanced role for the private sector in the funding and provision of social and health services; a commitment to reducing state expenditure in these areas; a privileging of marketized relationships between the state and service providers and between service providers and those receiving services; and the infusion of corporate business practices and norms into the work of government and service delivery organizations (Brodie 1999, 2002; Larner 2000; Baines 2004a). Although not an inevitable outcome of neoliberalization, policy debates regarding the appropriate configuration of health care and social services in many high-income countries have thus come to be permeated with discourses of cost efficiency and accountability; those receiving such services are framed as 'consumers,' and so-called free choice is invoked repeatedly as a normative good (Beardwood et al. 1999; Henderson & Petersen 2002).Within this policy framework, considerations of equity in working conditions and access to care are marginalized.

A number of related trends in the provision of health care and social services, and the nature of the work performed within these sectors, flow from neoliberal practices and discourses. One of the most significant trends involves moving responsibility for the provision and funding of services away from the public realm, assigning it instead to private service providers, communities, and families (Armstrong et al. 2002; Gilmour 2002; Ad Hoc Working Group on Women 2006). These shifts have important implications for the health and social care sectors, not least in terms of their impact on the ability of workers to provide quality care to patients and clients and to secure equitable working conditions that are supportive of their own well-being (McDaniel 2002b). All of these trends have important gender dimensions that often go unremarked but nevertheless have enormous consequences for care providers, their families, and for those for whom they care. It is to these gendered dimensions of public policy and policy reform and their implications for intimate labour that we now turn our attention.

Downloading of Care Work along Gendered Pathways

Several of the chapters in this collection describe the transfer of caring work/intimate labour from better-paid workers to those who are less generously compensated. This process reflects and reinforces an under-standing of the work being downloaded as increasingly deskilled, as it is moved along gendered hierarchies that constitute the relationships among different groups of care providers (physicians, nurses, home support workers, volunteers, family members). It is also important to note that, because of the diminishing rates of monetary compensation at lower levels of this hierarchy, the downward transfer of responsibil-ity also achieves cost savings for governments (Lilly 2008).

The chapters by Matthews-Sims and Gould and by Mellow illustrate the downloading of care along a gendered pathway wherein a natural-ization of intimate labour as reflecting women's innate capabilities, and a framing of such work as relatively unskilled, appear to go hand in hand. In their discussion of how home care services are experienced by those receiving it, Matthews and Sims-Gould note that women provid-ing such services are referred to as 'girls' or 'maids' and are assumed to be doing tasks that they should know intuitively how to do. Mellow sug-gests that an assumption that women volunteers working with patients in hospitals 'naturally' have the necessary skills may explain, at least in part, the lack of training provided for those taking up these roles.

Both chapters note how the relational – and gendered – work of lis-tening and engaging holistically with patients and clients has been to varying degrees stripped out of the jobs performed by those occu-pying higher-paid positions in the hierarchy (nurses in hospitals and home support workers in the community) and reassigned, implicitly or otherwise, to those providing support on an unpaid basis (volun-teers in hospitals and family members of those receiving home sup-port services). Purkis, Ceci, and Bjornsdóttir also note that relocating the provision of care from health care institutions to the homes of frail elderly people involves a cost shift to both (underpaid) home support workers and (unpaid) family members to whom caring responsibilities are transferred.

The chapters in this volume, however, offer two interesting counter-points to these trends. It is interesting to consider Benoit, Wrede, and Einarsdóttir's discussion of the reassignment of responsibilities for heath care work from doctors to Primary Health Care Centres (PHCs) in Finland. They suggest that, in this case, the transfer of work down the occupational hierarchy need not undermine the quality of services or result in greater inequity. Thus, they argue that, in Finland, the transfer of tasks from doctors to PHCs actually supports their expert roles.

Furthermore, along with the recent legislation governing the roles and responsibilities of midwives and nurse practitioners in some Canadian provinces, these developments signal the potential for positive change that can result from greater professional autonomy and expanded scope of practice for health care occupations that are considered to involve 'women's work.' Second, Eni's discussion of the work of Aboriginal peer support workers illustrates that there are contexts where the professionalization of care work offers neither dignity nor equity for either the provider or the recipient. Her example of prenatal care provided by peer support workers in Aboriginal communities points to a set of circumstances in which lay care provision is both more appropriate and more effective. Nevertheless, both Benoit et al.'s analysis and Eni's discussion of the challenges apparent in the circumstances they are analysing – including the need for appropriate levels of compensation that adequately recognize the work being accomplished – resonate with the discussion in many of the other chapters regarding the gendered dimensions of the provision of intimate labour.

Deteriorating Conditions of Work and Shortages of Workers

Several contributors point to the poor or deteriorating conditions under which nurses practice, both in Canada and internationally. Benoit et al. comment that currently there are high levels of dissatisfaction among the health care workforce in Iceland, particularly among nurses working in hospital settings. Similarly, Bourgeault and Wrede suggest that inadequate resources and heavy patient loads have resulted in poor working conditions for nurses in Canada, leading many to relocate in search of a more positive context for nursing practice. Although Bourgeault and Wrede point to the role of organizational policies in generating these circumstances (and see also Martin-Matthews & Sims-Gould, this volume), other research has highlighted the intimate connection between what managers within organizations have to work with and the public policies that shape the fiscal and other resources available to staff (Rankin & Campbell 2006). Baines (2004a), for example, has noted the significant cuts to government spending on social services and the growing presence of corporate management practices in the public sector in a number of Canadian provinces throughout the past two decades. She argues that, as a result of these shifts in public policy, the care that can be provided becomes 'thinner,' as reduced workforces are dispatched to complete 'efficiently' a narrowly specified set of tasks instead of being encouraged to consider and respond to the needs of the person as a whole. These developments shape the conditions under which care is provided in institutional settings, as well as in private homes, serving to undermine the health and well-being of both care providers and those receiving care (Aronson & Neysmith 1996).

Trends such as these are discussed in several of the chapters and are not confined to the Canadian context. In their account of changes to the provision of health care in hospital settings in Iceland, Benoit et al. find that a number of corporate management practices discussed by Baines (2004a, 2004b) have been emphasized as part of an attempt to enhance productivity and efficiency in Finland and Iceland, though not to the degree found in Canada. In this volume, Purkis et al., Martin-Matthews, and Sims-Gould point to similar developments in the home care field, including pressures on nurses and other support workers to become more 'efficient' practitioners by spending less time with those receiving care and standardizing their approach to the work. Purkis et al. also suggest that this intense focus on efficiency 'distracts' managers and policy makers from considering a set of fundamental issues that ought to be addressed prior to questions of efficiency, including how to ensure effective and supportive services that adequately address the needs of both care providers and care recipients. In this, they echo Janice Stein's argument that we cannot assess the efficiency of public services until we have decided what they are to be efficient at accomplishing, rather than assuming a simple equation between 'efficiency' and 'spending less money' (2001).

Bourgeault and Wrede identify a link between the undesirable working conditions facing Canadian nurses and the gendered nature of the profession. They also note that nursing work is similarly gendered and devalued in the Philippines, which along with the existence of training programs explicitly designed to equip nurses to work in North American contexts and other factors, creates a pool of nurses who are willing to relocate to Canada to practice. Increasing the supply of nurses available for employment works to reduce the incentive to address problematic features of the working environments in which hospital nurses must practice in Canada. The data that the authors present from the Finnish case confirms the importance of working conditions as an influence on nurses' decisions about where to practise. When these conditions deteriorated in Finland, the number of nurses migrating to work elsewhere increased; as they have improved, more and more Finnish nurses have returned to their home country. This points to the historical mutability of dignified working conditions for health care providers within and across countries.

The geographical mobility of nurses and other service workers across national borders also draws our attention to a significant – and troubling – implication of the analysis, presented by Thien and Dolan, concerning the consequences of shifts in government policies designed to introduce 'efficiencies' and 'cost savings' into the health care system. These include the closure of hospitals and health centres in rural areas, with facilities and services consolidated in hubs at some distance from many communities. In addition to complicating access to quality health care for residents of impacted communities (see also Hanlon et al. 2007), these consolidation strategies have implications for access to employment for health care providers. The closure of health care facilities in many communities means that health care workers must face unemployment, relocation, or longer commutes to places where employment opportunities are available, and the attendant effects on their personal as well as professional lives.

Familialization and Responsibilization of Intimate Labour

A number of the chapters draw attention to the central place occupied by processes of responsibilization and familialization in contemporary reconfigurations of health care services. As we have seen, responsibilization involves 'shifting the responsibility for social risks such as illness, unemployment, poverty, etc. ... into the domain for which the individual is responsible,' which 'leads to areas of social responsibility becoming a matter of personal provision'(Lemke 2001: 201; see also Burchell 1993).

Familialization, comprising the naturalization of 'the family' and its gendered division of labour, entails a complementary set of framings whereby women in families are constituted as the obvious and appropriate source of care for family members who are unwell or otherwise in need of support. Familialization and responsibilization both reinforce the gendered pathways by which intimate labour is downloaded to unpaid family members.

The chapters by Thien and Dolan, Mackenzie et al., and Treloar and Funk all highlight the complex and variable mix of love and obligation that holds family caregivers – generally women – in place. These chapters note the ways in which, at various points in time and place, governments and service providers, operating with limited financial resources, come to rely heavily on this pool of unpaid and poorly supported 'care workers' who absorb individually not only responsibility for care but also the costs. There is no shortage of such workers: compared with the internationally educated nurses discussed by Bourgeault and Wrede, family members who are providing care are less able to move on – geographically or emotionally – in search of more supportive working conditions. Thus, the image of 'serial caregiving' presented by these authors is an evocative one, capturing as it does, the constraints on women's life choices, as they move from one unpaid position (caring for children), to the next (caring for aging parents), to yet another (caring for grandchildren); see also Funk and Kobayashi (this volume).

Here, as in the paid health and social care workforce, the distribution of this work is strongly gendered, so that – as many of the contributors to this volume note – when we refer to care provided 'closer to home' the reality is that this is care provided by women for their family members. Where this work is carried out without appropriate supports, the health consequences for women can be serious. As Treloar and Funk suggest, when the health of family caregivers is jeopardized in such circumstances it constitutes a significant *public health* issue. In addition to generating health challenges for the care providers, these developments can also undermine their ability to continue to meet adequately the needs of their ill, incapacitated, or dependent family members.

For example, Mackenzie et al. demonstrate that even though grandmothers find much that is positive in the experience of caring for their grandchildren – including, for Aboriginal grandmothers, ensuring that the children in their extended families are raised within their own communities – doing so puts their own health and well-being at significant risk. Like Purkis et al. in their discussion of home care, Mackenzie et al. note that grandmothers' willingness to take up this work involves a cost shift from the state to the women providing care and that this serves a neoliberal interest in reducing public spending. By relying on grandmothers to provide care without ensuring that they have access to adequate social support, including support for their own health needs, kinship care policies may not in fact result in care arrangements that support the well-being of children or their family members.

The analysis presented by Purkis et al. highlights the complex interconnections between care policies and ideas of familialization and responsibilization. They illustrate the manner in which fiscal and organizational imperatives constraining the resources available to a Canadian case manager result in the positioning of a 70-year-old woman as a principal resource for her frail and unwell mother. This ideological privileging of family as a site of love, support, and good care removes from view fraught relationships between parent and child that may be intensified by the introduction of new responsibilities and vulnerabilities that a caring relationship entails. The health of both mother and daughter are thus placed at risk. Interestingly, the analysis of circumstances in Iceland in the early 2000s presented by Purkis et al., demonstrates an alternative view of family members as being potentially, but *not necessarily*, available to assist in the care of relatives. By considering both cases together, we are able to see how crucial the presence or absence of public resources can be in shaping the experiences – and health – of women with family members requiring care.

Intimate Labour and Inequities among Women

One of the most striking findings made apparent through the comparative perspective afforded by the chapters in this volume is that many of the effects of neoliberal policy on intimate labour are quite heterogeneous. A large part of this heterogeneity is the result of policy shifts that have been superimposed onto health care workplaces and health care practices already marked by inequities associated with racialized identities, social class, and spatial location, in addition to those flowing from gender. Indeed, many of the chapters here note the multiple ways in which marginalized groups – including low-income populations, those living in rural areas, members of Aboriginal communities, other racialized groups, and women – are more vulnerable to poor health and inequity in their access to health and social care and face multiple challenges in their efforts to secure better access to equitable care. Scholars working in a number of disciplines have argued for the need for an intersectional analysis, that is, one that attends to the complex effects of marginalization along more than one dimension of inequity (Benoit et al. 2009; Hankivsky 2004; Browne et al. 2007; Hankivsky & Christoffersen 2008). Many of the contributors to this volume, in noting the uneven effects on different groups of women of neoliberal policies and the caring practices that they foster, underscore the importance of an intersectional approach to developing and analysing policies that shape the provision of health and social care.

For example, several of the authors show how neoliberal policy shifts tend to exacerbate already-existing inequities. Eni notes that rationalization and efficiency as hallmarks of prenatal care serve to further marginalize both Aboriginal pregnant women as well as their peer support workers, while both Purkis et al. and Mackenzie et al. highlight the problematic consequences for older women's health when government policies reflecting an interest in reducing government spending on the provision of care erase the particular needs that such women may be developing as they age, and reframe them instead as potential sources of unpaid care for their (even more elderly) parents or their grandchildren.

Another intersection that emerges as significant for the health and well-being of both care provider and care recipient is that between gender and social class. Treloar and Funk note the deleterious consequences for mothers' health and for the well-being of their children that flow from the absence of appropriate policy supports for women raising children without a partner and without adequate economic resources. They also argue the need for policy makers to attend to other dimensions of inequity, in addition to gender and economic disadvantage, when assessing how public policies affect single mothers' capacity to provide adequate care to their children and to protect their own health. Phillips et al. advance similar arguments in discussing the manner in which neoliberal policies undermine opportunities for dignified and equitable working conditions for those providing caring services to members of a highly stigmatized group – sex workers – who often experience discrimination on the basis of several aspects of their social location. Government disinterest in developing generous and responsive public services to support sex workers reinforces their marginal economic status, and the underresourcing of the services that are available creates challenging working environments for those providing care in this context.

Finally, race, ethnicity, and immigration status also emerge as factors that serve to deepen inequities in intimate labour. Bourgeault and Wrede draw attention to how race and ethnicity shape international mobility circuits so that women of colour are channelled into practical reproductive care work, such as food preparation and cleaning, and poorly paid intimate labour, such as child care and elder care. This crucial service work, frequently distanced from more highly valued affective work, such as nursing (Duffy 2005), is typically performed by vulnerable immigrant women and women of colour in poorly paid and often insecure positions in hospitals, nursing homes, and private homes (CDC 2002; Litt & Zimmerman 2003; Armstrong et al. 2006). These are sites where multiple dimensions of marginalization – gender, racialized identity, economic vulnerability, and devalued work – intersect to sustain inequitable and unhealthy working conditions (Benoit et al. 2009).

Comparative Insights

The chapters included in this volume draw our attention to the different profiles of health care services and health care work in Canada, Iceland, and Finland. Together, they suggest the significance of the prevailing political culture and welfare state practices in each country as crucial mediators of how neoliberal policy trends shape access to health and social care, and the quality of the working environments within which it is provided. In all three countries, access to health care and social services came to be understood as a social right ensured through the welfare state during the latter part of the twentieth century. However, there have been important differences among the three countries in terms of the specific policies through which this understanding has been expressed, reflecting variations in historically rooted patterns of state development, gender relations, and engagement with international economic developments as noted in other places (McDaniel 2002b; Sandall et al. 2009). Similarly, current policy discussions regarding the provision of services involving intimate labour are shaped in each case by nationally specific framings of social problems and social solutions (Vallgarda 2007). As a result, the normative commitments associated with neoliberalism, and policies flowing from them, have been variably visible in the contemporary policy landscape in these three countries: most prominent in Canada and least established in Finland, with Iceland occupying a middle ground – albeit a ground that is rapidly shifting – between the two. Although recognizing that policy orientations and practices cannot be simply uprooted from one context and transplanted untransformed into another, there may nevertheless be useful lessons from the cases of Finland and Iceland for Canadians, as well as aspects of recent experiences in Canada that policy makers, practitioners, and care recipients in Finland and Iceland may wish to consider.

Perhaps most importantly, the analyses of the Finnish and Icelandic cases presented by the contributors to this volume suggest that even as neoliberal trends in the health and social care sectors emerge, alternative ways of conceptualizing and implementing the provision of care remain possible. For example, Benoit et al. note that alongside movements in a neoliberal direction in the health care sector in Finland, there has also been enhanced support for the provision of preventive health care as a public service in recent years. Treloar and Funk similarly point to Finland as a jurisdiction where, despite neoliberal trends in recent times, public policy has been more supportive of employed women (and men) who are parents, whether single or partnered, than has been the case in Canada. Purkis et al. show us that while there are a number of similarities between home care practice in Canada and Iceland, policies in the latter context have – at least until recently – provided more generous public resources to support the work so that it is characterized by a flexible responsiveness to those who need their service and their families and their members who need care. Echoing a point raised in a number of the other chapters (Martin-Matthews & Sims-Gould Mellow; Phillips et al.), Purkis et al.'s analysis confirms that 'quality time and public resources' are essential to ensuring dignity in both providing and receiving care.

Although these features of the health and social care sectors in Finland and Iceland usefully underscore for a Canadian audience the importance of thinking broadly about how to shape policy and services, recent experience in Canada provides food for thought for policy makers, practitioners, and citizens in Finland and Iceland who are contemplating – or implementing – further movement in a neoliberal direction. In particular, the Canadian case illustrates the consequences of a failure to consider *simultaneously* the organization of intimate labour *and* the quality of care being provided when conceiving and implementing reforms. Creating equitable, dignified working conditions within formal organizational contexts, as well as ensuring appropriate supports for family caregivers, requires conscious effort and a commitment to ensuring adequate resources on the part of policy makers. On the other hand, policies and practices that do not address the working environment – including the gender inequities embedded within it – have detrimental effects on both those providing care services and those receiving them.

These insights are particularly relevant during the current global economic downturn. Between the time when the authors of the chapters in this volume first developed their analyses and the point at which we are finalizing this concluding chapter, Iceland has experienced a complete economic collapse. As a result, that country has gone from being one of the economic stars of the Organisation for Economic Co-operation and Development (OECD) to having had to take on a considerable loan from the International Monetary Fund, with many concomitant conditions regarding the direction of domestic fiscal and social policy. Thus, those aspects of social care arrangements in Iceland that have supported dignity in both the provision and the receipt of care work are confronting significant challenges and their future remains an open question. Here, as well as in other jurisdictions, the historical analysis *across* cases that the chapters in this volume facilitate can make a significant contribution to thoughtful assessments of the advantages and drawbacks of a broad range of policy options.

The comparative perspective afforded by the chapters in this volume, taken as a whole, also illustrates a more general point: the particulars of the context within which intimate labour is provided will shape both how policy developments – such as downloading, deteriorating work conditions, familialization, and responsibilization – are experienced and the responses they provoke. For example, Bourgeault and Wrede indicate that Canadian nurses, who are the most professionalized and unionized group within the country's feminized health care sector, are essentially 'voting with their feet' by choosing to either go elsewhere to pursue their profession or to exit from nursing entirely. And, as Benoit et al. point out, the recent establishment of certified midwives and nurse practitioners as constituting autonomous, recognized fields of practices in some Canadian provinces creates important resources for these practitioners in seeking a more democratic, gender equitable relationship with physicians. However, as the context of care moves closer to the home in Canada, workers have access to fewer resources with which to resist and respond to the developments noted above. As several of the contributors to this volume have pointed out, those providing care in less professionalized, autonomous, and formal contexts have fewer opportunities to express, or act on, their dissatisfaction with working conditions.

Summary and Conclusions

A central aim of this edited book has been to draw on cross-national evidence in order to produce contextually sensitive analyses of social policy in countries where neoliberal policy orientations have emerged to varying degrees and over different periods of time. Such an approach is meant not only to add needed nuance in terms of understanding how the normative assumptions associated with neoliberalism shape social policy but also to develop an empirical basis on which diverse audiences – scholars, students, practitioners, and policy makers – can draw in reconsidering the range of policy possibilities within a particular sociopolitical context.

An additional goal of bringing together the chapters included in this volume was to take up Zelizer's (2002, 2007) challenge to attempt to understand the heterogeneity of care work, or intimate labour, and the importance of the context in which it occurs for understanding dignity and equity in care work. The contributors have examined both paid and unpaid intimate labour carried out in both formal organizational settings, such as hospitals, as well as in intimate settings, such as people's private homes. However, by demonstrating how these types of intimate labour are shaped by broader welfare state developments, including recent neoliberal policies, we have also attempted to go beyond Zelizer's challenge, which is largely focused on the organization of care work in the present-day United States, to look also at the impact of the wider historical, social, and political context (local, national, and international) on intimate labour for both the workers and the recipients of care. Thus, this volume nuances the current debate on care work within the welfare state by showing, first, that the context (micro, meso, and macro) within which that care work occurs is of foremost importance in order to understand both the general quality of the work as well as the extent to which it provides for dignity and equity for the care provider as well as the care recipient. We believe that this multilevel contextualized approach provides a useful framework for conceptualizing care work/intimate labour and we invite other scholars to embark on other empirical studies to test to what extent the preliminary findings of our contributors hold firm or are in need of revision.

One of the key themes emerging from this book is that policies associated with the neoliberal turn have had a range of adverse effects on health and social care services, and the conditions under which intimate labour is provided and received. The chapters have drawn our attention to the ways in which the development and implementation of these policies have been associated with a radical transformation in the concept of the citizen, and in particular, of the social citizen. The post-Second World War welfare state conceived of citizens primarily in terms of their relation to a constellation of rights: civil, political, and social (Marshall 1965). Social rights are those that apportion to citizens a share of the social good. In countries where the welfare state includes a publicly funded health care system, access to primary health care is then an important part of social citizenship, as is access to a range of rights associated with employment, including fair wages, safe working conditions, and sickness and unemployment benefits.

However, the concept of the citizen and understandings of the rights of citizenship are being profoundly transformed in countries where neoliberal policies and discourses are dominant, or are in the process of becoming so. As Ilcan and Basok have argued 'the post-war emphasis on rights that was echoed by many welfare states ... has now become overshadowed by the centrality given to notions of responsibilities and obligations' so that 'government today is no longer engaged in traditional planning [of services] but is more involved in enabling, inspiring, and assisting citizens to take responsibility for social problems in their community' (2004: 132). In the context of health care, this displacement of the notion of social citizenship has been associated with strategies of downloading responsibility for illness to the individual (despite the fact that poor health is often rooted in features of their environment over which individuals have little or no control), and of downloading responsibility for care to the family, community agencies, and the formal and informal private care sector.

In closing, we suggest that returning to the ideal of social citizenship as a cornerstone of public policy provides a foundation on which policy makers and practitioners can build in developing strategies for improving health and social care services in diverse social, geographical, and organizational settings. The contributors to this volume have pointed to what such strategies entail: the provision of public resources that are sufficiently generous to ensure that services are available and accessible to people in diverse geographical and social locations, removing gender inequities between fields of practice, and supporting the health and well-being of care providers in both formal and informal settings. Equity and dignity in access to health and social care are inseparable from equity and dignity in the economic, social, and organizational conditions under which that care is provided. There is an urgent need to envision possible paths to achieving these social goods and to understand the high costs of failing to do so.

The preceding chapters have made a case for scholarship comparing the organization of intimate labour in three understudied high-income countries – Canada, Finland, and Iceland. These latter two countries, like Canada, have hybrid welfare states that in recent decasdes have been the subject of structural reforms in the delivery health care. However, there are also important differences between all three countries related to the institutional arrangements of the state and the public health care system. In particular, compared with Canada, neoliberal health care strategies in Finland and, to a lesser extent, Iceland, have been less intense and also shorter-lived. Continuous government support in Finland and Iceland for 'women-friendly' policies (Henriksson et al. 2006), including publicly funded health care and, at the same time, a stronger emphasis on primary care services and democratic professionalism among health professionals have resulted in more opportunities for dignity in health care and health care work than has been possible to date in Canada.

The aim of our edited book has been to use cross-national comparison in order to produce contextually sensitive analyses of social policy in neoliberal policy regimes. Such an approach is meant not only to add needed nuance in terms of understanding how the normative assumptions associated with neoliberalism shape social policy but also to give us comparative cases from which we can examine the range of policy possibilities that are available at any given time and during a given sociopolitical context.

Limitations and Directions for Future Research

There are, of course, limitations to our context-sensitive comparative analysis of intimate labour that should be pointed out. As discussed in previous chapters, the historical conditions that have given rise to the types of welfare states and system of professions found in Finland and Iceland are different from those found in Canada. Similarly, geographical proximity to the United States, a country where neoliberalism has been entrenched, affects the politics of formal and informal care work in Canada, while Finland's and Iceland's strong ties with the other Nordic countries (Sweden, Norway, and Demark) foster policies that support generous welfare states aimed at enhancing citizenship rights for all members. Thus, we are not able to generalize to other high-income countries with different historical trajectories as well as present-day welfare state configurations and legal protections for personal service workers in the formal economy as wells in the home. This is especially the case in middle- and low-income countries that are comparatively less resourced, and where democratic institutions are only partly established or even non-existent.

Finally, the contributions in this volume do not cover all forms of care work/intimate labour that can be found today in the three countries.

We have focused primarily on intimate labour that is sanctioned by governments as legitimate work worthy of a fare wage/salary. This is a significant limitation as there exists a considerable amount of personal service work in high-income countries – including self-employed child care providers (Karman & Elleithy 2006), as well as care workers who are reimbursed 'under the table' or in the 'shadow economy' – such as home care, cleaning, and sex work (Hallgrímsdóttir et al. 2008) – where workers have access to few if any social rights, as well as low prestige because of the kind of work they perform for a living, as well as discrimination because of their gender and race (Hallgrímsdóttir et al. 2006; Benoit et al. 2009).

For these and other reasons, care must be exercised before making generalizations from our three-country comparison. The analyses presented in the preceding chapters point to, but do not address, important questions regarding the types of policies that support, and those that undermine, dignity, safety, and equity in the provision and receipt of care work in these less visible and unregulated sectors of the economy.

REFERENCES

Ad Hoc Working Group on Women, Mental Health, Mental Illness and Addictions. (2006). *Women, Mental Health and Mental Illness and Addiction in Canada: An Overview.* Retrieved 17 Oct. 2006 from http://www.cwhn.ca/PDF/womenMentalHealth.pdf.

Armstrong, P., C. Amaratunga, J. Bernier, K. Grant, A. Pederson, & K. Willson. (2002). *Exposizing Privatization: Women and Health Care Reform in Canada.* Aurora: Garamond Press.

Armstrong, P., M. Boscoe, B. Clow, K. Grant, & A. Pederson. (2003). *Reading Romanow: The Implications of the Final Report of the Commission on the Future of Health Care in Canada for Women.* Retrieved 26 March 2007 from http://www.cewhcesf.ca/healthreform/publications/summary/reading_romanow.html.

Armstrong, P., H. Armstrong, & K. Scott-Dixon. (2006). *Critical to Care: Women and Ancillary Work in Health Care.* Retrieved 15 April 2006 from www.cewhcesf/ca/healthreform/.

Armstrong, P., H. Armstrong, & K. Scott-Dixon. (2008). *Critical to Care: The Invisible Women in Health Services.* Toronto: University of Toronto Press.

Aronson, J., & S.M. Neysmith. (1996). 'You're not just in there to do the work': Depersonalizing policies and the exploitation of home care workers' labor. *Gender and Society* 10(1): 59–77.

Baines, D. (2004a). Caring for nothing: Work organization and unwaged labour in social services. *Work, Employment and Society* 18(2): 267–95.

Baines, D. (2004b). Seven kinds of work – only one paid: Raced, gendered and restructured work in social services. *Atlantis: A Women's Studies Journal* 28(2): 19–28.

Balka, E., S. Mason, et al. (2004). 'You think it is turning but it is the multiple small stuff': Gender, the division of labour and musculoskeletal injury among nursing staff. *Canadian Woman Studies* 24(1): 145–52.

Beardwood, B., V. Walters, et al. (1999). Complaints against nurses: A reflection of the 'new managerialism' and consumerism in health care? *Social Science and Medicine* 48: 363–74.

Benoit, C., L. Shumka, R. Phillips, H. Hallgrímsdóttir, K. Kobayashi, O. Hankivsky, C. Reid, & E. Brief. (2009). Explaining the health gap between girls and women in Canada. *Sociological Research Online.* 14(5). Retrieved from http://www.socresonline.org.uk/14/5/9.html.

Blomquist, P. (2004). The choice revolution: Privatization of Swedish welfare services in the 1990s. *Social Policy and Administration* 38: 139–55.

Brenner, N., J. Peck, & N. Theodore. (2010). Variegated neoliberalization. *Global Networks* 10: 182–222.

Brodie, J. (1999). The politics of social policy in the twenty-first century. In D. Broad & W. Antony, eds., *Citizens or Consumers? Social Policy in a Market Society,* 37–45. Halifax: Fernwood.

Brodie, J. (2002). The great undoing: State formation, gender politics, and social policy in Canada. In C. Kingfisher, ed., *Western Welfare in Decline: Globalization and Women's Poverty,* 90–110. Philadelphia: University of Pennsylvania Press.

Browne, A., V.L. Smye, & C. Varcoe. (2007). Postcolonial feminist theoretical perspectives and women's health. In *Women's Health in Canada: Critical Perspectives on Theory and Policy,* 124–42. Toronto: University of Toronto Press.

Burchell, G. (1993). Liberal government and techniques of the self. *Economy and Society* 22(3): 267–82.

Burke, R.J. (2003). Healthcare restructuring in Canada. *International Journal of Sociology and Social Policy* 23: 1–7.

CDC. (2002). *Hand Hygiene in Health Settings.* Retrieved 26 March 2007 from http://www.cdc.gov/handhygiene/materials.htm.

Chouinard, V., & V.A. Crooks. (2008). Negotiating neoliberal environments in British Columbia and Ontario, Canada: Restructuring of state-voluntary sector relations and disability organizations' struggles to survive. *Environment and Planning C: Government and Policy* 26: 173–90.

Coburn, D. (2004). Beyond the income inequality hypothesis: Class, neoliberalism, and health inequalities. *Social Science and Medicine* 58: 41–56.

Denton, M., I.U. Zeytinoglu, S. Davies, & J. Lian. (2002). Job stress and job dissatisfaction of home care workers in the context of health care restructuring. *International Journal of Health Services* 32(2): 327–57.

Duffy, M. (2005). Reproducing labor inequalities: Challenges for feminists conceptualizing care at the intersections of gender, race, and class. *Gender and Society* 19: 66–82.

Duncan, S., & L. Reutter. (2006). A critical policy analysis of an emerging agenda for home care in one Canadian province. *Health and Social Care in the Community* 14(3): 242–53.

England, P. (2005). Emerging theories of care work. *Annual Review of Sociology* 31: 381–99.

England, P., M. Budig, & N. Folbre. (2002). Wages of virtue: The relative pay of care work. *Social Problems* 49(4): 455–73.

Esmail, N., & M. Walker. (2006). *How Good Is Canadian Health Care? An International Comparison of Health Care Systems.* Vancouver: Fraser Institute.

Gilmour, J.M. (2002). Creeping privatization in health care: Implications for women as the state redraws its role. In B. Cossman & J. Fudge, eds., *Privatization, Law, and the Challenge to Feminism,* 267–310. Toronto: University of Toronto Press.

Hallgrímsdóttir, H., R. Phillips, & C. Benoit. (2006). Fallen women and rescued girls: Social stigma and media narratives of the sex industry in Victoria, B.C., from 1980 to 2005. *Canadian Review of Sociology and Anthropology* (Special Issue) 43: 265–80.

Hankivsky, O. (2004). *Social Policy and the Ethics of Care.* Vancouver: UBC Press.

Hankivsky, O., & A. Christoffersen. (2008). Intersectionality and the determinants of health: A Canadian perspective. *Critical Public Health* 18(3): 271–83.

Hanlon, N., G. Halseth, R. Clasby, & V. Pow. (2007). The place embeddedness of social care: Restructuring work and welfare in Mackenzie, B.C. *Health and Place* 13: 466–81.

Henderson, S., & A. Petersen. (2002). *Consuming Health: The Commodification of Health Care.* London and New York: Routledge.

Henriksson, L., S. Wrede, & V. Bureau. (2006). Understanding professional projects in welfare service work: Revival of old professionalism? *Gender, Work and Organisation* 13: 174–92.

Ilcan, S., & T. Basok. (2004). Community government: Voluntary agencies, social justice, and the responsibilization of citizens. *Citizenship Studies* 8(2): 129–44.

Karman, Z., & A. Elleithy. (2006). Self-employed women's work-life imbalance: An urgent need for policy response. *Horizons* 8: 19–23.

Larner, W. (2000). Neoliberalism: Policy, ideology, governmentality. *Studies in Political Economy* 63: 5–25.

Lemke, T. (2001). 'The birth of bio-politics': Michel Foucault's lecture at the College de France on neoliberal governmentality. *Economy and Society* 30(2): 190–207.

Lilly, M.B. (2008). Medical versus social work-places: Constructing and compensating the personal support worker across health care settings in Ontario, Canada. *Gender, Place and Culture* 15(3): 295–9.

Litt, J.S., & M.K. Zimmerman. (2003). Global perspectives on gender and care work: An introduction. *Gender and Society* 17: 156–65.

Marshall, T.H. (1965). *Class, Citizenship, and Social Development*. New York: Anchor Books.

McDaniel, S. (2002a). Intergenerational interlinkages: Public, family, and work. In D. Cheal, ed., *Aging and Demographic Change in Canadian Context*, 22–71. Toronto: University of Toronto Press.

McDaniel, S. (2002b). Women's changing relations to the state and citizenship: Caring and intergenerational relations in globalizing Western democracies. *Canadian Review of Sociology and Anthropology* 39: 125–50.

McKie, L. (2001). Gender, caring and employment in Britain. *Journal of Social Policy* 30(2): 233–58.

McMahon, F., & M. Zelder. (2002). *Making Health Spending Work*. Vancouver: Fraser Institute.

Neysmith, S.M. (Ed.). (2000). *Restructuring Caring Labour: Discourse, State Practice, and Everyday Life*. Don Millls: Oxford University Press.

Noseworthy, T.W., J.J. McGurran, & D.C. Hadorn. (2003). Waiting for scheduled services in Canada: Development of priority-setting scoring systems. *Journal of Evaluation in Clinical Practice* 9(1): 23–31.

Rankin, J.M., & L. Campbell. (2006). *Managing to Nurse: Inside Canada's Health Care Reform*. Toronto: University of Toronto Press.

Sandall, J., C. Benoit, E. Van Teijlingen, S. Wrede, R. Westfall, & S. Murray. (2009). Social service professional or market expert? Maternity care relations under neoliberal healthcare reform. *Current Sociology* 57: 529–53.

Shamian, J., L. O'Brien-Pallas, D. Thomson, C. Alksnis, & M.S. Kerr. (2003). Nurse absenteeism, stress and workplace injury: What are the contributing factors and what can/should be done about it? *International Journal of Sociology and Social Policy* 23: 81–103.

Stein, J.G. (2001). *The Cult of Efficiency*. Toronto: Anansi Press.

Stinson, J., N. Pollak, & M. Cohen. (2005). *The Pains of Privatization: How Contracting Out Hurts Health Support Workers, Their Families, and Health Care.* Vancouver: Canadian Centre for Policy Alternatives – B.C. Office.

Vallgarda, S. (2007). Health inequalities: Political problematizations in Denmark and Sweden. *Critical Public Health* 17: 45–56.

White, L.E. (2001). Closing the care gap that welfare reform left behind. *Annals of the American Academy of Sciences* 577: 131–43.

Zelizer, V.A. (2002). How care counts. *Contemporary Sociology* 31: 115–19.

Zelizer, V.A. (2007). Caring everywhere. Keynote Address, Conference on Intimate Labors, University of California, Santa Barbara, 4–6 Oct.